AGEING AND INTERGENERATIONAI RELATIONS

Family reciprocity from a global perspective

Edited by Misa Izuhara

This edition published in Great Britain in 2010 by

The Policy Press
University of Bristol
Fourth Floor
Beacon House
Queen's Road
Bristol BS8 1QU
UK

Tel +44 (0)117 331 4054
Fax +44 (0)117 331 4093
e-mail tpp-info@bristol.ac.uk
www.policypress.co.uk

North American office:
The Policy Press
c/o International Specialized Books Services (ISBS)
920 NE 58th Avenue, Suite 300
Portland, OR 97213-3786, USA
Tel +1 503 287 3093
Fax +1 503 280 8832
e-mail info@isbs.com

British Library Cataloguing in Publication Data
A catalogue record for this book is available from the British Library.

Library of Congress Cataloging-in-Publication Data
A catalog record for this book has been requested.

ISBN 978 1 84742 204 0 paperback
ISBN 978 1 84742 205 7 hardcover

Cover design by The Policy Press
Front cover: image kindly supplied by www.sxc.hu/profile/andreyutzu
Printed and bound in Great Britain by TJ International, Padstow

For my family

Contents

List of tables and figures

Tables

Figure

Notes on contributors

Marilyn Coleman is a Curators' Professor of Human Development and Family Studies at the University of Missouri, US. Her research interests are primarily post-divorce relationships, especially remarriage and stepfamily relationships. She has co-authored eight books, published well over 150 journal articles and book chapters and garnered over four million dollars in grants, most with her colleague and husband, Dr Lawrence Ganong. She was the first female editor of the leading family journal in the world, *Journal of Marriage and Family*, from 1992 to 1996, and is on the editorial boards of six journals. Dr Coleman has won numerous national and campus awards for teaching, research and service.

Pascale F. Engelmajer is currently finishing her PhD in Buddhist Studies at the University of Bristol, UK. Her research interests include filial relationships and gender in the Pâli canon, and the way religious norms shape intergenerational relationships in contemporary Thailand. She holds a Master of International Affairs degree from Columbia University, US, and a Master of Arts in Buddhist Studies from the University of Bristol. She taught Political Science and Gender Studies at Webster University in Thailand for several years.

Lawrence H. Ganong, PhD, is Professor of Nursing and Human Development and Family Studies at the University of Missouri, US. With Dr Coleman, he has co-authored over 175 articles and book chapters, as well as seven books, including *Stepfamily relationships* (Springer, 2004), *Handbook of contemporary families* (Sage Publications, 2004), and *Family life in 20th-century America* (Greenwood Press, 2007) with Kelly Warzinik. His primary research programme has focused on stepfamilies, particularly addressing what stepfamily members do to develop satisfying, effective relationships. For the past few years, Ganong and Coleman have investigated normative beliefs about intergenerational obligations following divorce and remarriage. Dr Ganong was an associate editor of the *Journal of Social and Personal Relationships* and serves on the editorial boards of several journals.

Misa Izuhara is a senior lecturer in the School for Policy Studies and the Director of the Centre for East Asian Studies at the University of Bristol, UK. Her research interests focus primarily on housing and social change, ageing and intergenerational relations, and also comparative policy analysis between the East and the West. She is the author of *Housing, care and inheritance* (Routledge, 2009), and editor of *Comparing social policies: Exploring new perspectives in Britain and Japan* (The Policy Press, 2003). She is the past editor of refereed international journal, *Policy & Politics* (2005–08).

Ricky Joseph is a research fellow at the Centre for Urban and Regional Studies (CURS) at the University of Birmingham, UK, where he also completed his PhD in 2007. His doctoral thesis used life histories to gain insights into the housing wealth experiences of two generations of Caribbean migrants, and was funded under the Economic and Social Research Council (ESRC)/Office of the Deputy Prime Minister (ODPM) Sustainable Communities Research Programme. His research interests are wide ranging, covering minority ethnic homeownership, housing wealth, return migration and Caribbean land development. As a housing practitioner prior to joining CURS, he has extensive experience of governance and policy development within the housing association sector in the UK.

Ruth Katz is a professor at the Department of Human Services and a senior researcher at the Centre for Research and Study of Aging and the Centre for Research and Study of Family, Faculty of Social Welfare and Health Sciences at the University of Haifa, Israel. She has received research grants (with Ariela Lowenstein) from the European Commission (5th framework), the Bi-national US–Israel Science Foundation and the Israel Science Foundation. She has published articles about intergenerational family relations, quality of life and life satisfaction of old family members, familial norms and elder care, migration and support systems, work–family conflict, divorce and cohabitation, and family patterns in various sectors of Israeli society in professional journals and books.

Ariela Lowenstein is a full professor in the Department of Gerontology and the Director of the Centre for Research and Study of Aging, Faculty of Social Welfare and Health Sciences at the University of Haifa, Israel. In 2009, she was nominated as the head of the Health Services Management Department at Max Stern Academic Yezreel College, Israel. Her research areas cover intergenerational family relations, elder abuse, quality of life, family caregiving and gerontological education. She has published extensively on ageing issues in close to 200 publications, having written two books in Hebrew and co-edited three books in English. Lowenstein has a reputation as one of the leading national and international experts in social gerontology, and is active in central roles in different ageing organisations.

Akpovire Oduaran is a professor at the Department of Adult Education at the University of Botswana, Botswana. His current research interests include lifelong learning, intergenerational relationships, adult literacy, training and development. He has published widely, served as a consulting editor to several international journals, and also given keynote speeches at various international conferences in his fields. Professor Oduaran served on the International Expert Panels organised by the United Nations (2007) and UNESCO (2006 and 2007).

Choja Oduaran gained her doctoral degree in Counselling and Human Services from the University of Botswana in 2003. She was the first person and the first woman ever to have been awarded the doctoral degree in education by the university. Dr Oduaran is a practising guidance counsellor and taught several courses at the University of Botswana. She currently serves in the capacity of consultant to the Marang Child Care Network Trust.

Chris Phillipson is Professor of Applied Social Studies and Social Gerontology at Keele University, UK. His current research interests include globalisation and ageing, social exclusion and older people, and transitions from work to retirement. He is a past president of the British Society of Gerontology. His books include *Reconstructing old age* (Sage Publications, 1998), *The family and community life of older people* (co-authored, Routledge, 2001), *Aging, globalization and inequality* (co-edited, Baywood, 2006) and *Futures of old age* (co-edited, Sage Publications, 2006).

Foreword

Judith Phillips

Globalisation has resulted in, and has implications for, new and diverse patterns of family and intergenerational relations and support. The traditional patterns of reciprocity are increasingly being challenged by the changing dynamics of ageing and family life; across the world such patterns and processes require revision and reframing. These are the themes developed within this book.

The international contributors, all well known in this field, provide a comparative insight to established concepts such as reciprocity and new themes such as intergenerational ambivalence. They address both theoretical frameworks for making sense of the new dynamics of ageing as well as providing a series of case studies illustrating the key issues. Students, academics, professionals and policy makers will find this text of particular value with its synthesis of current research and fresh analytical lens on intergenerational relations.

ONE

Introduction

Misa Izuhara

Changing social contexts

At the turn of the millennium, relations between generations continue to evolve, shift or even be reinforced in order to cope with the increasing domestic and global pressures which individuals and families are now facing in a globalising world. Relationships between generations have never been static, but the dynamic nature of such social ties within families has always attracted ample research interests. In Western academic circles, the 1990s was a recent period in social gerontology when a substantial and influential body of work on intergenerational relations involving older people was produced, making a significant contribution to the knowledge and understanding of contemporary adult relationships within families (see for example Kendig et al, 1992; Bengtson and Harootyan, 1994; Bengtson et al, 1995; Walker, 1996; Arber and Attias-Donfut, 1999). More than a decade later, when pressures on family and public resources have continued to rise nationally and globally, intergenerational relations now require new scrutiny.

There are a number of explanations for such general shifts occurring in relationships between generations. First and foremost, however, it must be emphasised that generalising on the shifts in intergenerational relations is deceptive with conceptual and empirical difficulties, since the pace and shape of relationships per se, let alone the speed and direction of such shifts, varies enormously in a global context. The conventional arrangements that had existed previously, from which such shifts were made, could also be very different. Nevertheless, in many societies there are shared driving forces contributing to the processes of change in family systems and support. Especially since the mid- to late 1980s, for example, the speed of economic, societal and demographic shifts appears to have accelerated in combination with a pervasive ideological shift, which is often referred to in terms such as 'globalisation', 'neoliberalisation' and 'social fragmentation' (see Sassen, 1998; Held and McGrew, 2003; Vincent et al, 2006). The development of public policy has also contributed to this transformation.

Economic restructuring, demographic changes and shifting social norms have put greater strains on family life, and have helped produce a greater diversity in family and household structures, which in turn has led to varied attitudes, functions as well as relations between generations. Some of the common opportunities and pressures shaping the current trends are identified here. First, *changing economic cycles* are a distinctive driver for leading intergenerational relations to change. Medical and technological changes also form part of such a societal dimension of intergenerational relations (Lang and Perrig-Chiello, 2005). Indeed, economic booms accompanying rising real incomes and living standards shape family structures and relations in a number of ways. For example, modernisation, brought by postwar economic growth in many 'traditional' societies, helped transform household structures towards more of a nuclear model. Increased female participation in the formal labour market is reducing the pool of family resources available to care for dependent members. In more recent years, with globalisation, changes in economies and labour markets have tended to produce greater uncertainty for families and institutions. The current global financial crisis has added further strain on families, institutions and thus societies, with increasing precariousness in the labour market including job losses, reduced household incomes and reduced employment security as well as social protection (Doogan, 2009). One impact of the economic downturn on family relations has been the prolonged dependency of adult children on their parents.

Second, another well-debated factor is *demographic change*. Global ageing has brought the diversification of individual lifecourses as well as family forms (Lowenstein, 2005; see also Chapter Two in this volume for details). Population ageing is one part of the significant contemporary social processes impacting on human lives, existing institutions and also intergenerational ties (Lowenstein and Bengtson, 2003). There are a few converging as well as polarising trends in intergenerational relations influenced by the processes of societal ageing globally. A combination of increased longevity and declining fertility has meant a shift from a vertical to a more horizontal structure, which Bengtson and Harootyan (1994) call the 'beanpole family' (see also Lowenstein, 2005). Under the current demographic shift there are more living generations ('*inter*generational extension') but fewer members in each generation ('*intra*generational contraction') (Bengtson et al, 1996). This type of family is forming in many advanced economies, where adults have more ageing parents (generations above) than children. Moreover, as the average age of women or couples having babies has risen in these societies, the gap between generations has also widened. Some scholars (for example Lowenstein, 2005) argue that such 'age-gapped' families may hinder the development of affective bonds and shared values across generations. And such families co-exist with 'age-condensed' families in the same society, which may sometimes illustrate a 'class' divide. In 'age-condensed' families, there is a blurring of boundaries between generations, especially when early fertility occurs across multiple generations, which is the case among many Black families in North American society and also among working-class British families (Bengtson and Harootyan, 1994).

Demographic shifts alter people's expectations, roles and lengths of time spent in the conventional lifecourse. For example, the length of time spent in specific family roles has been altered (Lowenstein, 2005). Low fertility has also meant that more pressure has been placed on a smaller pool of younger resources to provide support for a longer period of time if family members are to continue to play conventional caring roles. In some advanced nations, however, this coincides with a privileged position of children whose share of the resources from above could be greater due to having fewer siblings and to the greater financial resources of their parents' generations. Moreover, rapidly ageing societies, including most East Asian societies, tend to exhibit a much more profound generational gap regarding social norms, expectations and cultural practices. Such consensus–conflict models between generations may highlight significant East–West differences (Izuhara, 2009). Overall, intergenerational relations need to be understood within a lifecourse approach (Rossi and Rossi, 1990), but the age 'cohort' may no longer represent 'generational' role within the family. And so age cohort may not be a useful measurable unit for comparative international analysis regarding family systems and support, since people in the same cohort may share less of their lifecourse-related experiences at a point in time within and across societies.

The emergence of reconstituted families following divorce, separation, remarriage and repartnering is another phenomenon illustrating diversified family formation and structure that is increasingly common in Western societies. For those families, the line of responsibilities may become unclear and need constant negotiation. Divorce, separation and forming step relations seem to affect the ability of adult children to care for their older parents, and at the same time divorce and separation could reinforce a strong desire for older parents to remain independent (Dimmock et al, 2004). Such patterns are not necessarily consistent across families, because divorce and remarriage can bring families closer together, but can also create more distance between members both physically and emotionally. Indeed, this is likely to produce different patterns of family support exchanges, and intergenerational relations as a whole, between different family ties (for example biological or step relations, resident or absent) within and beyond households (for a more detailed discussion, see Chapter Eight of this volume).

Furthermore, in an era of globalisation, increasing geographic mobility of individuals and families within and beyond national boundaries requires the re-evaluation of intergenerational relations (Bryceson and Vuorela, 2002; Castles and Miller, 2008). In many urbanised/urbanising societies, urban migration and the accompanying social change have created a geographic distance between generations of families which has impacted on living arrangements, transforming the traditional family support network and making support exchange more problematic in old age. Changes that have taken place within a localised society over time and over generations are likely to become more exaggerated when family members cross national and cultural boundaries (see for example Ackers, 1998; Izuhara and Shibata, 2002; Baldassar et al, 2007). Linking migratory movements to some of the issues regarding family relations, this volume addresses how migration affects traditional norms and practices; in Chapter Four, Ricky Joseph looks at whether new patterns regarding ageing Caribbean migrants in the UK are emerging, and in Chapter Seven, Pascale Engelmajer and I look at female urban migration in Thailand.

The macro-level domestic and global changes described above are likely to shape interpersonal relationships within families. This volume draws on both theoretical perspectives and empirical analysis in relation to contemporary exchange rationales and practices of family support, and the changing nature and patterns of intergenerational relations. It addresses these issues in diverse national and cultural contexts.

Defining 'intergenerational relations'

The concept of 'intergenerational relations' overlaps with that of 'family relations', and the two terms are occasionally used interchangeably in this volume, especially given the main focus on interpersonal relationships 'within families'. However, the two terms have some distinctive differences in meaning. The former can be applied to the different levels of relationships including those between generations in a primary institution of families and also the interactions between age cohorts in a wider social structure. 'Family relations', on the other hand, includes various ties within the same generation ('*intra*generational relations'), as spousal and sibling ties are an integral part of family relations (Connidis, 2005).

Indeed, 'intergenerational relations' cover different levels of social units, and micro-level interpersonal relations do not exist alone but are influenced by and interact with macro-level social economic structure and policies (see Giddens, 1991; Walker, 1996). Such interaction between 'structure' and 'agency' – 'individuals as actors exercise agency as they negotiate relationships within the constraints of social structure' (Connidis and McMullin, 2002, p 558) – offers another useful theoretical framework when analysing intergenerational relations (see Chapter Nine of this volume for further analysis). Such micro–macro interactions shape the distinctive exchange patterns that exist in each national context since intergenerational solidarity and transfers are partly in response to differences in welfare state policies such as pension systems, health and social care. Due to the recent trend in population ageing, for example, the issue of 'generational equity' as a source of conflict forms one of the major debates in welfare states (see, for example, Hills, 1996; Becker, 1999; Hill, 2007). Variations in cohort size, such as baby boomers, changes in economic performance and shifts in policy and politics over time are all likely to generate inequalities among generations around, for example, access to and returns from pension funds (Evandrou and Falkingham, 2006).

The responsibilities of long-term care for vulnerable adults are another area within which state–family boundaries are often contested. They have shifted over time in many welfare states, attracting considerable academic as well as popular debate (Izuhara, 2009). As Finch (1989) argues, 'any government wishing to restrict public expenditure is likely to explore how family ties can be strengthened either explicitly or implicitly by defining such obligations'. The availability (and lack) of policy measures and thus accompanying benefits and services does influence the nature and level of support that families provide to their older members. In this context, the development of public policy such as the 'social insurance scheme on long-term care' in Japan in 2000 is able to dramatically transform the conventional norms and practices of family support exchanges over generations. Under Japan's 'socialisation of care' approach, for example, various players – public, private or voluntary – now supplement and complement care traditionally provided by family members, with newly established social insurance funds.

It is therefore important to locate the analysis of family relations in the context of the wider national and global political economy and public policies. In this context, distinctiveness in the cohorts in terms of socioeconomic advantages tends to exist across different periods in postwar history in different societies (see for example Forrest, 2008). Demographic location of wealth over age cohorts shifts along with the modernisation process and global economic change, which may also alter the direction of support flow. Current older people are able to have more resources than their preceding cohorts, and in some cases, more than successive cohorts in some national contexts. The availability of public funds and services does not necessarily replace family support, but it is likely to contribute to altering how generations relate to each other and support one another.

Exploring several underlying 'key concepts' will, to a certain extent, help us better understand the logic behind relationships between generations as well as the rationales for such practices. A concept that this volume is largely concerned with (as found in the sub-title) is 'family reciprocity', which is a vital characteristic of the 'generational contract', although there are many key theories explaining contemporary intergenerational relationships in this field (see Chapter Three of this volume for a more detailed discussion).

The 'generational contract' forms the backbone of a wider social contract defined in each national context. Unlike the social contract mediated by the state, the micro-level contract usually involves a direct exchange of goods and services between generations within families. It is not usually written nor necessarily abides by the law but is often bound by strong social norms defining such family practices of providing support. There is a deep-rooted cultural significance in generational contracts. A particular 'generational contract' tends to be negotiated within families in each society, reflecting the different national contexts such as cultures, laws and institutions (Walker, 1996; Izuhara, 2002, 2004). Furthermore, individuals within and across societies are likely to possess wide variations in their conceptual understandings of such a 'generational contract' – how it should be or how it is implemented in their own family lives.

One of the vital characteristics of the 'generational contract' is the norm of 'reciprocity', which governs how individuals accept and provide support involving rights and responsibilities, and credits and debts within the institution of families (Akiyama et al, 1997; Izuhara, 2009). For example, parents bring up children by providing financial and material resources, and in return that serves as a credit for them to receive care and support from their children in their old age. There are some exchange rules applied to family members and again such rules usually vary in different cultures and societies (and even in different regions and groups within the same society). In general, between generations, it is possible for the exchange to be one way over the long term, if it is somehow reciprocated in the end. For example, parents may be net 'providers' at a particular point in time due to a reasonable expectation that they may be net 'receivers' at a later date. Due to affluence brought to the parents' generations in many advanced economies, older people may possess more 'exchangeable' commodities including time, financial and real estate assets without many other competing responsibilities. In this scenario, older parents could remain as net providers for a prolonged period of time since support often flows from the wealthier generation to the less fortunate one, which evens out any inequalities.

The term 'reciprocity' implies 'equal or comparable exchange' of various kinds of resource between individuals and groups (Akiyama et al, 1997). As long as it is 'comparable' in conceptual values, different commodities such as financial resources, actual goods, time and in-kind personal and practical help, information and advice, or more symbolic expressive resources such as love and status, could be exchanged between individual family members. Exchanging different kinds of resource is quite common in some cultures, while in others exchange rules are defined in a more symmetrical pattern. The exchange of different kinds of resources such as money and affection is, for instance, quite common in Japanese families (although 'symmetrical reciprocity' is the norm between non-family members). As Akiyama and her colleagues (1997) point out, in a Japanese context, expressive resources such as love, status and affection hold high currency and broad exchangeability. The high level of, and commitment towards the provision of, long-term care by daughters-in-law has been traditionally driven by such moral values in exchange for their 'good' reputation. In contrast, the US family system prescribes 'symmetrical reciprocity' as an exchange rule. In this context, reciprocity is firmly a two-way exchange of goods and services and needs to be maintained in order to secure a good relationship even within intimate family relations (Akiyama et al, 1997). In this scenario, resources tend to be exchanged in a short space of time in order not to be indebted to others for a long time.

Although reciprocal arrangements feature strongly in intergenerational support practices, reciprocal arrangements alone do not dictate support provision in the micro-level contract. As Marshall et al (1987) argue, the nature of the caring relationship 'rests on a delicate balance between reciprocity, affection and duty'. In this context, previous research has also confirmed that reciprocity (and its affect) are not necessarily conditions for the provision of practical support to ageing parents, but instead feature significantly in the ideological construction of the caring relationship (see for example Qureshi and Walker, 1989). The degree of reciprocity may therefore vary widely from society to society, and also over time within a society.

Finally, the notion of family has changed dramatically, particularly over the past three decades in many contemporary societies. There is no longer such a thing as 'the family' – a conventional form or relations to describe this primary social unit. Instead, there is now a range of ways in which people live their lives which might be considered as families, such as cohabitation, single parenthood and stepparenthood, same-sex relationships and so on (Silva and Smart, 1999; Beck-Gernsheim, 2002; Carling et al, 2002; Williams, 2004). In other words, the concepts of family practices have moved away from the fixed boundaries of co-residence, legal marriage, blood ties, ethnicity and obligations which once defined the family. With the blurring of such boundaries, it is indeed increasingly difficult to articulate what is or is not a 'family'. Family forms and ties have become diverse, with increasingly fluid and negotiated relationships, especially when examining intimacy, care and commitments around families. In some instances, friends and neighbours also perform what might traditionally have been family roles. Today many studies on family lives and personal relationships have started to focus on more 'individualised relationships' (rather than the family as a unit), beyond the normative boundary of families (Williams, 2004).

Social policy has a role to play in family transformation. There is always a debate as to whether policy is a follower or a facilitator of such family transformation. In order to respond to changes already taking place in families, governments often introduce new policies – for example, providing services to fill a gap vacated by families or removing restrictions for non-conventional families to claim benefits and services. At the same time, new policy measures can also facilitate or even accelerate transformations of family forms and functions. Although this volume does not cover alternative social ties beyond family relations, it explores some of the newly emerging relationships such as post-divorce stepfamily relations (see Chapter Eight of this volume).

Continuity and change: new patterns of reciprocity?

The structure and function of family relations has multiple dimensions. Solidarity or conflict (and somewhere in between) in family relations are demonstrated in various ways, including financial support, structural support (providing accommodation), personal and practical support, emotional and moral support, associational support (contact among family members), consensual support (sharing opinions) and also expressive support (offering love, pride and status) (see for example Finch, 1989; Lawton et al, 1994). Indeed, within families generations exchange not only material and financial resources but also instrumental and expressive resources, although different societies have different social norms and practices and also each family or an individual tie within the family practises their own exchange mechanism. Caregiving in old age is thus just one dimension.

This chapter has already identified some of the driving forces – external opportunities and pressures – contributing to the transformation of family forms, ideologies as well as functions. Since these dimensions are interrelated but independent, strong structural and functional family relations (such as extended family living arrangements) do not necessarily indicate strong emotional ties in some families and social contexts. Neither do changes observed in one area such as residential separation of generations necessarily suggest the erosion of other spheres of family support. Urbanisation, for example, may separate family households, but it is possible that recent globalisation and advanced technologies such as discount airlines and skype calls help facilitate more frequent contact and can bring family members closer in different ways (although it is also undeniable that face-to-face contact, providing an 'opportunity structure' for interaction, tends to strengthen other aspects of solidarity; see Lawton et al, 1994). Associational, financial and expressive support, for example, can be maintained or even strengthened at a distance. Financial support gained through economic opportunity of migration can outweigh the loss of physical support in the original households in developing national contexts. Indeed, structural changes do not necessarily erode the family support network but can alter intergenerational relations.

This raises a fundamental question as to whether any new patterns of family reciprocity are emerging in national or global contexts. The evidence may not be conclusive and it is likely to be a mixed picture of continuity and change. In some developmental states, visible changes have been witnessed in areas such as the decline in co-residency and increase in female labour force participation that has helped shrink the conventional pool of informal family carers. Some case study chapters in this volume demonstrate the fragmentation of conventional relations between generations. In these scenarios, it could be argued that over time intergenerational relations are in a process of continual transformation as they respond to social and demographic change. Despite social change and the development of public policies, however, some areas of family support still remain strong and some practices are even reinforced further because of recent external pressures and the lack of alternative resources in some national contexts. Many exchanges of support in families are indeed not 'new' as, for example, grandparents, especially grandmothers, have always been involved in such exchanges. In this context, what looks like new patterns could in fact be the re-discovery or re-emphasis of existing relationships. It could also be an adaptation of culturally and institutionally ascribed norms of family relations. We return to evaluate this vital question later in Chapter Nine.

Structure of the volume

This volume offers an interdisciplinary approach to the study of intergenerational relations, drawing analysis from a wide range of expertise within and beyond social gerontology. It offers a global perspective that reflects the wide-ranging geographic locations examined. This chapter introduces the rationale and background, and sets the context for the volume. The first part of the volume (Chapters Two and Three) then reviews key theoretical and conceptual debates. The second part (Chapters Four to Eight) consists of case study chapters, and offers new insights and an understanding of exchange practices based on studies from different regions and different relationships. Many of the chapters are based on the long-standing research of the contributing authors – in particular, Chapters Three, Four, Five, Seven and Eight include original empirical/textual research.

In Chapter Two, Chris Phillipson explores the interaction between demography and globalisation. Population ageing has been a major factor influencing changes in intergenerational relations, and such a demographic shift is firmly located in broader social and economic developments, including processes associated with globalisation. By linking those two key issues together, Phillipson also examines how demographic shifts and globalisation are currently influencing the nature of intergenerational relations, and asks, are any new forms of contact and reciprocity across generations emerging within and beyond national boundaries?

In Chapter Three, Ruth Katz and Ariela Lowenstein advance analysis of two key competing theoretical debates in adult intergenerational relations – the solidarity–conflict model and the intergenerational ambivalence model. These paradigms tend to offer different conceptual lenses for understanding complex family relationships in societies that have been undergoing significant social change. Katz and Lowenstein also examine the impact of these models on well-being in later life.

The case study chapters that follow draw from a wide range of authors from various disciplines and geographic locations. Chapter Four provides a case study on migration, transnational kinship networks and intergenerational wealth transmission among Caribbean elders in the UK. Ricky Joseph provides life history accounts of Caribbean elders engaging in complex financial exchanges with kinship networks in countries of both origin and residence. These exchanges are often used to help younger family members onto the housing ladder at the start of their housing careers. However, Joseph also explores some of the issues and tensions inherent in inheritance planning made more problematic not only by the fact that properties are located across a wide geographic span, but also by the cultural desire to balance the need to preserve the 'family home'.

In Chapter Five, I examine the changing nature and patterns of East Asian practices on family support and reciprocity. I use the housing dimension to explore the flow of support, but look beyond the conventional nuclear family households to include three interrelated generations within families. I identify changing strategies and practices of family relations to cope with the wider and rapid structural changes taking place in the region. Analysis of the empirical data is focused on a comparison of two dynamic cities in East Asia – Tokyo and Shanghai.

The focus of the analysis in Chapter Six is the role of grandparents in ageing Sub-Saharan Africa. Confronted by the endemic problem of HIV/AIDS, Africa is beginning to re-discover and apply what had worked in the past in terms of building tacit intergenerational relationships in an era of globalisation. Akpovire and Choja Oduaran focus on emerging patterns of distorted family relations and their coping strategies with the 'missing generation' in the middle as a result of the HIV/AIDS epidemic. While the pandemic is decimating the region's human capital, introducing new trends in grandparenting is the main focus of this chapter.

In many societies, intergenerational relations include not only material and moral support but also spiritual and religious dimensions and they carry high currency in some cultures. Parents and grandparents are responsible for transmitting faith and religion, and in return children carry out the beliefs and practices of their ancestors. In Chapter Seven, Pascale Engelmajer and I examine such religious dimensions of intergenerational debts and obligations. We explore in particular how the religiously defined debts that children owe impact on the lives of women in Thailand. In this context, we examine the motivations and outcomes of female migration to urban areas.

In Chapter Eight, Lawrence Ganong and Marilyn Coleman examine research and clinical writing on intergenerational relations in stepfamilies. They draw on over 24 studies that they have conducted in the US about intergenerational responsibilities following divorce and remarriage, and illustrate the various ways in which reciprocity is perceived in post-divorce stepfamilies as well as other factors that influence beliefs about intergenerational transfers in stepfamilies. Although older step relationships have not been widely studied, they are increasingly important given the increases in both life spans and marital transitions in industrialised nations.

Chapter Nine concludes the volume with some reflections on policy issues, covering the debate and analysis on state–family interaction (intergenerational relations and welfare states) and identifying the themes that have emerged throughout the volume – 'are new patterns of reciprocity emerging?'.

References

Ackers, L. (1998) *Shifting spaces: Women, citizenship and migration within the European Union*, Bristol: The Policy Press.

Akiyama, H., Antonucci, T.C. and Campbell, R. (1997) 'Exchange and reciprocity among two generations of Japanese and American women', in J. Sokolovsky (ed) *The cultural context of aging: Worldwide perspectives* (2nd edn), London: Bergin & Garvey, pp 163-78.

Arber, S. and Attias-Donfut, C. (eds) (1999) *The myth of generational conflict: The family and state in ageing societies*, London and New York, NY: Routledge.

Baldassar, L., Baldock, C.V. and Wilding, R. (2007) *Families caring across borders*, London: Palgrave Macmillan.

Beck-Gernsheim, E. (2002) *Reinventing the family: In search of new lifestyles*, Cambridge: Polity Press.

Becker, H. (1999) 'Discontinuous change and generational contracts', in S. Arber and C. Attias-Donfut (eds) *The myth of generational conflict: The family and state in ageing societies*, London and New York, NY: Routledge, pp 114-32.

Bengtson, V.L. and Harootyan, R.A. (1994) *Intergenerational linkages: Hidden connections in American society*, New York, NY: Springer.

Bengtson, V.L., Rosenthal, C.J. and Burton, L.M. (1996) 'Paradoxes of families and aging', in R.H. Binstock and L.K. George (eds) *Handbook of aging and the social sciences* (4th edn), San Diego, CA: Academic Press, pp 253-82.

Bengtson, V.L., Warner Schaie, K. and Burton, L.M. (1995) *Adult intergenerational relations: Effects of societal change*, New York, NY: Springer.

Bryceson, D. and Vuorela, U. (eds) (2002) *The transnational family: New European frontiers and global networks*, Oxford: Berg.

Carling, A., Duncan, S. and Edwards, R. (eds) (2002) *Analysing families: Morality and rationality in policy and practice*, London: Routledge.

Castles, S. and Miller, M.J. (2008) *The age of migration: International population movements in the modern world* (4th edn), Basingstoke: Palgrave Macmillan.

Connidis, I.A. (2005) 'Sibling ties across time: the middle and later years', in M.L. Johnson (ed) *The Cambridge handbook of age and ageing*, Cambridge: Cambridge University Press, pp 429–36.

Connidis, I.A. and McMullin, J.A. (2002) 'Sociological ambivalence and family ties: a critical perspective', *Journal of Marriage and Family*, vol 64, pp 558–67.

Dimmock, B., Bornat, J., Peace, S. and Jones, D. (2004) 'Intergenerational relationships among stepfamilies in the UK', in S. Harper (ed) *Families in ageing societies: A multi-disciplinary approach*, Oxford: Oxford University Press, pp 82–94.

Doogan, K. (2009) *New capitalism? The transformation of work*, Cambridge: Polity Press.

Evandrou, M. and Falkingham, J. (2006) 'Will the baby-boomers be better off than their parents in retirement?', in J.A. Vincent, C. Phillipson and M. Downs, *The futures of old age*, London: Sage Publications.

Finch, J. (1989) *Family obligations and social change*, Cambridge: Polity Press.

Forrest, R. (2008) 'Globalisation and the housing asset rich: geographies, demographies and policy convoys', *Global Social Policy*, vol 8, no 2, pp 167–87.

Giddens, A. (1991) *Modernity and self-identity*, Oxford: Polity Press.

Held, D. and McGrew, A. (2003) *The global transformations reader* (2nd edn), Cambridge: Polity Press.

Hill, M. (2007) *Pensions: Policy and politics in the twenty-first century*, Bristol: The Policy Press.

Hills, J. (1996) 'Does Britain have a welfare generation?', in A. Walker (ed) *The new generational contract: Intergenerational relations, old age and welfare*, London: UCL Press, pp 56–80.

Izuhara, M. (2002) 'Care and inheritance: Japanese and English perspectives on the "generational contract"', *Ageing & Society*, vol 22, no 1, pp 61–78.

Izuhara, M. (2004) 'Negotiating family support? The "generational contract" between long-term care and inheritance', *Journal of Social Policy*, vol 33, no 4, pp 649–65.

Izuhara, M. (2009) *Housing, care and inheritance*, London: Routledge.

Izuhara, M. and Shibata, H. (2002) 'Breaking the chain of the generational contract? Japanese migration and old-age care in Britain', in D. Bryceson and U. Vuorela (eds) *The transnational family: New European frontiers and global networks*, Oxford: Berg, pp 155–69.

Kendig, H.L., Hashimoto, A. and Coppard, L.C. (eds) (1992) *Family support for the elderly: The international experience*, Oxford: Oxford University Press.

Lang, F.R. and Perrig-Chiello, P. (2005) 'Editorial to the special section on intergenerational relations', *European Journal of Ageing*, vol 2, no 3, pp 159-60.

Lawton, L., Silverstein, M. and Bengtson, V.L. (1994) 'Solidarity between generations in families', in V.L. Bengtson and R. Harootyan (eds) *Intergenerational linkages: Hidden connections in American society*, New York, NY: Springer.

Lowenstein, A. (2005) 'Global ageing and challenges to families', in M.L. Johnson (ed) *The Cambridge handbook of age and ageing*, Cambridge: Cambridge University Press, pp 403-12.

Lowenstein, A. and Bengtson, V.L. (2003) 'Challenges of global aging to families in the twenty-first century', in V.L. Bengtson and A. Lowenstein (eds) *Global aging and challenges to families*, Hawthorne, NY: Aldine de Gruyter, pp 371-9.

Marshall, V.W., Rosenthal, C. and Dacink, J. (1987) 'Older parents' expectations for filial support', *Social Justice Research*, vol 1, no 4, pp 405-24.

Qureshi, H. and Walker, A. (1989) *The caring relationships: Elderly people and their families*, Basingstoke: Macmillan.

Rossi, A.S. and Rossi, P.H. (1990) *Of human bonding: Parent–child relations across the life-course*, New York, NY: Aldine de Gruyter.

Sassen, S. (1998) *Globalization and its discontents*, New York, NY: New Press Settlements.

Silva, E.B. and Smart, C. (eds) (1999) *The new family?*, London: Sage Publications.

Vincent, J.A., Phillipson, C. and Downs, M. (eds) (2006) *The futures of old age*, London: Sage Publications.

Walker, A. (ed) (1996) *The new generational contract: Intergenerational relations, old age and welfare*, London: UCL Press.

Williams, F. (2004) *Rethinking families*, London: Calouste Gulbenkian Foundation.

TWO

Globalisation, global ageing and intergenerational change

Chris Phillipson

Introduction

Population ageing has been a major factor influencing changes in intergenerational relationships. Some of the key questions explored in research over the past two decades have concerned issues relating to generational equity, the emergence of new forms of multigenerational support, the characteristics of intergenerational solidarity and changing roles and relationships within families (Bengtson, 1993; Fokkema et al, 2008). This literature has raised important issues about changes affecting the lives of older people both within and without the sphere of family relationships. At the same time, demographic change must itself be nested in broader social and economic developments, with the processes associated with globalisation among the most important. For the purpose of this chapter, the issues for discussion can be identified at three levels: first, the characteristics associated with global ageing and the underlying changes in mortality and fertility; second, developments associated with globalisation and its impact on formal and informal relationships; and third, the influence of both on the nature of intergenerational ties, and new forms of contact and reciprocity across generations.

Following a brief overview, a summary of the key changes associated with global ageing on the one side and globalisation on the other are presented, followed by a detailed consideration of the characteristics of intergenerational ties placed within this wider context. The discussion then moves to explore links between globalisation and family change, ending with a return to assess the nature of intergenerational ties and the possibility of these contributing to conflict or cohesion in the 21st century.

Generations, ageing and globalisation

The relationship between generations and ageing raises a number of complex issues for social analysis. Bengtson and Putney (2006, p 20) make the point that: 'The problem of generations and ageing, and the resulting problems of generational succession, support, stability and change, represents one of the most enduring puzzles about social organization and behaviour'. They see the issues as threefold:

first, the problem of families or societies ensuring continuity given changes in membership through birth, ageing and generational succession; second, the question of how generations can adapt to a changing social and environmental context; third, the issue of dealing with conflicts or tensions between generations. The idea of generations has often in fact been taken as an entry point for discussions about influences on social behaviour, whether as a means of understanding political upheaval (for example Mannheim, 1952), cultural change (Gilleard and Higgs, 2005) or conflict between age groups (Foner, 2000).

Yet despite the richness of the debates, some caution is necessary at the outset. In the first place, the conceptual language surrounding that of generations is itself confusing. Hagestad and Uhlenberg (2007) highlight the fact that three types of phenomena have been assigned the term *generation*: first, *age groups* or individuals at given life stages, such as youth, adulthood and old age; second, *historical generations*, defined as birth cohorts with particular characteristics; and third, *family generations*, that is, locations in a system of ranked descent. This chapter follows Hagestad and Uhlenberg (2007) in using the last of these to define generations. The authors point out that: 'In focusing on these three, one is examining people who not only are anchored differently in dimensions of time, primarily biographical time/chronological age and historical time, but also the rhythm of family time.... A host of challenging, yet neglected issues lies in the intersection of these three phenomena' (Hagestad and Uhlenberg, 2007, pp 239-40).

An additional feature to be added is that of 'ageing', this implying movement across biological, psychological and social levels. A familiar concept for handling some of the issues here is the notion of the 'lifecourse', which itself has three levels of analysis: the *individual level* which traces changes as a consequence of the prior experiences of individuals; *collective analyses* which consider outcomes for birth cohorts of social changes experienced over the lifecourse; and *socio-cultural/symbolic analyses* which consider the lifecourse and associated transitions as socially constructed (Dannefer and Miklowski, 2006).

Finally, in this chapter the above terms are located within the conceptual language associated with globalisation, or the idea of 'nation-states ... enmeshed in and functionally part of a larger pattern of global transformations and global flows' (Held et al, 1999, p 49). The theme of globalisation became highly influential in the social sciences during the 1990s, notably in sociology and political science (Held et al, 1999), and subsequently in social policy (George and Wilding, 2002) and social gerontology (Vincent, 2006). Globalisation is now viewed as an influential force driving changes in later life, for example, through the role of international organisations influencing aspects of social policy (Estes and Phillipson, 2002) or through the impact of acceleration migration and urbanisation on family life in old age (UN-HABITAT, 2008).

The conceptual framework elaborated above will be used to examine what Hagestad and Uhlenburg (2007, p 240) refer to as a neglected question in the study of the changing age composition of populations, namely, 'the consequences of population ageing for social relationships'. This chapter gives particular emphasis to questions relating to intergenerational patterns of reciprocity and exchange, setting these within the broader context of globalisation and associated changes affecting the lifecourse. We begin first with a consideration of the demography of global ageing, highlighting relevant changes over the course of the 20th and early part of the 21st century.

Global ageing and the 'first demographic revolution'

As the broad features of population ageing are well known, they will only receive a bare summary in this chapter. In the UK, the 2001 Census showed that for the first time the number of people aged 60 and over in England and Wales was greater than the number below the age of 16. The figures among the 'oldest old' illustrate the extent of demographic change. In 1951 there were 0.2 million people aged 85 and over in the UK, a figure which had increased to 1.3 million by 2007. Populations across most of the world are ageing: the proportion of the global population aged 65 and over in 1900 was one per cent (UK: five per cent); in 2000 it was seven per cent (UK: 16 per cent); and by 2050 it is estimated that it will be 20 per cent, a figure that the UK is likely to reach in 2020 (House of Lords, 2005). Kalache et al (2005, p 30) make the point that developing countries will experience the steepest increase in the older population, at least up to the period 2050. Already over 60 per cent of the population aged 60 and over live in developing countries, increasing to around 75 per cent by 2025 and 85 per cent in 2050. Countries such as Brazil, China and Nigeria will double their absolute number of older people from the beginning of the 21st century to 2025.

The factors driving what has come to be termed 'the first demographic transition' have been declining mortality followed by declining fertility, these elements transforming the shape of populations and the generational groups within them. Fewer deaths and fewer births result in intergenerational structures less pronounced at the bottom, and much more so at the top. Horizontal ties (to siblings, cousins) are reduced in number; vertical ties are expanded (for example from grandparent to grandchild) in scope and complexity. This pattern has been strengthened by the continuing falls in mortality affecting most countries of the global North. Age-standardised mortality rates in the UK over the 40-year period 1967–2007 show declines of 38 per cent for men and 29 per cent for women (Dunnell, 2008).

Demography and changing social relationships

The above developments have increased the availability of extended intergenerational kin (Bengtson et al, 2003), with grandparents, to take one example, now more prominent within family relationships. Hagestad and Uhlenberg (2007, p 244) highlight this point with data from the US giving the number of living grandparents for 10- and 30-year-olds: the proportion of 10-year-olds with all four grandparents alive increased from six per cent in 1900 to 41 per cent in 2000; at age 30 just one per cent had between two and three grandparents alive in 1900, this increasing to 31 per cent in 2000 (see Grundy et al, 1999, for similar UK data). The co-longevity of different generations is now an important dimension of family life. A study of the first wave UK baby boom generation (that is, those born during 1945–52), using data from the English Longitudinal Study of Ageing (ELSA), found 43 per cent of those aged 50–57 still had a mother alive in 2002 (average age 79.8 years), and 20 per cent had a father alive (average age 80.7 years) (Leach et al, 2008). Multigenerational ties now occupy a considerable part of people's lives, with, for example, 40 to 50 per cent of those 80 and over in Continental and Northern European countries living in four generational groups (Kohli et al, 2005).

Evidence for what Bengtson et al (2003) refer to as 'longer years of shared lives' appears matched by the extent of contact and support across generations (see also Katz and Lowenstein, Chapter Three, this volume). Research suggests that the majority of older people remain part of a substantial kin network comprising spouses/partners, children, grandchildren and siblings (Phillipson et al, 2001). Close relationships may be more geographically dispersed but even here the extent of change can be exaggerated. A survey conducted in Britain in 1999 found that around half those aged 50+ had non-resident children living within 30 minutes' travel time (Grundy et al, 1999). Levels of interaction between older people and their children and other relatives remain extensive. A UK survey published in 2004 reported that three quarters of older people (77 per cent) saw relatives at least weekly, with around one in ten seeing relatives less than once a year (Victor et al, 2004). Fokkema et al (2008), drawing on data from the Survey of Health and Retirement in Europe (SHARE) carried out in 11 European countries, reported that '… no more than one per cent of parents had completely lost touch with their children'. Summarising the state of European families and links between parents and adult children, the same study concluded that '… the majority of European later-life families are characterised by (1) having a child nearby; (2) being in frequent contact with at least one of their children; (3) having strong family care obligations; and (4) regular exchange of help in kind from parents to children' (p 83).

Given the above findings, the first demographic transition might be said to have transformed the structure of populations (creating more living generations) but maintained existing patterns of reciprocity and support. Indeed, one argument might be that with older adults (that is, grandparents) in greater supply but with fewer grandchildren (given declining fertility), the possibilities for support across generations has never been greater. At the same time, it is important not to isolate demographic change from the social and economic structures with which it intersects. In this respect, it might be argued that in the 'first transition' exchange across generations was supported both through the *demographic capital* of increased vertical ties and through the *social capital* produced through the organisation of the lifecourse and the development of the welfare state.

For most Western societies, the period stretching from the 1950s through to the late 1970s/early 1980s produced significant changes in policies directed at older people. During these decades, with varying degrees of emphasis, responses to ageing were formed around the institutions and relationships associated with, first, state-supported public welfare; second, the institution of retirement; and third, what came to be known as the 'intergenerational contract' (Phillipson, 1998). In general terms, this period is associated with the emergence of retirement as a major social institution, buttressed by the growth of entitlements to pensions. Roles such as grandparenting emerged as part of this development, becoming an important element in the range of activities pursued following the ending of employment. Retirement, along with the development of social security and pensions, provided the basis for a reconstructed and standardised lifecourse built around what Best (1980) termed as the 'three boxes' of education, work and leisure. This arrangement was reinforced by the theme of 'intergenerational reciprocity', with older people receiving care and support as part of the 'moral economy' underpinning an extended lifecourse (Arber and Attias-Donfut, 2000). Kohli (1987, p 129) summarised this development as follows:

> It is by the creation of lifetime continuity and reciprocity that the welfare system contributes to the moral economy of the work society. This becomes especially clear when we look at retirement. The emergence of retirement has meant the emergence of old age as a distinct life phase, structurally set apart from active life and with a clear chronological boundary. But the other parts of the welfare system can be viewed in this perspective as well: as elements in the construction of a stable lifecourse, covering the gaps ('risks') that are left open by the organization of work.

The welfare state in fact played a vital role in moderating the relationship between generations. Indeed, research from the mid-1990s onwards confirmed that public transfers in no way 'crowded out' support from within the family; rather there was an element of 'crowding in', with older generations 'retaining a crucial role in distributing financial and material resources within the family' (Hoff and Tesch-Römer, 2007, p 77).

The issue now to be considered is the extent to which the structure and assumptions underpinning intergenerational reciprocity are presently being challenged. To what extent is a period of rapid globalisation transforming traditional relationships across generations? What other factors can be cited which might be interacting with the political and social forces generated by global change? To what degree are generations being redefined in the context of familial, social and global transformations?

Globalisation and family change

The argument to be explored in this section is that aspects of change already apparent among some groups of older people will become much more prominent as younger cohorts (for example the 'baby boomers') move into early old age. Three interlocking aspects of change can be identified: first, changes to family life in areas such as marriage and divorce, this leading to what some commentators have termed 'the second demographic transition'; second, the period of economic and social instability which developed from the early to late 1970s/1980s; and third, the gathering intensity of globalisation and its impact on social and family life.

The various developments affecting family life have been viewed as having equally profound consequences to those that followed the 'first demographic transition'. Writing from a North American perspective, Hughes and Waite (2007, p 179) summarise the issues as follows:

> In the last four decades, the … family has been transformed. People now marry later in life and are quite likely to cohabit prior to marriage, an almost unheard of arrangement 40 years ago. Divorce is common and much less stigmatized than in the past. A sizeable fraction of births occur to unmarried women, and many children grow up without sustained contact with their biological fathers. These changes have occurred to varying degrees in all developed nations. They are so profound that some scholars refer to them as the Second Demographic Transition, granting them the same significance as the declines in mortality and fertility that began in the 18th century and accelerated world population growth.

In the UK, these changes have been reflected in the marriage and divorce patterns of 'first wave' baby boomers, marking a distinct change from preceding cohorts. They provide early indicators of the growth of divorce and repartnering characteristic of the postwar family, with ELSA data showing 35 per cent of those born between 1945 and 1952 in a category other than 'first and only marriage' or 'widowed'; this reduces to 31 per cent and 23 per cent for those born in 1937–44 and 1929–36 respectively. First wave baby boomers also indicate a distinct break from these preceding cohorts in the proportion who have lived at some point with a partner without being married, with nearly one in five among those born during 1945–54 compared with an average of less than one in ten in the preceding cohorts (Leach et al, 2008). SHARE data, analysed by Fokkema et al (2008), highlighted the impact of these changes, and noted social class as well as demographic variables influencing contact and support within the family. The researchers found, for example, parental divorce and higher social class contributing to a weakening of parent–child ties: '… divorced single parents and the more highly educated and wealthier parents are living at a greater distance from their children and having less frequent contact and weaker feelings of family care obligations than their counterparts. Moreover, divorced mothers and fathers and parents with higher incomes are less likely to receive help in kind from their children than widows/widowers and those with low incomes, respectively' (Fokkema et al, 2008, p iv).

Hughes and Waite (2007, p 196) suggest that more recent cohorts such as the 'baby boomers' look very different from earlier ones: 'Members of later cohorts are less likely to be currently married, more likely to be living alone, and more likely to be living in a complex household. The incidence of cohabitation, multiple marriages, and non-marital childbearing and childlessness will all be greater in these cohorts than in earlier ones.... Along with these differences in family structures have come both new and altered family roles and relationships. Most importantly, these changes appear to have challenged people's ideas of what constitutes a family and what family members may or may not owe each other' (see also Chambers et al, 2009).

This change in the characteristics of *demographic capital* has been reinforced through developments in the wider social context influencing generational ties. Previously, intergenerational relations were underpinned by the notion of an institutionalised lifecourse buttressed by expectations of an expanding welfare state. From the mid-1970s, however, a number of changes can be identified arising from rising levels of unemployment and reflecting structural changes affecting the manufacturing industry. The retirement transition itself became more complex with the emergence of different pathways (for example unemployment, long-term sickness, redundancy, disability, part-time employment, self-employment) which people follow before they describe themselves or are officially defined as 'wholly retired' (Marshall et al, 2001; Chiva and Manthorpe, 2009). This period also brought instability in respect of the images and institutions associated with supporting older people. The context here was the new political economy shaping old age. This development has been variously analysed as reflecting a move from 'organised' to 'disorganised capitalism', to a shift from 'simple' to 'reflexive modernity', or to the transformation from mass assembly ('Fordist') to flexible/service-driven ('post-Fordist') economies. Lash and Urry (1987) identify the period from 1970 as marking the 'end of organised capitalism', the latter characterised by full employment and expanding welfare states (the core elements underpinning the growth of retirement). With the period of 'disorganised capitalism' comes the weakening of manufacturing industry and the creation of a 'mixed economy of welfare'. Industrial de-concentration was followed by spatial de-concentration, as people (the middle classes in particular) moved in accelerating numbers from the older industrial cities. These developments reflected what many commentators viewed as a heightened degree of instability running through capitalist social relations. Lash and Urry (1987) coined the term 'disorganised capitalism' to refer to the way in which:

> ... [the] fixed, fast-frozen relations of organized capitalist relations have been swept away. Societies are being transformed from above, from below, and from within. All that is solid about organized capitalism,

class, industry, cities, collectivity, nation state, even the world, melts
into air. (Lash and Urry, 1987, cited in Kumar, 1995, p 49)

The social problems associated with this form of capitalism became progressively
more acute with the move into economic recession towards the latter end of the
first decade of the 21st century. The key issue here is the undertow of instability
and crisis running through the system and the resulting consequences for older
workers and older people. A 'disorganised system' is one with greater job insecurity
and a deterioration in the quality of work (Green, 2005; Sennett, 2006); where
incomes at work become subject to larger fluctuations 'so that both poor and
moderately affluent people are increasingly exposed to the risk of a large ...
drop in income from one year to the next' (Solow, 2008, p 79); where companies
close their pension plans to new employees, wishing to withdraw from the
'responsibility of providing pensions' (Munnell, cited in Greenhouse, 2008); and
where governments press to 'extend working life' even while drastically reducing
the employment options available to older people (Phillipson, 2009).

Adding to this new context for intergenerational relations has been the social
and economic changes arising from globalisation. For much of the period from
the 1970s through to the 1990s, critical perspectives in gerontology focused on
national concerns about policies and provision for older people. Scholars worked
within the boundaries of the nation state in developing perspectives around issues
such as dependency and inequality in later life. The significant change over the
past five years, reflecting, as argued above, developments within core disciplines
such as politics and sociology, has been the link between critical gerontology and
broader questions arising from the pressures and upheavals associated with living
in a global world (Hutton and Giddens, 2000).

Globalisation and generational ties

In respect of intergenerational relations two important effects of globalisation
might be noted: the first relating to the economic dimension, the second arising
from international migration. On the first of these, globalisation can be said to
exert unequal and highly stratified effects on the lives of older people (Yeates,
2001; Vincent, 2006). In the developed world, the magnitude and absolute
size of expenditure on programmes for older people has made these the first
to be targeted with financial cuts (just as older people were one of the first
beneficiaries of the welfare state). An additional dimension has been the way in
which intergovernmental organisations (IGOs) feed into what has been termed
the 'crisis construction and crisis management' of policies for older people (Estes
and Associates, 2001). Bob Deacon (2000) argues that globalisation generates a
global discourse within and among global actors on the future of social policy,
especially in areas such as pensions and health and social services. Yeates (2001), for
example, observes that 'both the World Bank and IMF have been at the forefront
of attempts to foster a political climate conducive to [limiting the scope of] state

welfare ... promoting [instead] ... private and voluntary initiatives' (p 122). In fact globalisation has provided fresh impetus to transforming the financing of old age from a social to an individual responsibility. On the one side, growing old has come to be viewed as a global problem and concern; on the other side has come the individualising of risks through the lifecourse (O'Rand, 2000). These are no longer seen as requiring the collective solutions of a mature welfare state. Indeed, as Blackburn (2006, p 4) suggests, individuals and institutions have now to be 'weaned from the teat of public finance and learn how to be "responsible risk takers" ... rejecting the old forms of dependence of which the old age pension was a prime example'. Globalisation has, in fact, introduced a new paradox to the experience of ageing. Growing older seems to have become *more* secure, with longer life expectancy and the potential of enhanced life styles in old age. Set against this, the pressures associated with the achievement of security are themselves generating fresh anxieties among cohorts of all ages. The language of social insurance, established during the 1940s, appears to have been displaced in the 21st century by the 'mantra of personal responsibility' and risk taking (Hacker, 2008). The likely impact of these developments on intergenerational ties is as yet unclear, although some possible implications will be reviewed in the concluding section of this chapter.

Globalisation also influences intergenerational ties through the impact of international migration and the rise of transnational communities. Glick Schiller and her colleagues have defined transnationalism as the process by which: '... immigrants build social fields that link together their country of origin and their country of settlement. Immigrants who build such social fields are designated "transmigrants". Transmigrants develop and maintain multiple relations – familial, economic, social, organizational, religious, and political that span borders. Transmigrants take actions, make decisions, and feel concerns, and develop identities within social networks that connect them to two or more societies simultaneously' (1992, p 5).

In similar vein, Basch et al (1994, p 6) further define this relationship as follows:

> ... "transnationalism" [is] the process by which immigrants forge and sustain multi-stranded social relations that link together their societies of origin and settlement. We call these processes transnationalism to emphasize that many immigrants build social fields that cross geographic, cultural and political borders ... an essential element is the multiplicity of involvements that transmigrants sustain in home and host societies.

Transnational communities may themselves be said to reflect both the growth of a global economy and the impact of this on the construction of family and community ties. This new political economy is creating what may be described as 'global families' – these arising from the communities that emerge from international migration. A significant group comprise those who came as labour migrants (or as the wives thereof) to countries such as Britain and who have subsequently 'aged in place' (Warnes et al, 2004). Many of these, however, even among the very poor, and especially among the first generation of migrants, may return at regular intervals to their country of origin (Gardner, 1995). As a consequence, globalisation is producing a new kind of ageing in which the dynamics of family and social life may be stretched across different continents and across different types of societies.

Global migration is also producing considerable diversity in respect of the social networks within which growing old is shaped and managed. Typically, older people's networks have been examined within national borders, and their experiences of care and support assessed within this context (Phillipson, 1998). But migrants bring important variations with responsibilities that may cover considerable physical as well as cultural distances. King and Vullnetari (2006), for example, explored the impact of the mass migration of young people from Albania, notably on those older people living in rural parts of the country. They report feelings of separation and abandonment among the older generation, heightened by the realisation that their children were unlikely to return (Vullnetari and King, 2008). The Albanian case illustrates problems of maintaining ties with relatives who may have entered a destination country without having any legal position, with their 'undocumented status making it difficult for them to return' to their homeland country (Vullnetari and King, 2008, p 788).

In contrast to the above, there are numerous examples in the literature of migrants moving 'backwards and forwards' between their 'first' and 'second' homeland, subject to financial and domestic constraints. Goulbourne (1999) (see also Bauer and Thompson, 2006) highlights the 'back and forth' movement of his Caribbean families living in Britain (also see Chapter Four in this volume). Similar descriptions have been linked to first generation Bangladeshi migrants in the UK (Gardner, 2002; Phillipson et al, 2003); to Italian migrants in Perth, Western Australia (Baldassar et al, 2007); and to members of the Turkish community living in Germany (Naegele, 2008). All of this movement reflects what Christine Ho (1991) has described, in her research on Anglo-Trinidadians living in Los Angeles, as 'the concerted effort [of migrants] to sustain connections across time and geography' (p 179). The implication of these ties for changing patterns of reciprocity and support is addressed in the next section of this chapter.

This type of movement, across time and space, raises complex issues for the maintenance of intergenerational reciprocity. On the one hand, Baldassar (2007) challenges traditional assumptions that support is necessarily grounded in physical proximity between the individuals concerned. She goes on to note that: 'Empirically, the general preoccupation with geographic proximity means that very little research has been done on the relationships between ageing parents and adult children who live at a distance ..., with the result that transnational practices of care have remained largely invisible or assumed to be unfeasible' (p 276). Following this, if we recognise the different dimensions associated with care and support – practical, financial, personal, emotional and moral – then distinctive possibilities emerge for maintaining a caring relationship of one kind or another across national boundaries.

At the same time, it is important to recognise the pressures and constraints affecting families dispersed across the globe as a consequence of migration. Bauer and Thompson (2006, p 5), in their study of Jamaican migrants, suggest that there is: '… a kind of grief intrinsic in migration itself, even when made in a spirit of betterment. Some migrants for years continued to feel a general sense of loss, which they expressed in terms of feeling physically isolated. Migrant women were particularly likely to feel the absence of family and close local community at times of child birth, but sometimes men spoke of similar feelings of loss'. Baldassar (2007) suggests, however, that such feelings will vary across different groups, reflecting for example whether coming from earlier or later cohorts of migrants and the stage of the family life cycle. She studied three cohorts of migrants from Italy to Perth (Western Australia): those who left in the 1950s and 1960s; in the 1970s and 1980s; and in the 1990s. It was the intermediate group, who had migrated in the 1970s and 1980s, and who were now mostly in their fifties, who were experiencing the greatest difficulties in supporting parents in their first homeland:

> [This group] expressed the greatest concerns for ageing parents and providing care from a distance. Many have parents who can no longer speak on the phone due to dementia or who can no longer write due to disability…. Even those parents who are in good health consider visiting Perth too hazardous or are busy caring for an ailing spouse. This state of affairs generally results in this group being engaged in more intense 'distant thinking' and more frequent visits than the post-war cohort, whose parents are now deceased. Women, in particular, struggle with feelings of guilt about their inability to provide more support for their parents and to their siblings who are caring for parents. (Baldassar, 2007, p 290)

These experiences will almost certainly increase given the accelerated migration of people from rural to urban areas, this occurring across all continents of the world. The consequences of these shifts in population will be an important factor contributing to changes in the nature of support within families and generations.

Globalisation and the future of intergenerational relations

As noted at the beginning of this chapter, ideas about exchange and reciprocity continue to exert considerable force – within and beyond research into ageing. They have been especially important in the debate about intergenerational equity, and have been used to explain a number of findings from research in the area of family sociology (Arber and Attias-Donfut, 2000; Katz et al, 2003). At the same time, this approach may need some modification given a context of greater fluidity and instability in personal relationships (Chambers et al, 2009). Reciprocity in the 'risk society', as advanced by Beck (1992) and Giddens (1998), may have a different quality when compared with the 'environment of kin' (Frankenberg, 1966) into which older people's lives have traditionally been absorbed. Gouldner's (1960) view about the universality of reciprocity may still apply, but the associated mechanisms – given accelerated geographical and social mobility – are likely to produce different outcomes for kin as well as non-kin relations.

The impact of this new social environment on intergenerational ties remains somewhat uncertain. Bengtson and Putney (2006, p 21), in their review of this area, suggest that relations between age groups have indeed become more problematic, given a context of globalisation and rapid social change. Yet they suggest that intergenerational relations may be the key to resolving many of the associated problems:

> This is because the essential characteristics of multi-generational families – relatedness, interdependence and solidarity, and age integration – can influence and transform societal practices and policies and mitigate potential for conflicts between age groups. In matters of relations between generations and age, there are strong common characteristics between multigenerational families, age groups and society. A viable social contract between generations will remain a characteristic of human society in the future – at both the micro and macro levels of age group interactions.

But the possibilities for tensions and divisions should also be noted. At the micro level there is increasing fluidity as well as diversity in family life. Morgan (1999), for example, makes the point that rather than simply following established cultural principles or norms governing ways of doing and being a family, individuals are active in creating their own modes of living. These may or may not meet principles of solidarity and interdependence, but will almost certainly reflect the outcome of actions 'negotiated' (to use Finch and Mason's 1993 phrase) between family members. And the level of existing age integration can itself be over-emphasised, with studies by Uhlenberg and de Jong Gierveld (2004, p 22) suggesting 'a deficit of young adults in the networks of older people' (see further, Hagestad and Uhlenberg, 2007). At a macro level, relations between generations may come under pressure from a variety of directions. Problems with pension funding, given the long-run decline in the working population and the (at least) short-run economic recession, may lead to a re-run of debates concerning generational equity. And globalisation has the capacity to arouse more generalised fears that may themselves corrode trust between generations. Tony Judt (2008, p 20) expresses this point as follows:

> Fear is reemerging as an active ingredient of political life in Western democracies. Fear of terrorism, of course; but also and perhaps most

insidiously, fear of uncontrollable speed of change, fear of the loss of employment, fear of losing ground to others in an increasingly unequal distribution of resources, fear of losing control of the circumstances and routines of one's daily life. And, perhaps above all, fear that it is not just we who can no longer shape our lives but that those in authority have lost control as well to forces beyond their reach.

Given the above context, intergenerational relationships may be entering a period of major uncertainty and potential upheaval. Ageing populations, and the vulnerable groups within them, need the certainty of predictable incomes and services. Yet these are not yet available to the mass of older people in developing countries, and their supply appears increasingly precarious to those in the developed world. Making the intergenerational contract work to resolve these issues will be increasingly important in the years ahead. Strengthening intergenerational relations given the insecurities arising from global change remains an essential social and public policy objective.

References

Arber, S. and Attias-Donfut, C. (eds) (2000) *The myth of generational conflict: The family and state in ageing societies*, London and New York, NY: Routledge.

Baldassar, L. (2007) 'Transnational families and aged care: the mobility of care and migrancy of ageing', *Journal of Ethnic and Migration Studies*, vol 33, no 2, pp 275-97.

Basch, L., Schiller, N. and Blanc-Szanton, C. (1994) *Nations unbound: Transnational projects, post-colonial predicaments and de-territorialised nation-states*, Langhorne, PA: Gordon and Breach.

Bauer, E. and Thompson, P. (2006) *Jamaican hands across the Atlantic*, Kingston, Jamaica: Ian Randle Publishers.

Beck, U. (1992) *The risk society*, London: Sage Books.

Bengtson, V.L. (1993) 'Is the "contract across generations" changing? Effects of population aging on obligations and expectations across age groups', in V.L. Bengtson and W.A. Achenbaum (eds) *The changing contract across generations*, Hawthorne, NY: Aldine de Gruyter, pp 3-24.

Bengtson, V.L. and Putney, N.M. (2006) 'Future "conflicts" across generations and cohorts?', in J. Vincent, C. Phillipson and M. Downs (eds) *The futures of old age*, London: Sage Publications, pp 20-9.

Bengtson, V.L., Lowenstein, A., Putney, N. and Gans, D. (2003) 'Global aging and the challenge to families', in Bengtson, V.L. and Lowenstein, A. (eds) *Global aging and challenges to families*, New York: Aldine de Gruyter, pp 1-26.

Best, F. (1980) *Flexible life scheduling*, New York, NY: Praeger.

Blackburn, R. (2006) *Age shock: How finance is failing us*, London: Verso.

Chambers, P., Allan, G., Phillipson, C. and Ray, M. (2009) *Family practices in later life*, Bristol: The Policy Press.

Chiva, A. and Manthorpe, J. (eds) (2009) *Older workers in Europe*, Maidenhead: McGraw Hill.

Dannefer, D. and Miklowski, C. (2006) 'Developments in the life course', in Vincent, J., Phillipson, C. and Downs, M. *Futures of old age*, London: Sage, pp 30-40.

Deacon, B. (2000) *Globalisation and social policy: The threat to equitable welfare*, Occasional Paper No 5, GASPP (Globalism and Social Policy Programme), Geneva: UNRISD (United Nations Research Institute for Social Development).

Dunnell, K. (2008) 'Ageing and mortality in the UK: National Statistician's annual article on the population', *Population Trends*, vol 134, pp 6-23.

Estes, C. and Associates (2001) *Social policy and aging*, Thousand Oaks, CA: Sage.

Estes, C. and Phillipson, C. (2002) 'The globalisation of capital, the welfare state and old age policy', *International Journal of Health Services*, vol 32, no 2, pp 279-97.

Finch, J. and Mason, J. (1993) *Negotiating family responsibilities*, London: Routledge.

Fokkema, T., ter Bekke, S. and Dykstra, P.A. (2008) *Solidarity between parents and their adult children in Europe*, NIDI (Netherlands Interdisciplinary Demographic Institute) Report No 76, Amsterdam: KNAW Press.

Foner, A. (2000) 'Age integration or age conflict as society ages?', *The Gerontologist*, vol 40, pp 272-6.

Frankenberg, R. (1966) *Communities in Britain*, London: Penguin Books.

Gardner, K. (1995) *Global migrants, local lives*, Oxford: Oxford University Press.

Gardner, K. (2002) *Age, narrative and migration*, Oxford: Berg.

George, V. and Wilding, P. (2002) *Globalization and human welfare*, London: Palgrave.

Giddens, A. (1991) *Modernity and self-identity*, Cambridge: Polity Press.

Gilleard, C. and Higgs, P. (2005) *Contexts of ageing*, Cambridge: Polity Press.

Goulbourne, H. (1999) 'The transnational character of Caribbean kinship in Britain', in S. McRae (ed) *Changing Britain: Families and households in the 1990s*, Oxford: Oxford University Press, pp 176-99.

Gouldner, A. (1960) 'The norm of reciprocity: a preliminary statement', *American Sociological Review*, vol 25, no 2, pp 161-78.

Green, F. (2005) *Understanding trends in job satisfaction: final report*, Report to the Economic and Social Research Council (ESRC), Swindon: ESRC.

Greenhouse, S. (2008) *The big squeeze: Tough times for the American worker*, New York, NY: Knopf.

Grundy, E., Murphy, M. and Shelton, N. (1999) 'Looking beyond the household: intergenerational perspectives on living kin and contacts with kin in Great Britain', *Population Trends*, vol 97, pp 19-27.

Hacker, J. (2008) *The great risk shift*, New York, NY: Oxford University Press.

Hagestad, G. and Uhlenburg, P. (2007) 'The impact of demographic changes on relations between age groups and generations: a comparative perspective', in K.W. Schaie and P. Uhlenburg (eds) *Social structures: Demographic change and the well-being of older adults*, New York, NY: Springer, pp 239-61.

Held, D., McGrew, A., Goldblatt, D. and Perraton, J. (1999) *Global transformations*, Oxford: Polity Press.

Ho, C. (1991) *Salt-water trinnies: Afro-Trinidadian immigrant networks and non-assimilation in Los Angeles*, New York, NY: AMS Press Inc.

Hoff, A. and Tesch-Römer, C. (2007) 'Family relations and aging: substantial changes since the middle of the last century', in H.-W. Wahl, C. Tesch-Römer and A. Hoff (eds) *New dynamics in old age: Individual, environmental and societal perspectives*, New York, NY: Baywood Publishing Company, Inc, pp 65-84.

House of Lords (2005) *Ageing: Scientific aspects, vol 1*, First Report of Session 2005–06, London: The Stationery Office.

Hughes, M.E. and Waite, L. (2007) 'The aging of the second demographic transition', in K.W. Schaie and P. Uhlenburg (eds) *Social structures: Demographic change and the well-being of older adults*, New York, NY: Springer, pp 179-212.

Hutton, W. and Giddens, A. (eds) (2000) *On the edge: Living with global capitalism*, London: Jonathan Cape.

Judt, T. (2008) *Postwar: A history of Europe since 1945*, London: Heinemann.

Kalache, A., Barreto, S. and Keller, I. (2005) 'Global ageing: the demographic revolution in all cultures and societies', in M. Johnson, in association with V. Bengtson, P. Coleman and T. Kirkwood (eds) *The Cambridge handbook of age and ageing*, Cambridge: Cambridge University Press, pp 30-46.

Katz, R., Daatland, S.O., Lowenstein, A., Bazo, M.T., Ancizu, I., Herlofston, K., Mehlausen-Hassoen, D. and Prilutzky, D. (2003) 'Family norms and preferences in intergenerational relations: a comparative perspective', in V.L. Bengtson and A. Lowenstein (eds) *Global aging and challenges to families*, Hawthorne, NY: Aldine de Gruyter, pp 305-26.

King, R. and Vullnetari, J. (2006) 'Orphan pensioners and migrating grandparents: the impact of mass migration on older people', *Ageing and Society*, vol 26, pp 783-816.

Kohli, M. (1987) 'Retirement and the moral economy: an historical interpretation of the German case', *Journal of Aging Studies*, vol 1, pp 125-44.

Kohli, M., Künemund, H. and Lüdicke, J. (2005) 'Family structure, proximity and contact', in A. Börsch-Supan, A. Brugiviavini, H. Jürges, J. Mackenbach, J. Siegrist and G. Weber (eds) *Health, ageing and retirement in Europe: First results from the Survey of Health and Retirement in Europe*, Mannheim, Germany: MEA.

Kumar, K. (1995) *From post-industrial to post-modern society*, Oxford: Basil Blackwell.

Lash, S. and Urry, J. (1987) *The end of organised capitalism*, Cambridge: Polity Press.

Leach, R., Phillipson, C., Biggs, S. and Money, A. (2008) 'Sociological perspectives on the baby boomers: an exploration of social change', *Quality in Ageing*, vol 9, pp 19-26.

Mannheim, K. (1952) 'The problem of generations', *Essays on the sociology of knowledge*, London: Routledge and Kegan Paul.

Marshall, V., Heinz, W., Krüger, H. and Verma, A. (eds) (2001) *Reconstructing work and the lifecourse*, Toronto, Canada: University of Toronto Press.

Morgan, D.H.J. (1999) 'Risk and family practices: accounting for change and fluidity in family life', in E. Silva and C. Smart (eds) *The new family?*, London: Sage, pp 13-30.

Naegele, G. (2008) 'Age and migration in Germany: an overview with a special consideration of the Turkish population', Paper to the 56th Snnual Scientific Meeting of the Gerontological Society of America, Washington, DC.

O'Rand, A.M. (2000) 'Risk, rationality and modernity: social policy and the aging self', in K.W. Schaie, *Social structures and aging*, New York, NY: Springer, pp 225-49.

Phillipson, C. (1998) *Reconstructing old age*, London: Sage Publications.

Phillipson, C. (2009) 'Pensions in crisis: aging and inequality in a global age', in L. Rogne, C. Estes, B. Grossman, B. Hollister and E. Solway (eds) *Social insurance and social justice*, New York, NY: Springer, pp 319-40.

Phillipson, C., Ahmed, N. and Latimer, J. (2003) *Women in transition: A study of the experiences of Bangladeshi women living in Tower Hamlets*, Bristol: The Policy Press.

Phillipson, C., Bernard, M., Phillips, J. and Ogg, J. (2001) *The family and community life of older people*, London: Routledge.

Schiller, N.G., Basch, L. and Blanc-Szanton, C. (1992) *Towards a transnational perspective on migration, class, ethnicity and nationalism*, New York, NY: New York Academy of Sciences.

Sennett, R. (2006) *The culture of the new capitalism*, Yale: Yale University Press.

Solow, R. (2008) 'Trapped in the new "You're on your own" world', *The New York Review of Books*, vol LV, no 18, pp 79-81.

Uhlenberg, P. and de Jong Gierveld, J. (2004) 'Age segregation in later life: an examination of personal networks', *Ageing and Society*, vol 24, no 1, pp 5-28.

UN–HABITAT (2008) *State of the world's cities 2008/2009*, London: Earthscan.

Victor, C.R., Scrambler, S., Bond, J. and Bowling, A. (2004) 'Loneliness in later life: preliminary findings from the Growing Older Project', in A. Walker and C. Hennessey (eds) *Quality of life in old age*, Maidenhead: Open University Press, pp 107-26.

Vincent, J. (2006) 'Globalization and critical theory: political economy of world population issues', in J. Baars, D. Dannefer, C. Phillipson and A. Walker (eds) *Aging, globalization and inequality: The new critical gerontology*, Amityville, NY: Baywood Publishing Company, Inc, pp 245-72.

Vullnetari, J. and King, R. (2008) '"Does your granny eat grass?" On mass migration, care drain and the fate of older people in rural Albania', *Global Networks*, vol 8, no 2, pp 139-71.

Warnes, A.M., Freidrich, K., Kellaher, L. and Torres, S. (2004) 'The diversity and welfare of older migrants in Europe', *Ageing and Society*, vol 24, no 3, pp 307-26.

Yeates, N. (2001) *Glabalization and social policy*, London: Sage.

THREE

Theoretical perspectives on intergenerational solidarity, conflict and ambivalence

Ruth Katz and Ariela Lowenstein

Introduction

The aim of this chapter is to highlight the development of the conceptual and theoretical bases on which the intergenerational solidarity–conflict and ambivalence paradigms were shaped. Further analysis of the two paradigms can provide insight for understanding the complex social phenomenon of intergenerational family relations in later life. In this chapter we will address and analyse the two models and discuss empirical evidence regarding their impact on quality of life, based on OASIS[1] (Old Age and Autonomy: The Role of Service Systems and Intergenerational Family Solidarity).

Changes in the structure of society caused by global ageing (Kinsella, 2000), and new ideologies, resulted in changed family structures and patterns of behaviour. Some scholars perceived disengagement and isolation from the large family as adaptive and functional strategies, not only for the young but for the older generation as well (Ogburn, 1938; Sussman, 1991). However, most studies of intergenerational family relationships revealed that adult children were not isolated from their parents but frequently interacted with them and exchanged assistance, even when separated by large geographic distances (Silverstein and Bengtson, 1997; Katz et al, 2005). The strength of obligation and positive regard across generations was hardly diminished by geographic separation.

Family sociologists showed that the extended family maintains cross-generational cohesion through modern communications and transportation. It became clear that the family, and not the welfare system, continues to take responsibility and provides most of the care for older parents (Abel, 1991; Lowenstein et al, 2008). Data from cross-national studies (for example OASIS, SHARE [Survey of Health and Retirement in Europe], VOC [Value of Children]) indicate that family relations and exchange of support between family generations is still strong but may seek other expressions when circumstances change (Silverstein and Bengtson, 1997; Boersch-Supan et al, 2005; Katz et al, 2005; Lowenstein and Daatland, 2006; Lowenstein, 2007).

Burgess (1926) defined the family as a 'unity of interacting personalities' (p 3). Bourdieu's (1996) perspective on the family was based on the central theme of capital and habitus, focusing on intergenerational transmission of different types of capital, referring to three types – economic, social and cultural: economic – income and inheritance; social – knowledge and specific identities of individuals; and cultural – embodied cultural capital – the legitimation for preferences, practices and behaviours based on past experiences within the family. He characterises the family as a specific objective and subjective social unit that organises the way individual family members from different generations perceive social reality. Attias-Donfut and Wolff (2005), Arber and Attias-Donfut (1999) and Kohli (2007) introduced the need to define a generation with regard to both society and the family (the lineage position). The sequence of generations in the family directly conditions the position of the individual in economic, political and cultural spheres (Biggs and Lowenstein, forthcoming).

Several theoretical paradigms were advanced to capture the complexity and multifaceted nature of intergenerational family relations in later life. A central paradigm during the past four decades has been the intergenerational solidarity paradigm that guided much of the research on the topic. In this chapter we will describe and analyse the roots and development of this paradigm, looking at its transformation to the solidarity–conflict paradigm, as well as to the recently renewed and challenging model of intergenerational ambivalence. Finally, we will examine the association between the components' paradigms and the quality of life of older people.

Theoretical traditions

The historical background outlined above provides the context for the development of the intergenerational solidarity framework. Lowenstein et al (2001) described the development of the solidarity paradigm and introduced the contrasting perspectives of conflict and ambivalence. This part of the chapter is based on that review.

The solidarity model first proposed in the 1970s is a comprehensive scheme for describing sentiments, behaviours and attitudes in parent–child and other family relationships (Roberts et al, 1991). The first attempt to use and develop the model was by Bengtson, Olander and Haddad (1976), followed by others (for example Atkinson et al, 1986; Rossi and Rossi, 1990). The term 'solidarity' itself reflects various theoretical traditions, including (1) classical theories of social organisation; (2) the social psychology of group dynamics; and (3) the developmental perspective in family theory (Bengtson and Roberts, 1991). This theoretical background, which shaped the perspective of the intergenerational solidarity concept, is reviewed below.

Classical theories of social organisation

Understanding the nature of the bonds that create cohesion between individuals has long occupied sociology researchers. Durkheim (1933) made an important distinction between two types of solidarity. The first, which he termed 'mechanical solidarity', refers to traditional family cohesion that characterised ties between individuals in the pre-industrial revolution era that was based on internalisation and endorsement of traditional norms and customs. This type of bond, he held, was weakened by industrial society and was replaced by 'organic solidarity', which was typified by mutual dependence of individuals, as imposed by their relations to the division of labour. The differences between traditional and industrial societies, in Durkheim's view, form the basic normative solidarity that leads to cohesion. Parsons (1973) contributed to this by suggesting that several types of solidarity can exist simultaneously in various social interactions.

The central contribution of the classical sociological theories to later models of solidarity lay therefore in describing the relevant bases of group solidarity: normative perceptions internalised by group members, functional interdependencies among group members and consensus between members over rules of exchange (Roberts et al, 1991).

Social psychology of group dynamics

Research on group dynamics includes a cogent theoretical taxonomy of the elements of group solidarity developed by Homans (1950) and expanded by Heider (1958) and by McChesney and Bengtson (1988). Homans identified four components of group solidarity: (1) interactions between group members (based on functional interdependence as described by Durkheim [1933] in organic solidarity conception); (2) extensive activity involving group members; (3) the affective dimension – sentiment – between members of the group; and (4) norms. The more cohesive the group, the more its members interact, like each other and share similar normative commitments to group activities (Roberts et al, 1991). Heider (1958), expanding this theory, emphasised the importance of 'contact' and 'liking', and added the component 'similarity'.

The social exchange framework was applied as a starting point for explanations of parent–adult child relationships characterised by multidimensional resources, costs and benefits, emotional and financial exchanges (Hogan et al, 1993; Dwyer et al, 1994). The basic assumption underlying much of the research collectively known as exchange theory is that interaction between individuals or collectivities can be characterised as attempts to maximise rewards (both material and non-material). Drawing on economic cost-benefit models of social participation, Thilbaut and Kelley (1959), Homans (1961) and Blau (1964) expanded this perception into a view of social behaviour as an exchange. As in economic exchange, the profit that the individual derives from social exchange is equivalent to the difference between rewards and costs (Homans, 1961). Participants in a behavioural exchange will continue their exchange only so long as the exchange is perceived as being more rewarding than it is costly. Power resides implicitly in the dependence of the other. If both parties in the exchange relationships are equally dependent on each other, the relationship is considered balanced. When the exchange relations are unbalanced, the exchange partner who is the more dependent – hence the less powerful – will attempt to rebalance the relationship and thereby reduce the costs he/she incurs from the exchange. The relationship can be balanced in one of four possible ways: withdrawal, extension of power network, emergence of status and coalition formation (Emerson, 1962).

Dowd (1975) and Bengtson and Dowd (1981), using exchange theory to explain the decrease in social interaction and activity with age, maintained that withdrawal and social isolation are not the result of system needs or individual choice, but rather of an unequal exchange process between older people and other members of society. The shift in opportunities, roles and skills that accompanies advancing age typically leaves older people with fewer resources with which to exert power in their social relationships, and their status declines accordingly (Hendricks, 1995).

The intergenerational solidarity framework integrates exchange theory, suggesting that individuals with resources to exchange are those who can provide various types of help and support, while the recipients of help and support are made dependent on the providers, thereby weakening their power in the relationship (Hirdes and Strain, 1995). The family members who provide more assistance than they receive may perceive the supportive exchange as less desirable over time. In turn, the family member receiving assistance may want to avoid feeling dependent on the support provider and may seek to reciprocate with other forms of assistance, such as emotional support or advice, thus 'balancing' the support exchange in an effort to reciprocate (Parrott and Bengtson, 1999).

The contribution of social psychologists to the development of the intergenerational solidarity paradigm is in extending the classic definition of consensus over rules of exchange to incorporate the notion of similarity among members of the group. Combining the classical and the social psychological definitions of family solidarity, five elements may be identified: normative integration, functional interdependence, similarity or consensus, mutual affection and interaction.

Family sociology approaches

The conceptual development of the intergenerational solidarity paradigm has been highly influenced by the classical and social psychological approaches (Roberts et al, 1991). Early research in family studies described solidarity in terms of family integration, which was variously defined as involving common interests, affection and interdependence (McChesney and Bengtson, 1988).

In the 1960s, when interest in defining and measuring the components of intergenerational solidarity emerged (for example Rogers and Sebald, 1962; Strauss, 1964), a conceptual framework was proposed (Nye and Rushing, 1969) in which findings from both previous and future research could be integrated. Predicated on the conception of the family as an integrative structure, it included many of the components that were identified in the classical sociological and psychological traditions, positing six dimensions of family cohesion to be developed and measured: associational integration, affectual integration, consensual integration, functional integration, normative integration and goal integration.

Bengtson and Schrader (1982), refining these components, defined intergenerational solidarity as a multidimensional structure with six elements: associational solidarity, affectual solidarity, consensual solidarity, functional solidarity, normative solidarity and intergenerational family structure. Table 3.1 summarises the theoretical bases that contributed to the development of the intergenerational solidarity paradigm.

Table 3.1: Development of theoretical bases contributing to family cohesion

Classic sociological theories	Social psychology	Family sociology approach
Mechanical solidarity (normative) Organic solidarity (functional) Consensus over rules of exchange *Durkheim (1933)*	Interactions Activity Affection Norms *Homans (1950)*	Structural integration Affectual integration Consensual integration Functional integration Normative integration Goal integration *Nye and Rushing (1969)*
Possible existence of several forms of solidarity simultaneously *Parsons (1973)*	Similarity (consensus) Sentiment *Heider (1958)*	Associational solidarity Affectual solidarity Consensual solidarity Functional solidarity Normative solidarity Structural solidarity *Bengtson and Schrader (1982)*

The intergenerational solidarity paradigm for understanding family relationships in later life emerged from these theories as a response to concern about the isolation of the nuclear family. Based on the classical theories of social organisation, the social psychology of group dynamics and the developmental perspective in family theory, research on solidarity between generations codified six principal dimensions (Bengtson and Schrader, 1982; Roberts et al, 1991). The building blocks of solidarity included emotional cohesion (affect), social contact (association), geographic distance (structure), supportive behaviours (function), filial obligations (norms) and attitudinal agreement (consensus). Later works used this basis in examining interrelationships of the elements and the contribution of each to family solidarity.

Six elements of the intergenerational solidarity paradigm

The six components of the intergenerational solidarity framework reflect behavioural, affectual, cognitive and structural dimensions of the larger family, as outlined in Table 3.2.

Table 3.2: The six elements of intergenerational solidarity with nominal definitions and examples of empirical indicators

Construct	Nominal definition	Empirical indicators
Associational solidarity	Frequency and patterns of interaction in various types of activities in which family members engage	1. Frequency of intergenerational interaction (ie, face-to-face, telephone, mail) 2. Types of common activities shared (ie, recreation, special occasions, etc)
Affectual solidarity	Type and degree of positive sentiments held about family members, and the degree of reciprocity of these sentiments	1. Ratings of affection, warmth, closeness, understanding, trust, respect, etc, for family members 2. Ratings of perceived reciprocity in positive sentiments among family members
Consensual solidarity	Degree of agreement on values, attitudes and beliefs among family members	1. Intrafamilial concordance among individual measures of specific values, attitudes and beliefs 2. Ratings of perceived similarity with other family members in values, attitudes and beliefs
Functional solidarity	Degree of helping and exchange of resources	1. Frequency of intergenerational exchange of assistance (eg, financial, physical, emotional) 2. Ratings of reciprocity in the intergenerational exchange of resources
Normative solidarity	Strength of commitment to performance of familial roles and to meeting familial obligations (familism)	1. Ratings of importance of family and intergenerational roles 2. Ratings of strength of filial obligations
Structural solidarity	Opportunity structure for intergenerational relationships reflected in number, type and geographic proximity of family member	1. Residential propinquity of family members 2. Number of family members 3. Health of family members

Source: Adapted from Bengtson and Schrader (1982); McChesney and Bengtson (1988)

Interrelationships of its elements

Classic sociological theories assumed the possibility of opposed elements of solidarity (for example Durkheim's distinction between organic and mechanic solidarity). In the literature of social psychology, both Homans (1950) and Heider (1958) held that affection, association and consensus are related. Heider suggested that similarity (consensus) and contact (association) reflect mutual affection. Hence, higher rates of consensus and association predict higher rates of affection (Roberts et al, 1991).

The first attempt to construct a model of intergenerational solidarity (Bengtson et al, 1976) was based on and expanded by Heider's perception of the three elements of affection, association and consensus as interrelated and positively correlated to such solidarity. However, two empirical tests (Atkinson et al, 1986; Roberts and Bengtson, 1990) failed to support the model's central proposition that the three elements are interdependent (for example feelings of affection, association and consensus between parents and their adult children mutually strengthened intergenerational solidarity).

Research by Bengtson and Roberts (1991) found a moderate to high correlation between affectual solidarity and associational solidarity, but consensual solidarity was found to be independent of any interdependence with the other two elements. Mangen and McChesney (1988) found a high correlation between associational, functional and structural solidarity, but a low correlation between these three elements and affectual solidarity. Moreover, they found no correlation between affection, proximity and exchange of help.

A new effort to create a model for intergenerational solidarity predicted that (1) high rates of normative solidarity will lead to high rates of affectual solidarity, associational solidarity and exchange, and (2) high rates of normative solidarity will result in strategies that parents and adult children will develop to overcome negative attitudes and conflicts in their lives and maintain affectual solidarity, association and exchange (Bengtson and Roberts, 1991). The model assumed that high rates of affectual solidarity would lead to high rates of associational solidarity (Schulman, 1975), but that some components of structural solidarity would either facilitate or hinder mutual activities and exchange (Sussman, 1965).

Rossi and Rossi (1990) developed yet another intergenerational solidarity model, in which the component of consensus between parents and adult children was not independent, but was expected to lead to higher rates of affectual solidarity. Normative solidarity in this model was associated with rates of association and exchange, but was not expected to lead to higher rates of affectual solidarity.

Research findings supported the assumption that norms, affective feelings and structural situations influence associational solidarity and exchange. Positive relations were found between rates of subjective agreement regarding values and rates of affectual solidarity. Affectual solidarity directly influenced intergenerational exchange relations.

Silverstein and Bengtson (1997), examining the structure of intergenerational relations based on three dimensions – affectual solidarity, structural solidarity and functional solidarity – found, inter alia, that the use of these three dimensions improved the ability of describing the entire range of family cohesion in comparison to using the six original dimensions codified by Bengtson and

Roberts (1991). The model has reflected statistically independent components that divide substantially into two general dimensions: (1) structural–behavioural (associational solidarity, functional solidarity and structural solidarity); and (2) cognitive–affective (affectual, consensus and normative solidarity) (Bengtson and Roberts, 1991; Silverstein and Bengtson, 1997).

Significance of the paradigm

Intergenerational solidarity is viewed as an important component in family relations, especially for successful coping and social integration in old age (McChesney and Bengtson, 1988; Silverstein and Bengtson, 1991). The existence or absence of intergenerational solidarity affects the individual's self-esteem and psychological well-being and the giving and receiving of help and support. Intergenerational relationships generally contribute to the psychological well-being of the individual throughout his/her lifecourse (Bachman, 1982; Roberts and Bengtson, 1988; Rossi and Rossi, 1990).

Research has demonstrated several advantages of the model. It focuses on family cohesion as an important component of family relations, particularly for enhancing psychological well-being in old age (Silverstein and Bengtson, 1994) and even increasing longevity (Silverstein and Bengtson, 1991). The model emphasises that intergenerational relations are multidimensional (Silverstein and Bengtson, 1997). It has been widely used to study variations in parent–adult child relations in various ethnic groups (for example Kauh, 1997), in multicultural societies (Katz, 2009) and in cross-national contexts (for example Lowenstein and Ogg, 2003).

Studies of the effect of family solidarity on coping with situations of crisis have revealed that higher family solidarity contributes to better adjustment in crisis like widowhood or immigration (Silverstein and Bengtson, 1991; Katz and Lowenstein, 1999). Negative effects of intergenerational solidarity, however, were found in several studies. High family solidarity created heavy demands in time and family resources in families of low economic status (Belle, 1986). In other families, too, much affinity suppressed feelings of individuality (Minuchin, 1974; Beavers, 1982).

The conceptual framework of intergenerational solidarity represents one of several enduring attempts in family sociology to examine and develop a theory of family cohesion (Mancini and Blieszner, 1989). The paradigm is a comprehensive scheme for describing sentiments, behaviours, attitudes, values and structural arrangements in parent–child relationships and has guided much of the research on adult intergenerational relationships over the past three decades of the last century (for example Atkinson et al, 1986; Rossi and Rossi, 1990; Lee et al, 1994; Starrels et al, 1995).

Two notable advantages stand out in this conceptual framework as used in research: (1) measures based on the dimensions of solidarity provide a reliable and valid instrument to evaluate the strength of family relationships; and (2) the structure of intergenerational solidarity is wide enough to include extant latent forms of solidarity. Although the solidarity paradigm became the 'gold standard' for assessing intergenerational relations, its component dimensions were not indicative of a unitary construct (Atkinson et al, 1986; Roberts and Bengtson, 1990).

Intergenerational conflict and ambivalence

Some scholars have criticised the overly positive and consensual bias of the solidarity perspective. Research within the solidarity framework typically assumes that individuals' personal feelings such as affection, attraction and warmth serve to maintain cohesion in the family system (Sprey, 1991). The very term 'solidarity' implies an emphasis on consensus among family members (Marshall et al, 1993). Negative aspects of family life are interpreted in this view as an absence of solidarity (Lowenstein, 2007). Research along these lines has tended to emphasise shared values across generations, normative obligations to provide help and enduring ties between parents and children (Luescher and Pillemer, 1998). The concept of intergenerational solidarity contains normative implications that easily lend themselves to idealisation (Luescher, 1999). Based on empirical findings, as well as on changes that occurred in family relations and patterns in different cultures, scholars observed and emphasised additional aspects of intergenerational relationships: conflictual relationships and relationships that reflect ambivalence.

Continuing efforts to refine the construct validity of solidarity resulted in the inclusion of conflict as a principle dimension (Clarke et al, 1999), leading to questions of whether conflict was the antithesis of affection (that is, high conflict implied the absence of affection) or an independent construct. Still this begged the question of whether intergenerational relationships that were both emotionally close and conflicted (or emotionally distant with little conflict) were meaningful and empirically discernable types within the solidarity design. This impasse was bridged by parallel conceptual and empirical developments brought about by the integration of conflict within a more general approach to social cohesion, renewed interest in the concept of ambivalence and the use of person-centred approaches to study intergenerational relationships.

Conflict perspective

Conflict has long been considered intrinsic to social relationships, but became formally integrated within mainstream sociological thought with Georg Simmel's classic essay on social conflict, and later in Coser's reappraisal of Simmel (Coser, 1956). Both Simmel and Coser reasoned that conflict might serve an integrative function in intimate social relationships and be important to their successful maintenance. As Simmel (1955, p 19) noted, conflict may be the 'only means for making life with actually unbearable people at least possible'.

In his work *The origin of the family, private property and the state*, Engels (1884/1972) was the first to relate the terms 'family' and 'conflict', while discussing conflicts between genders. This approach, however, was seldom used as a conceptual framework in family studies in general, and in intergenerational relations in particular (Marshall et al, 1993; Clarke et al, 1999). The main argument against applying the conflict theory to family research was that the conception of human interactions as a series of conflicts, as Karl Marx viewed it (Gollnik, 1990), is applicable to the macro sociological level but not to the micro level, where affect motivates human behaviour. Farrington and Chertok (1993), however, argue that being conflicted by nature, the individual interacts in a similar way in society and within the family. They also point out that in Freud's psychoanalysis approach conflict is integrated as a part of the intrapsychic process. Thus, studying the family based on the conflict approach enables the simultaneous exploration of processes in the family and its environment (Farrington and Chertok, 1993).

Clarke et al (1999) note that research on later-life family relationships has not adequately addressed questions about conflict. One of the reasons is that conflicts in later-life families are often perceived as relatively unimportant, particularly when compared to levels of conflict reported earlier in the family lifecourse. Related to this is the fact that parents' reports of their relationships with their children tend to be more positive than their children's reports, at all stages of the lifecourse (Giarrusso et al, 1995). Clarke et al's (1999) work, however, revealed that two thirds of parents and children in the sample reported strife in their relationships.

Conflict theory views the 'superstructure' as containing religious, moral, legal and familial values which are created, implemented and modified in accordance with the vested interests of those in control of the economy. Theorists in this tradition maintain that a capitalistic economy makes each family responsible for providing for its own members, and that the levels and intensities of family violence, when observed, are directly associated with social stress (Gelles, 1980; Witt, 1987). In terms of gender, Lehr (1984) found that women's conflicts tended to be over family matters while men tended to have less frequent conflicts, and those were related to occupation, leisure time or political events.

Conflict theory focuses on isolation, caregiver stress, family problems and abuse. Straus (1979) notes that conflict has been used to describe three different phenomena in analyses of family interaction and violence: (1) the collision of individuals' agendas and interests; (2) individuals' tactics or responses to conflict of interest; and (3) hostility toward others.

Several studies, especially in the area of caregiving, show that the ability of the family to cope with conflicts arising from caregiving responsibilities affect the quality of the care provided, and the quality of relations between the caregiver and the care receiver (Merrill, 1996; Lieberman and Fisher, 1999). Studies on family relations, caregiving and well-being of family members living in multigenerational households also present the issue of family conflict (Strawbridge and Wallhagen, 1991; Montgomery and Kosloski, 1994; Brody et al, 1995; Pruchno et al, 1997; Lowenstein and Katz, 2000). Findings by Webster and Herzog (1995) reveal that memories of early family conflict have an enduring effect on family relations, and frustration and conflict over parental favoritism has been shown to predict the quality of adult children's bonds with their parents (Bedford, 1992).

The family solidarity paradigm was modified to become the 'family solidarity–conflict' model, which incorporates conflict and considers the possible negative effects of too much solidarity (Silverstein et al, 1996). Since 1985, the Longitudinal Study of Generations (LSOG) included conflict items, which have continued to appear in the survey. Thus, Bengtson and others have incorporated conflict into the study of intergenerational family relations, arguing that as a normative aspect of these relations it is likely to influence the perception of the relationship, and the willingness of family members to assist each other. Conflict, however, also allows for resolving issues, thereby enhancing the overall quality of the relationship rather than harming it, and should actually be integrated into the intergenerational solidarity framework (Parrott and Bengtson, 1999). However, these two dimensions of solidarity and conflict do not represent a single continuum, from high solidarity to high conflict. Rather, intergenerational solidarity can exhibit both high solidarity and high conflict, or low solidarity and low conflict, depending on family dynamics and circumstances (Bengtson et al, 2000). Their view is related to the basic assumption inherent in conflict theory, that conflict is natural and inevitable to all human life. Social interaction, such as experienced within family units, always involves both harmony and conflict; groups cannot exist in total harmony, or they would be completely static (Klein and White, 1996).

In formulating the 'family solidarity–conflict' model, Bengtson and Silverstein joined a group of contemporary theorists of ageing who view conflictual relations as an important element in understanding ageing as part of a system of age stratification, where relations between different age groups are not only based on norms of reciprocity or equality of exchange. There are conflicts between generations over resources such as access to labour markets, income and occupational prestige. Given this conflict of interests between young and old, within the setting of an impersonal, highly differentiated society with an emphasis on young and new occupations, older people are eventually pushed out of the labour market (Turner, 1999).

These revisions of the solidarity model, which was developed as an inductive approach, exemplify the scientific process of theory building that aspires to build cumulative knowledge and uses empirical testing as a means of assessing the utility of a model or theory (Katz et al, 2005). Currently, Bengtson et al (2005) advocate multidimensional typologies based on the solidarity and conflict dimensions.

Ambivalence perspective

Modernity is characterised by the depth and pervasiveness of a 'dilemmatic' attitude, namely structural contradictions built into societal organisations that result in cognitive dilemmas at the common sense and ideological levels (Billing et al, 1988). Weigert (1991) speaks of modernity in terms of pluralism and multivalence. People born into a slow-changing traditional society based on clear kinship roles, with authoritative cultural rules and shared religious rituals, know what to feel, how to define it, how to display it and to whom. On the other hand, people positioned in a multiverse of intersecting circles of roles and rituals are faced with the task of arranging feelings into a meaningful whole. People in modern developed societies face a characteristically modern dilemma: the ambiguity of competing meanings and the ambivalence of conflicting feelings.

Sigmund Freud (1913/1964) used ambivalence to interpret the psychodynamics between son and father within reconstructed family dramas. In later writings, Freud widened ambivalence to interpret large-scale cultural phenomena as well as interpersonal dynamics, such as client–therapist relations. Psychologists view ambivalence technically in terms of 'cathexis' in which positive and negative feelings toward an object are present simultaneously. A person who is ambivalent is torn between conflicting feelings, desires or alternatives for action (Murray and Kluckhohn, 1959).

In interaction with people of different opinions, there is some evidence that ambivalent attitudes lead to over-reaction. These reactions suggest that the ambivalent condition is stressful and motivates search for resolution through a variety of responses: punitive (Katz, 1981), joking (Coser, 1966), counter-cultural (Yinger, 1982), religious (Otto, 1985) or 'normally neurotic' (Putney and Putney, 1972).

Based on the conceptual force of ambivalence presented by Freud, sociological ambivalence was given its classic formulation in an article by Merton and Barber (1963). In their view, sociological ambivalence focuses on incompatible normative expectations of attitudes, beliefs and behaviour. These incompatible expectations may be assigned to or incorporated into a particular status within a society or even within a single role of a single status. In his expansion of Merton and Barber's argument, Coser (1966) notes that sociological ambivalence is built into the structure of statuses and roles. Coser (1956, p 64) elaborated that 'converging and diverging motivations may be so commingled in the actual relationship that they can be separated only for classificatory or analytical purposes, while the relationship actually has a unitary character *sui generis*'. Merton's sociological analyses (1976) suggest that ambivalence can result from contradictory normative expectations within a role, role set or status, and that it can be functional for the social system within which it occurs.

Postmodernism and feminist theories of the family have the potential to capture the sociological ambivalence (Luescher and Pillemer, 1998). In Stacey's (1990) explicitly postmodern perspective, contemporary family relationships are diverse, fluid and unresolved. Feminist theory challenges the assumption that a harmony of interests exists among all members of the family. Evidence of sociological ambivalence comes, for example, from the feminist literature on household division of labour (Thorne, 1992) and on contradictions involved in women's caring activities versus their other family roles (Abel and Nelson, 1990).

Within the world of a family, the tension a person feels between individual and group needs takes on special intensity. Group members seek both autonomy and profit that the individualistic culture holds so central. They also need the security and commonwealth that the group provides (Weigert, 1991). Involvement in family throughout life means that members experience loss of deep identities and the reversal of relationships of power and dependency between parents and children (Weigert and Hastings, 1977).

Luescher (1999) has proposed ambivalence as an alternative to both the solidarity and conflict perspectives to serve as a model for orienting sociological research on intergenerational relations. Luescher and Pillemer (1998) proposed a working definition for intergenerational ambivalence and divided it into two dimensions: (1) contradictions at the structural level (statuses, roles and norms) – the objective level; and (2) contradictions at the psychological level (cognition, emotions and motivations) – the subjective level.

Based on his earliest work Luescher (1999) proposed a heuristic model which is an attempt to combine postulate of ambivalence with considerations concerning the two basic dimensions implied in the concept of generations: first, intergenerational relations are institutionally imbedded in a family system which is characterised sociologically by structural, procedural, and normative conditions in a society. These institutional conditions are, on the one hand, reinforced and reproduced by the way people act out their relations. On the other hand, these conditions can also be modified and can lead to innovations. Reproduction and innovation are two poles of the social field in which the family is realised as an institution. These two poles may be conceived as referring to structural ambivalence (see Figure 3.1). Second, parents and children share a certain degree of similarity that is reinforced by the intimacy of mutual learning processes, and contain a potential for closeness and subjective identification. At the same time similarity is also a cause of and reason for distancing. Consequently, on this intersubjective dimension as well, Luescher postulates an ambivalence polarity.

Ambivalence in a social science perspective, as defined by Luescher and Luescher and Pillemer, evolves when dilemmas and contradictions in social relations and social structures are interpreted as being basically irreconcilable. They argue that the concept of ambivalence is a good reference point because it avoids normative assumptions and moral idealisations. Moreover, it points to a pragmatic necessity for researching strategies that shape intergenerational relations.

Other research attempts to operationalise ambivalence have focused on the interplay between structural and individual ambivalence and the negotiation between the two. More recently, Connidis and McMullin (2002a, 2002b) have proposed that ambivalence can be viewed as a brokering concept between the solidarity model and the problematisation of family relations, and offered a critical perspective through their work on the impact of divorce on intergenerational relations. They go on to argue that ambivalence should be reconceptualised. One of their central tenets is that individuals experience ambivalence when social structural arrangements prevent them from their attempts to negotiate within relationships. For example, women have societal pressures to care and less opportunity to resist, despite the entry of women into the labour force. Hence they are more likely than men to experience ambivalence. Thus, women negotiate

Figure 3.1:The intergenerational ambivalence model

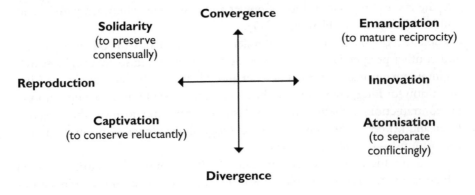

Source: Luescher (1999)

their caregiving situations and ambivalence created by competing demands on their time in order to manage work, family life and caring.

The sociological approach to ambivalence proposed by them is based on the connection between individual experiences, social relationships, social institutions and societal change (Connidis and McMullin, 2002b). Luescher, they point out, 'conflates institutions and social structures ... while they specify social structure' (Connidis and McMullin, 2002b, p 600). Luescher (2004, p 588), however, argues that ambivalence 'is based on attributions and as an interpretation of modes of behaviour, cognitions, and emotions which can be conditioned by social structures or located within them'. Given that ambivalence has its basis in the tension between autonomy and dependence, it is not surprising that intergenerational relations are among the most ambivalent, extending well beyond the more obvious applications to adolescent children and their parents (Fingerman et al, 2004). In mature parent–child relations, ambivalence levels are elevated when parental health is poor (Willson et al, 2003; Fingerman et al, 2006), as parents become increasingly reliant on their adult children to whom they were formerly providers (Willson et al, 2006).

Critics of Connidis and McMullin (Bengtson et al, 2002) question the validity of the reinterpretation of the term 'ambivalence'. In their view, as a concept it does not necessarily tie individual agency and social structure together, and it may be a motivator to doing nothing. Bengtson et al (2002) criticise the ambivalence concept on several counts. They ask how it differs from the decades-old symbolic interactionist approach to role conflict. They also wonder how it can predict or explain intergenerational family dynamics better. They view ambivalence as perhaps complementing the solidarity–conflict framework, which is conceptually adequate for exploring mixed feelings, namely 'From the intersection of solidarity and conflict comes ambivalence, both psychological and structural' (Bengtson et al, 2002, p 575). They argue that both the solidarity–conflict and the ambivalence models can be regarded as lenses 'through which one can look at family relationships' (p 575).

While conflict in the solidarity paradigm was originally conceptualised as a form of 'anti-solidarity', a repulsive force to the interpersonal 'glue' that was positive sentiments, more recent theorising has explicitly incorporated ambivalence into the model as the space where affection and conflict intersect. Detecting ambivalence within this more general solidarity framework extended an empirical approach to the study of families that classified relationships into meaningful categories that may consist of inconsistent elements (Hogan et al, 1993; Silverstein and Litwak, 1993; Giarrusso et al, 2005; van Gaalen and Dysktra, 2006). Over its historical development, the solidarity–conflict model has had as its goal to be a comprehensive, parsimonious and universal scheme for describing intergenerational family relationships. Yet despite its widespread application, there have been few cross-national comparisons of the model. However, the recent availability of multinational data, mostly in Europe, has provided the opportunity to explicitly test the universality of the solidarity–conflict paradigm and the potential to evaluate how nations differ in their intergenerational ties (Katz et al, 2005; Lowenstein and Daatland, 2006; Lowenstein, 2007; Lowenstein et al, 2007, 2008).

To summarise the above discussion: (1) the addition of conflict to the solidarity paradigm has allowed for the measurement and detection of ambivalence and other emergent properties of intergenerational relationships; and (2) incorporating solidarity–conflict into the protocols of multinational studies has provided the opportunity to formally test the universality of the solidarity–conflict model across diverse societies. Accordingly, the next section will present some empirical findings from the OASIS cross-national five countries study, testing the impact of solidarity, conflict and ambivalence on quality of life within different age groups and various social environments.

Associations between intergenerational family relations (solidarity, conflict and ambivalence) and quality of life in two age groups (OASIS)

In order to test empirically and compare the predictive potential of the intergenerational family relations models for quality of life we utilised data from the OASIS study that included five countries: Norway, England, Germany, Spain and Israel. These countries reflect a diverse range of welfare regimes (institutional, conservative, residual) (Esping-Andersen, 1990, 1997) and familial cultures (family-oriented, individualistic), differences that may be reflected in intergenerational family relationships and may impact on elders' quality of life.

Data collection was based on face-to-face interviews with an urban representative sample of 1,200 respondents (800 aged 25–74 and 400 aged 75+) in each of the participating five countries, totalling 6,000 respondents. Overall response rates in all countries varied from 70 to 76 per cent. All respondents lived in the community, and therefore people living in institutions were explicitly excluded. The present analysis focused on a two-generational exchange system between older parents (60+) and adult children (25–59). A complete account of the OASIS model, design and methodology is available in Lowenstein and Ogg (2003).

Measures of the main variables: quality of life, intergenerational relations and background attributes

Quality of life was measured by the WHOQOL-BREF (World Health Organization Quality of Life) inventory (WHO QOL scales), which focuses on evaluations of subjective living situations (WHO QOL Group, 1998). The instrument was designed for use in cross-cultural and cross-societal research and was developed, tested and validated by researchers from 15 culturally diverse research centres in Europe, Asia, North and South America and Africa. The scale is multidimensional, covering 24 facets of quality of life by single indicators relating to physical health, psychological well-being, satisfaction with social relationships and satisfaction with living conditions. All items are rated on a 5-point Likert scale, ranging from 1 = very dissatisfied, to 5 = very satisfied. Its reliability was 0.65–0.87. Performing a factor analysis on the 24 items revealed a one-factor structure, which was later used in the analysis (factor loadings 0.75–0.84). A mean score was computed.

Intergenerational family solidarity was measured by means of the Intergenerational Family Solidarity Measures for Survey Assessment (Mangen et al, 1988). Solidarity items were selected from LSOG, which asked respondents a series of questions about the nature of their relationship with their adult children or parents as follows:

1) *Proximity* refers to the geographic distance that might constrain or facilitate interaction, measured on a 6-point scale ranging from 1 = living at a travelling distance of 3 hours or more to 6 = living together.
2) *Association* indicates the frequency of face-to-face contact, coded as 1 = less than several times a year to 6 = daily or more often.
3) *Affection* describes feelings of emotional intimacy between family members, using three questions such as 'How close do you feel to [this child]?'. The questions are coded from 1 = not at all to 6 = extremely.
4) *Functional solidarity* refers to the instrumental assistance operationalised as receiving from or providing help to at least one child and/or parent in the following areas: shopping and transportation, household chores, house repair and gardening, personal care/childcare, financial assistance and emotional support. Affirmative responses were summed up for a total *help received* and *help given* score ranging from 0 to 6.
5) *Consensus* represents the degree of similarity in opinions and values, measured by means of one item: 'In general, how similar are your opinions and values about life to those of [this child]?'. The item was coded as 1 = not at all similar to 6 = extremely similar.

6) *Conflict*, measured with three items relating to the degree of conflict or tension, criticism and arguments between the generations such as 'How much does [this child] argue with you?'. The questions were coded as 1 = not at all to 6 = a great deal. A mean score was used.

A factor analysis performed for all countries (pooled samples) revealed a two-factor structure. The first reflects a structural–behavioural dimension (proximity and association); factor loadings 0.90 and 0.87, labelled Solidarity S, Cronbach alpha 0.84. The second reflects the affective–cognitive (affect and consensus); factor loadings 0.75 and 0.98, labelled Solidarity A, Cronbach alpha 0.69. This dual structure is somewhat similar to that noted by Bengtson and Roberts (1991) and Silverstein and Bengtson (1994). Receiving or providing help and conflict did not emerge in the factor structure and were thus used separately in the analyses.

Ambivalence: three questions measured ambivalence, adapted from the measurements developed by Luescher (1999). For example, 'Sometimes, family members can have mixed feelings in their relationships with one another. Thinking about this child, how often do you have mixed feelings in your relationship with him/her?' coded as 1 = never to 5 = very often. A mean score was used.

Background characteristics: gender 1 = male, 0 = female; marital status 1 = married, 0 = not married; number of living adult children older than 21; education, measured by the highest level attained on a 3-point scale: 1 = primary, 2 = secondary, 3 = higher; financial adequacy: 1 = comfortable, 0 = not comfortable; activities of daily living (ADL) functioning measured by the SF-12 version of the MOS 36-item Short Form Health Survey (SF-36) (Ware and Sherbourne, 1992), with a total score scale of 0-100 (a higher score indicating better functioning).

Findings

To examine the impact of the three main concepts of intergenerational family relations on quality of life we calculated two block-recursive regressions – the first is from the adult children's perspectives (see Table 3.3) and the second is from the older parents' point of view (see Table 3.4). Both regressions have three models: the first contains only family relations, in the second model country variables (Israel as the reference) were added and in the third model background characteristics were also included.

From the perspective of the adult children, aged 25–59, intergenerational family relations were not associated with quality of life, and Germany differed from the other four countries with higher quality of life. The only significant contribution was the third model with personal attributes, mainly health, financial adequacy and level of education. The overall explained variance of quality of life was 30 per cent and most of it was predicted by the three background attributes. It can be said that for relatively young people intergenerational family relations are not the main predictors of their self-evaluated quality of life. Apparently there are

Table 3.3: Standardised regression coefficients for overall quality of life including family relations towards parents, countries and background attributes (ages 25–59)

	Model 1		Model 2		Model 3	
Solidarity S (Prox+Contact)	0.04		0.08	*	0.04	
Solidarity A (Affec+Consensus)	0.02		0.03		0.03	
Help received	−0.03		−0.04		−0.05	
Help provided	−0.03		−0.01		0.03	
Conflict	−0.06		−0.05		−0.06	
Ambivalence	−0.13		−0.12		−0.08	
Norway			0.07		0.06	
England			−0.06		0.06	
Germany			0.17	***	0.12	***
Spain			0.03		0.06	
Respondent gender					−0.05	
Parent gender					−0.04	
Age group (25-39/40-59)					−0.02	
No of children					0.01	
Education					0.13	***
Financial					0.25	***
Health					0.35	***
n	1,123		1,123		1,123	
Total R²	0.037	*	0.074	***	0.301	***
R² change			0.038	***	0.227	***

Notes: *$p<0.05$, ***$p<0.001$

other important aspects of life like health and career (finance and education) that are strongly connected with it.

The findings of the second regression, which examined predictors of quality of life for the older parents, were quite different from those for the younger generation regarding intergenerational family relations. The overall explained variance was much higher than in the first regression (47 per cent) and family variables contributed 12 per cent to it. For older people, 60 and above, intergenerational family relations were more meaningful components when evaluating their quality of life. Three dimensions of solidarity contributed significantly – affectual solidarity and consensus, and both dimensions of functional solidarity – help received and provided. It is interesting to note that providing help was positively related to quality of life whereas receiving help had a negative impact. The ability to provide help to one's children can enhance feelings of independence that in turn positively affect quality of life. In contrast, the need for help from one's children might have adverse effects on self-esteem, which in turn negatively affects quality of life. Ambivalence had a significantly negative impact on quality of life in the

Table 3.4: Standardised regression coefficients for overall quality of life including family relations towards children, countries and background attributes (ages 60+)

	Model 1		Model 2		Model 3	
Solidarity S (Prox+Contact)	−0.03		0.03		0.01	
Solidarity A (Affect+Consensus)	0.14	***	0.16	***	0.10	***
Help received	−0.23	***	−0.26	***	−0.04	*
Help provided	0.22	***	0.22	***	0.08	***
Conflict	−0.03		0.00		0.01	
Ambivalence	−0.08	***	−0.08	***	−0.07	
Norway			0.23	***	0.14	***
England			0.18	***	0.18	***
Germany			0.34	***	0.23	***
Spain			0.02		0.05	*
Respondent gender					0.00	
Child gender					0.01	
Age group (60-74/75+)					0.00	
No of children					0.00	
Education					0.08	***
Financial					0.20	***
Health score					0.48	***
n	2,164		2,164		2,164	
Total R^2	0.120	***	0.215	***	0.471	***
R^2 change			0.095	***	0.256	***

Notes: *$p<0.05$, ***$p<0.001$

first two models but failed to contribute in the third model, and conflict had no effect at all.

Other variables that were associated with quality of life of older parents included countries that added 10 per cent showing that Israel and Spain were different from the other three countries, with lower perceived quality of life of the older people in those two countries. Background characteristics, although not the sole predictor as for the younger generation, had the strongest predictive power on quality of life and added another 26 per cent.

Conclusions

In this chapter we have presented and discussed the historical roots on which the long-established solidarity paradigm, later expanded to the solidarity–conflict model, that guided research on family intergenerational relations for more than three decades, was developed. Conflict, however, as a late addition to the intergenerational solidarity paradigm, has remained somewhat conceptually apart from the original dimensions of the model. The renewed conceptual framework of intergenerational ambivalence was further discussed and the effects of the two paradigms on quality of life of different generations examined in a cross-national context.

The OASIS design allowed for testing the more problem-oriented positivist model of solidarity–conflict, measured through the years by quantitative methods. We have to bear in mind, however, that some of the key components of ambivalence, such as contradictions in relationships that cannot be reconciled, may be easier to infer from qualitative data, as may be the case with conflict where a multiple domain approach might be more fruitful (Clarke et al, 1999).

Nevertheless, the OASIS study demonstrates the validity and utility of the three concepts of solidarity, conflict and ambivalence for expanding knowledge of the key dilemmas identified in the intergenerational relations literature. However, in order to fully understand the complexity of family relations, not only the perception of older parents but also the adult children's point of view was analysed. The empirical examination of the predictive power of intergenerational family relations – solidarity, conflict and ambivalence – on quality of life reveal that these relations were more important for the older generation than for the younger. For the older generation the solidarity dimensions, especially the emotional component of the relations and the ability to provide help, had a positive effect on quality of life. Ambivalence had little negative effect and conflict did not contribute to quality of life. Lowenstein (2007), who tested the same conceptual frameworks for people aged 75 and over, presented similar findings. She suggested that conflict and ambivalence are more prone to social desirability than solidarity, and that it is difficult to measure these two dimensions with quantitative methods. The ambivalence perspective, which was developed deductively, points to the need for new methods and measures.

Our data also revealed the differences between age groups in the predictive power of family relations – solidarity, conflict and ambivalence – to quality of life that probably reflects the different phases they experience in the lifecourse.

To sum, more creativity will be needed to capture the complicated and multidimensional concept of intergenerational family relations. Scholars might consider the possible paradigmatic changes in the social fabric of families, and in societal networks, which might impact on family relationships in the future.

Note
[1] OASIS was funded under the 5th programme of the European Union, Contract No QLK6-TC 1999-02182.

References
Abel, E.K. (1991) *Who cares for the elderly? Public policy and the experience of adult daughters*, Philadelphia, PA: Temple University Press.

———

Abel, E.K. and Nelson, M.K. (1990) *Circles of care: Work and identity in women's lives*, New York, NY: State University of New York Press.

Arber, S. and Attias-Donfut, C. (eds) (1999) *The myth of generational conflict: The family and state in an aging society*, London and New York, NY: Routledge.

Atkinson, M.P., Kivett, V.R. and Campbell, R.T. (1986) 'Intergenerational solidarity: an examination of a theoretical model', *Journal of Gerontology*, vol 41, no 3, pp 408-13.

Attias-Donfut, C. and Wolff, F.-C. (2005) 'Generational memory and family relationships', in M.L. Johnson (ed) *The Cambridge handbook of age and ageing*, Cambridge: Cambridge University Press, pp 443-54.

Bachman, J.G. (1982) 'Family relationships and self-esteem', in M. Rosenberg and H.B. Kaplan (eds) *Social psychology of self-concept*, Arlington Heights, IL: Harlam Davidson, pp 356-64.

Beavers, W.R. (1982) 'Healthy, midrange, and severely dysfunctional families', in F. Walsh (ed) *Normal family processes*, New York, NY: Guilford Press.

Bedford, V. (1992) 'Memories of parental favoritism and quality of parent–child ties in adulthood', *Journal of Gerontology: Social Sciences*, vol 47, s149-s155.

Belle, D.E. (1986) 'The impact of poverty on social networks', in L. Lein and M.B. Sussman (eds) *The ties that bind: Men's and women's social networks*, New York, NY: Haworth Press.

Bengtson, V.L. and Dowd, J.J. (1981) 'Sociological functionalism, exchange theory and life-cycle analysis: a call for more explicit theoretical bridges', *International Journal of Aging and Human Development*, vol 12, no 2, pp 55-73.

Bengtson, V.L. and Roberts, R.E.L. (1991) 'Intergenerational solidarity in aging families: an example of formal theory construction', *Journal of Marriage and the Family*, vol 53, pp 856-70.

Bengtson, V.L. and Schrader, S. (1982) 'Parent–child relations', in D. Mangen and W.A. Peterson (eds) *Research instruments in social gerontology*, Minneapolis, MN: University of Minnesota Press, vol 2, pp 115-86.

Bengtson, V.L., Olander, E.B. and Haddad, A.A. (1976) 'The generation gap and aging family members: toward a conceptual model', in J.E. Gubrium (ed) *Time, roles and self in old age*, New York, NY: Human Sciences Press, pp 237-63.

Bengtson, V.L., Giarrusso, R., Mabry, J.B. and Silverstein, M. (2002) 'Solidarity, conflict and ambivalence: complementary or competing perspectives on intergenerational relationships?', *Journal of Marriage and Family*, vol 64, pp 568-76.

Bengtson, V.L., Giarrusso, R., Silverstein, M. and Wang, H. (2000) 'Families and intergenerational relationships in aging societies', *Hallym International Journal of Aging*, vol 2, no 1, pp 3-10.

Bengtson, V.L., Acock, A.C., Allen, K.A., Dilworth-Anderson, P. and Klein, D.M. (2005) 'Theory and theorizing in family research', in V.L. Bengtson, A.C. Acock, K.A. Allen, P. Dilworth-Anderson and D.M. Klein (eds) *Sourcebook of family theory and research*, Thousand Oaks, CA: Sage Publications, pp 3-33.

Biggs, S. and Lowenstein, A. (forthcoming) 'Toward generational intelligence: linking cohorts, families and experience', in M. Silverstein and R. Giarousso (eds) *From generation to generation: Continuity and change in aging families*, Baltimore, MD: Johns Hopkins University Press.

Billing, M., Condor, S., Edwards, D., Gane, M., Middleton, D. and Radley, A. (1988) *Ideological dilemmas*, Beverly Hills, CA: Sage Publications.

Blau, P. (1964) *Exchange and power in social life*, New York, NY: Wiley.

Boersch-Supan, A., Brugiavini, A., Juerges, H., Mackenbach, J., Siegrist, J. and Weber, G. (eds) (2005) *Health, ageing and retirement in Europe – First results from the Survey of Health, Ageing and Retirement in Europe*, Mannheim: Mannheim Research Institute for the Economics of Aging, University of Mannheim.

Bourdieu, P. (1996) *The rules of art*, Cambridge, Polity Press.

Brody, E.M., Litvin, S.J., Hoffman, C. and Kleban, M.H. (1995) 'Marital status of caregiving daughters and coresidence with dependent parents', *The Gerontologist*, vol 35, pp 75-85.

Burgess, E.W. (1926) 'The family as a unity of interacting personalities', *The Family*, vol 7, pp 3-9.

Clarke, E.J., Preston, M., Raksin, J. and Bengtson, V.L. (1999) 'Types of conflicts and tensions between older parents and adult children', *The Gerontologist*, vol 39, no 3, pp 261-70.

Connidis, I.A. and McMullin, J. (2002a) 'Ambivalence, family ties, and doing sociology', *Journal of Marriage and Family*, vol 64, pp 594-601.

Connidis, I.A. and McMullin, J. (2002b) 'Sociological ambivalence and family ties: a critical perspective', *Journal of Marriage and Family*, vol 64, pp 558-67.

Coser, R.L. (1956) *The functions of social conflict*, New York, NY: Free Press.

Coser, R.L. (1966) 'Role distance, sociological ambivalence, and traditional status systems', *American Journal of Sociology*, vol 72, pp 173-87.

Dowd, J.J. (1975) 'Aging and exchange: a preface to theory', *Journal of Gerontology*, vol 30, no 5, pp 584-94.

Durkheim, E. (1933) *The division of labor in society* (translated by G. Simpson), New York, NY: Free Press.

Dwyer, J.W., Lee, G.R. and Jankowski, T.B. (1994) 'Reciprocity, elder satisfaction, and caregiver stress and burden: the exchange of aid in the family caregiving relationship', *Journal of Marriage and the Family*, vol 56, pp 35-43.

Emerson, R.M. (1962) 'Power dependence relations', *American Sociological Review*, vol 27, pp 31-41.

Engels, F. (1884/1972) *The origin of the family, private property and the state*, New York, NY: Pathfinder Press.

Esping-Andersen, G. (1990) *The three worlds of welfare capitalism*, Princeton, NJ: Princeton University Press.

Esping-Andersen, G. (1997) 'Hybrid or unique? The Japanese welfare state between Europe and America', *Journal of European Social Policy*, vol 7, no 3, pp 89-179.

Farrington, K. and Chertok, E. (1993) 'Social conflict theories of the family', in P.G. Boss, W.J. Doherty, R. LaRossa, W.R. Schuman and S.K. Steimetz (eds) *Sourcebook of family theories and methods: A contextual approach*, New York, NY: Plenum Press, pp 357-81.

Fingerman, K.L., Hay, E.L. and Birditt, K.S. (2004) 'The best of ties, the worst of ties: close problematic and ambivalent social relationships', *Journal of Marriage and Family*, vol 66, pp 792-808.

Fingerman, K.L., Chen, P.C., Hay, E.L., Cichy, K.E. and Lefkovitz, E.S. (2006) 'Ambivalent reactions in the parent and offspring relationship', *The Journal of Gerontology Series B*, vol 61, pp 152-60.

Freud, S. (1913/1964) *Totem and taboo*, London: Hogart.

Gelles, R.J. (1980) 'Violence in the family: a review of research in the seventies', *Journal of Marriage and the Family*, vol 42, pp 873-84.

Giarrusso, R., Stallings, M. and Bengtson, V.L. (1995) 'The "intergenerational stake" hypothesis revisited: parent–child differences in perceptions of relationships 20 years later', in V.L. Bengtson, K.W. Schaie and L.M. Burton (eds) *Adult intergenerational relations: Effects of societal change*, New York, NY: Springer, pp 227-63.

Giarrusso, R., Silverstein, M., Gans, D. and Bengtson, V.L. (2005) 'Ageing parents and adult children: new perspectives on intergenerational relationships', in M.L. Johnson (ed) *The Cambridge handbook of age and ageing*, Cambridge: Cambridge University Press, pp 413-22.

Gollnik, R. (1990) 'Stichwort: "Konflict"', in H.J. Sandkuhler (ed) *Europaisch Enzvklopadie Zu Philosophie und Wissenschaften*, Hamburg: Felix Meiner Verlag, p 850.

Heider, F. (1958) *The psychology of interpersonal relations*, New York, NY: John Wiley.

Hendricks, J. (1995) 'Exchange theory in aging', in G. Maddox (ed) *The encyclopedia of aging* (2nd edn), New York, NY: Springer.

Hirdes, J.P. and Strain, L.A. (1995) 'The balance of exchange in instrumental support with network members outside the household', *Journal of Gerontology: Social Sciences*, vol 50b, s134-s142.

Hogan, D.P., Eggebeen, D.J. and Clogg, C.C. (1993) 'The structure of intergenerational exchanges in American families', *American Journal of Sociology*, vol 98, pp 1428-58.

Homans, G.C. (1950) *The human group*, New York, NY: Harcourt, Brace & World.

Homans, G.C. (1961) *Social behavior: Its elementary forms*, New York, NY: Harcourt, Brace & World.

Katz, I. (1981) *Stigma*, Hillsdale, NJ: Erlbaum.

Katz, R. (2009) 'Intergenerational family relations and life satisfaction among three elderly population groups in transition in the Israeli multi-cultural society', *Journal of Cross-Cultural Gerontology*, vol 24, pp 77-91.

Katz, R. and Lowenstein, A. (1999) 'Adjustment of older Soviet immigrant parents and their adult children residing in shared households: an intergenerational comparison', *Family Relations*, vol 48, no 1, pp 43-60.

Katz, R., Lowenstein, A., Phillips, J. and Daatland, S.O. (2005) 'Theorizing intergenerational family relations. Solidarity, conflict and ambivalence in cross-national contexts'. in V.L. Bengtson, A.C. Acock, K.R. Allen, P. Dilworth-Anderson and D. Klein (eds) *Sourcebook of family theory and research*, Thousand Oaks, CA: Sage Publications, pp 393-402.

Kauh, T.O. (1997) 'Intergenerational relations: older Korean-Americans' experiences', *Journal of Cross-Cultural Gerontology*, vol 12, pp 245-71.

Kinsella, K. (2000) 'Demographic dimensions of global aging', *Journal of Family Issues*, vol 21, no 5, pp 541-58.

Klein, D.M. and White, J.M. (1996) *Family theories*, Thousand Oaks, CA: Sage Publications.

Kohli, M. (2007) 'The institutionalization of the lifecourse: looking back to look ahead', *Research in Human Development*, vol 4, nos 3-4, pp 253-71.

Lee, G.R., Netzer, J.K. and Coward, R.T. (1994) 'Final responsibility expectations and patterns of intergenerational assistance', *Journal of Marriage and The Family*, vol 56, pp 559-65.

Lehr, U. (1984) 'The role of women in the family generation context', in V. Garms-Homolova, E.M. Hoerning and D. Schaffer (eds) *Intergenerational relationships*, Gottingen, Germany: Hogrefe, pp 125-32.

Lieberman, M.A. and Fisher, L. (1999) 'The effects of family conflict resolution and decision making on the provision of help for an elder with Alzheimer's disease', *Gerontologist*, vol 39, no 2, pp 159-66.

Lowenstein, A. (2007) 'Solidarity–conflict and ambivalence: testing two conceptual frameworks and their impact on quality of life for older family members', *Journal of Gerontology Social Sciences*, vol 62B, S100-S107.

Lowenstein, A. and Daatland, S.O. (2006) 'Filial norms and family support in comparative cross-national context: evident from the OASIS study', *Ageing and Society*, vol 26, pp 203-23.

Lowenstein, A. and Katz, R. (2000) 'Rural Arab families coping with caregiving', *Marriage and Family Review*, vol 30, no 1, pp 179-97.

Lowenstein, A. and Ogg, J. (2003) '*Oasis-old age and autonomy: The role of service systems and intergenerational family solidarity*, Final Report, Haifa, Israel: Center For Research and Study of Aging, University of Haifa.

Lowenstein, A., Katz, R. and Gur-Yaish, N. (2007) 'Reciprocity in parent–child exchange and life satisfaction among the elderly in cross-national perspective', *Journal of Social Issues*, vol 63, no 4, pp 865-83.

Lowenstein, A., Katz, R. and Gur-Yaish, N. (2008) 'Cross national variations in elder care: antecedents and outcomes', in M.E. Szinovacz and A. Davey (eds) *Caregiving contexts*, New York, NY: Spring Publishing Co, pp 93-115.

Lowenstein, A., Katz, R., Prilutzky, D. and Mehlhausen-Hassoen, D. (2001) 'The intergenerational solidarity paradigm', in S.O. Daatland and K. Herlofson (eds) *Ageing, intergenerational relations, care systems, and quality of life – An introduction to the Oasis Project*, NOVA Rapport 14/01, Oslo, Norway: Norwegian Social Research.

Luescher, K. (1999) 'Ambivalence: a key concept for the study of intergenerational', in S. Trnka, *Family issues between gender and generations*, Seminar report, Vienna: European Observatory on Family Matters, pp11-25.

Luescher, K. (2004) 'Conceptualising and uncovering intergenerational ambivalence'. in K. Pillemer and K. Luescher (eds) *Intergenerational ambivalence: New perspectives on parent–child relations in later life*, Oxford: Elsevier Science, pp 23-62.

Luescher, K. and Pillemer, K. (1998) 'Intergenerational ambivalence: a new approach to the study of parent–child relations in later life', *Journal of Marriage and the Family*, vol 60, pp 413-25.

Mancini, J.A. and Blieszner, R. (1989) 'Aging parents and adult children: research themes in intergenerational relations', *Journal of Marriage and the Family*, vol 51, pp 275-90.

Mangen, D.J. and McChesney, V.L. (1988) 'Intergenerational cohesion: a comparison of linear and nonlinear analytical approaches', *Research on Aging*, vol 1, pp 12136.

Mangen, D.J., Bengtson, V.L. and Landry, P.H., Jr (1988) *Measurement of intergenerational relations*, Beverly Hills, CA: Sage Publications.

Marshall, V.W., Matthews, S.H. and Rosenthal, C.J. (1993) 'Elusiveness of family life: a challenge for the sociology of aging', in G.L. Maddox and M.P. Lawton (eds) *Annual review of gerontology and geriatrics: Focus on kinship, aging and social change*, New York, NY: Springer.

McChesney, K.Y. and Bengtson, V.L. (1988) 'Solidarity, intergeneration and cohesion in families: concept and theories', in D.L. Mangen, V.L. Bengtson and P.H. Lardy, Jr (eds) *Measurements of intergenerational relations*, Beverly Hills, CA: Sage Publications, pp 15-30.

Merrill, D.M. (1996) 'Conflict and cooperation among adult siblings during the transition to the role of filial caregiver', *Journal of Social and Personal Relationships*, vol 13, no 3, pp 399-413.

Merton, R.K. (1976) *Sociological ambivalence*, New York, NY: Academic Press.

Merton, R.K. and Barber, E. (1963) 'Sociological ambivalence', in E. Tityakian (ed) *Sociological theory: Values and sociocultural change*, New York, NY: Free Press, pp 91-120.

Minuchin, S. (1974) *Families and family therapy*, Cambridge, MA: Harvard University Press.

Montgomery, R.J. and Kosloski, K. (1994) 'A longitudinal analysis of nursing home placement for dependent elders cared for by spouses vs adult children', *Journal of Gerontology: Social Sciences*, vol 49, S62-S74.

Murray, H. and Kluckhohn, C. (1959) 'Outline of a conception of personality', in C. Kluckhohn, H. Murray and D.M. Schneider (eds) *Personality and nature, society and culture*, New York, NY: Knopf, pp 3-52.

Nye, F.I. and Rushing, W. (1969) 'Towards family measurement research', in J. Hadden and E. Borgatta (eds) *Marriage and family*, Illinois City, IL: Peacock.

Ogburn, W.F. (1938) 'The changing family', *Family*, vol 19, pp 139-43.

Otto, R. (1985) *The idea of The Holly*, New York, NY: Oxford University Press.

Parrott, T.M. and Bengtson, V.L. (1999) 'The effects of earlier intergenerational affection, normative expectations, and family conflict on contemporary exchange of help and support', *Research on Aging*, vol 21, no 1, pp 73-105.

Parsons, T. (1973) 'Some afterthoughts on Gemeinschaft and Gesellschaft', in W.J. Cahnman (ed) *Ferdinand Tonnies: A new evaluation*, Leiden: Brill, pp 140-50.

Pruchno, R.A., Burant, C.J. and Peters, N.D. (1997) 'Typologies of caregiving families: family congruence and individual well-being', *The Gerontologist*, vol 32, no 2, pp 157-67.

Putney, S. and Putney, G.J. (1972) *The adjusted American*, New York, NY: Perennial Library, Harper and Row.

Roberts, R.E.L. and Bengtson, V.L. (1988) 'Intergenerational cohesion and psychic well-being: implications over the adult lifecourse', Paper presented at the annual meeting of the American Sociological Association, San Francisco, August.

Roberts, R.E.L. and Bengtson, V.L. (1990) 'Is intergenerational solidarity a unidimensional construct? A second test of a formal model', *The Journal of Gerontology*, vol 45, s12-S20.

Roberts, R.E.L., Richards, L.N. and Bengtson, V.L. (1991) 'Intergenerational solidarity in families', in S.P. Pfeifer and M.B. Sussman (eds) *Families: Intergenerational and generational connections*, New York, NY: Haworth Press, pp 11-46.

Rogers, E.M. and Sebald, H. (1962) 'Familism, family integration, and kinship orientation', *Marriage and Family Living*, vol 24, p 27.

Rossi, A.S. and Rossi, P.H. (1990) *Of human bonding: Parent–child relations across the lifecourse*, Hawthorne, NY: Aldine de Gruyter.

Schulman, N. (1975) 'Life cycle variations in patterns of close relationships', *Journal of Marriage and the Family*, vol 37, pp 813-21.

Silverstein, M. and Bengtson, V.L. (1991) 'Do close parent–child relations reduce the mortality risk of older parents?', *Journal of Health and Social Behavior*, vol 32, pp 382-95.

Silverstein, M. and Bengtson, V.L. (1994) 'Does intergenerational social support influence the psychological well-being of older parents? The contingencies of declining health and widowhood', *Social Sciences & Medicine*, vol 38, no 7, pp 943-57.

Silverstein, M. and Bengtson, V.L. (1997) 'Intergenerational solidarity and the structure of adult child–parent relationships in American families', *American Journal of Sociology*, vol 103, no 2, pp 429-60.

Silverstein, M. and Litwak, E. (1993) 'A task specific typology of intergenerational family structure in later life', *The Gerontologist*, vol 33, no 2, pp 258-64.

Silverstein, M., Chen, X. and Heller, K. (1996) 'Too much of a good thing? Intergenerational social support and the psychological well-being of older parents', *Journal of Marriage and The Family*, vol 58, pp 970-82.

Simmel, G. (1955) *Conflict and the web of intergroup affiliations*, Glencoe, IL: Free Press.

Sprey, J. (1991) 'Studying adult children and their parents', in S.K. Pfeifer and M.B. Sussman (eds) *Families: Intergenerational and generational connections*, Binghamton, NY: Haworth Press, pp 221-35.

Stacey, J. (1990) *Brave new families: Stories of domestic upheaval in late twentieth century America*, New York, NY: Basic Books.

Starrels, M.E., Ingersoll–Dayton, B., Neal, M.B. and Yamada, H. (1995) 'Intergenerational solidarity and the workplace: employees' caregiving for their parents', *Journal of Marriage and the Family*, vol 57, no 3, pp 751-62.

Straus, M. (1979) 'Measuring intrafamily conflict and violence: the conflict tactics (CT) scales', *Journal of Marriage and the Family*, vol 41, pp 75-88.

Strawbridge, W.L. and Wallhagen, M. (1991) 'Impact of family conflict on adult caregivers', *The Gerontologist*, vol 31, pp 770-8.

Sussman, M.B. (1965) 'Relationships of adult children with their parents in the United States', in E. Shanas and G.F. Streib (eds) *Social structure and the family: Generational relations*, Englewood Cliffs, NJ: Prentice-Hall.

Sussman, M.B. (1991) 'Reflections on intergenerational and kin connections', in S.P. Pfeifer and M.B. Sussman (eds) *Families, intergenerational and generational connections*, New York, NY: Haworth Press.

Thilbaut, J.W. and Kelley, H. (1959) *The social psychology of groups*, New York, NY: Wiley.

Thorne, B. (1992) 'Feminism and the family: two decades of thought', in B. Thorne and M. Yalom (eds) *Rethinking the family*, Boston, MA: Northeastern University Press, pp 3-30.

Turner, B.S. (1999) 'Aging and generational conflicts: a reply to Sarah Irwin', *British Journal of Sociology*, vol 49, no 2, pp 299-304.

van Gaalen, R.I. and Dykstra, P.A. (2006) 'Solidarity and conflict between adult children and parents: a latent class analysis', *Journal of Marriage and Family*, vol 68, pp 947-60.

Ware, J.E. Jr and Sherbourne, C.D. (1992) 'The MOS-36 item short form health survey (SF-36): 1. Conceptual framework and item selection', *Medical Care*, vol 30, p 6.

Webster, P.S. and Herzog, A.R. (1995) 'Effects of parental divorce and memories of family problems on relationships between adult children and their parents', *Journal of Gerontology: Social Sciences*, vol 50B, s24-s34.

Weigert, A.J. (1991) *Mixed emotions*, New York, NY: State University Press.

Weigert, A.J. and Hastings, R. (1977) 'Identity loss, family, and social change', *American Journal of Sociology*, vol 82, pp 1171-85.

WHO QOL (World Health Organization Quality of Life) Group (1998) 'Quality of life assessment development and general psychometric properties', *Social Science and Medicine*, vol 46, pp 1569-85.

Willson, A.E., Shuey, K.M. and Elder, G.H. (2003) 'Ambivalence in the relationship of adult children to aging parents and in-laws', *Journal of Marriage and Family*, vol 65, pp 1055-72.

Willson, A.E., Shuey, K.M., Elder, G.H. Jr and Wickrama, K.A.S. (2006) 'Ambivalence in mother–adult child relations: a dyadic analysis', *Social Psychology Quarterly*, vol 69, pp 235-52.

Witt, D.D. (1987) 'A conflict theory of family violence', *Journal of Family Violence*, vol 2, no 4, pp 291-301.

Yinger, J.M. (1982) *Counter cultures*, New York, NY: Free Press.

FOUR

Globalised transmissions of housing wealth and return migration

Ricky Joseph

Introduction

There is increasing interest in intergenerational transmissions of housing wealth, inheritance planning and how these reflect shifting patterns of intergenerational relations (Finch and Mason, 2000; Rowlingson and McKay, 2005). The proliferation in this literature in the UK context reflects the fact that greater numbers of households have assets to pass on to other family members during the giver's lifetime and in death, and that the values of these financial exchanges are much greater than for previous generations. A key source of this reciprocity is housing wealth. The UK housing market, since the postwar period, has experienced a number of key developments. These have included higher rates of homeownership, rising properties values, the dominance of homeownership ideology in successive government policies, the liberalisation of financial markets giving homeowners easier access to a wider range of financial products and services, higher levels of consumption and debt. The statistics alone give an indication of the scale and importance of homeownership to households and the national economy – it is by far the most popular form of housing tenure. In 2007 there were 14.7 million homeowners accounting for 70 per cent of all housing tenures in England. A recent report on the state of the homeownership market revealed that the average national house price between the period 1994 to 2007 rose by 230 per cent, from £60,000 to £200,000 (Hamnett, 2009). The total gross mortgage lending in the UK in 2007 stood at £364 billion, a threefold increase from 1999. An earlier report by Smith for the Joseph Rowntree Foundation estimated that the level of unmortgaged housing equity stood at £2.2 trillion (Smith, 2005). Much of these changes reflect the complex relationship between the home as the locus of kinship ties, as a source of financial well-being for households and their families, and as a major driver of the national economy.

This literature, which has charted the complexities of financial exchanges and reciprocity, has tended to neglect the diversity of the UK's homeownership community and the global nature of kinship and financial networks. Despite the wealth of quantitative and qualitative data on the socioeconomic profile of households engaging in transmissions of housing wealth through intergenerational loans and inheritance, there is little understanding of the position of minority ethnic homeowners, particularly those from a migration background. The introduction of the new ethnicity strand of the United Kingdom Household Longitudinal Survey (UKHLS) will offer important new data for the research and policy communities as it will collect information on the economic well-being of households and individuals from an ethnic background, including income, asset consumption behaviour and migration background (UKHLS, 2008). This chapter makes tentative steps towards addressing this gap by discussing the position of first-generation Caribbean elders who have established and sustained homeownership careers since their arrival in the UK in the period 1950–70. It takes on a transnational perspective, focusing on transmissions of housing wealth overseas, primarily in the country of origin rather than within the UK context and kinship networks. It draws on qualitative life history accounts to explore how housing wealth leakage takes place in the Caribbean region. The notion of 'housing wealth leakage' is used in this context to describe the way that housing equity accumulated from UK homeownership careers is invested overseas in housing and non-housing consumption. Particular attention is paid to the way that Caribbean elders invest in second homes on the island of origin and the way that access to land assets that may have been inherited or purchased since their arrival in the UK is used in establishing second homes. Attention is also given to the way that housing wealth is used in supporting family networks in the Caribbean.

The choice of this cohort of UK homeowners, mainly aged 50 years and upwards, is significant in terms of the global transmission of housing wealth and intergenerational relationships. The Caribbean population over 60 years of age now constitutes the largest non-White ethnic elderly population and has the largest proportion of people aged 65 and over (11 per cent), reflecting the fact that they were the first large-scale migration of non-White groups to Britain in the 1950s (Plaza, 2001; National Statistics, 2009). The arrival of the Caribbean population in the period 1950–70 not only marked the high point of labour migration from the New Commonwealth[1] but also coincided with major restructuring of the postwar housing market (Phillips, 1987; Byron, 1994). Despite significant barriers faced by Caribbean and other New Commonwealth migrants in penetrating the labour and housing markets, which are well documented in the literature (Davison, 1966; Rex and Moore, 1967; Karn et al, 1985; Sarre et al, 1989), levels of homeownership among this group, in the mid-1960s, was at times higher than the indigenous White population (Byron, 1993). Table 4.1 shows homeownership levels among New Commonwealth households from 1961 to 1974.

There are two central arguments developed in this chapter that are important given the transnational nature of Caribbean communities and the region which has a long tradition of migration and re-migration.

First, the literature tends to ignore claims to inherited land, housing investments, financial networks and kinship obligations in the country of origin. A resource that has been a feature within some Caribbean families has been family land. The system of family land has existed in parts of the English-speaking Caribbean since

Table 4.1: Housing tenure for the Caribbean, Asian and White populations, 1961–74 (%, all households)

Tenure type	White	Caribbean	Asian
1961[a]			
Owner-occupation	42	29	47
Council tenant	22	3	8
Private tenant	3	22	58
1964[a]			
Owner-occupation	45	40	67
Council tenant	25	5	10
Private tenant	3	15	32
1971[a]			
Owner-occupation	45	45	58
Council tenant	28	22	10
Private tenant	5	20	21
1974[b]			
Owner-occupation	50	50	76
Council tenant	32	26	4
Private tenant	18	24	19

Sources: [a] Taken from Bhat et al (1988); [b] Taken from Modood et al (1997)

the 1800s. It is discussed fairly extensively in a wide body of Caribbean literature, from social anthropology and land development studies to economic development. It is viewed as an important economic and symbolic resource in Caribbean society (see for example Besson and Momsen, 2007). An important feature of family land is that it is owned and inherited communally across extended kinship. It is arguable, within some Caribbean families, that there is a much longer tradition of land and property ownership than is generally acknowledged in the UK housing literature. The process of outward migration from the Caribbean region in the postwar wave of labour migration has further extended these inheritance claims to families who settled in the UK. This first wave of postwar migrants, now mostly in their retirement, would have been the first to have inherited a share of family land in the UK. Moreover, there is emerging evidence that the availability of family land has been a key resource enabling this cohort to realise return migration plans and in establishing second homes in the Caribbean.

The second central argument developed in this chapter relates to the first by speculating on the implications that inheritance of overseas land assets has for this cohort of Caribbean elders who have entered homeownership since arriving in the UK. The chapter argues that this has created a complex mix of 'asset portfolios' in the UK and Caribbean. Evidence from case studies is used to illustrate some of the difficulties and tensions faced by informants when undertaking inheritance planning of property and land assets which are transnational in nature, located across a wide geographical span and embedded within competing symbolic and economic traditions in Caribbean society.

We begin the chapter with a review of the literature on family land and develop connections with the migration and re-migration literature that makes a number of references to it and its significance within housing plans of returnees. This is followed by a brief description of the methodology used in conducting the study. The findings and analysis pick up and develop these key themes that are then followed by the conclusions, reflecting on its wider implications to the literature.

Family reciprocity and financial exchanges

The long tradition of migration and transnationalism that have been key features of Caribbean society has influenced the way that family reciprocity and financial exchanges have developed. The use of remittances in supporting family members who remain in the Caribbean has been well documented in the literature (see Chamberlain, 1998; Goulbourne and Chamberlain, 2001). These financial exchanges were often seen as a symbol of 'success', signalling the fact that the sender had achieved a degree of financial security in the country of settlement. The practice of remittances is sometimes seen as a fading practice confined to first-generation Caribbean migrants rather than the UK-born second- and third-generation Caribbean population in Britain. This is partly due to the changing nature of kinship ties in the Caribbean and new and competing ones in the UK. However, there is emerging evidence that challenges this perception, by putting forward the argument that the nature of remittance exchanges has been transformed from a purely financial exchange to one that takes on a much broader cultural and financial form. A number of scholars have developed the notion of 'cultural remittance' (Levitt, 2001; Burman, 2002; Reynolds and Zontini, 2006). Reynolds and Zontini (2006, p 9) adopt this notion of 'cultural remittance' to describe the way that it represents migrants' emotional attachments, identity and the way they utilise family links between siblings, parents and children and grandparents and grandchildren to maintain cultural connections to their place of origin. Reynolds and Zontini also broaden this definition to incorporate the way that migrants own and build property in the country of origin.

Family land, 'new kinds' of overseas inheritance and (re)migration

Although there is a developing literature on the inheritance experiences of minority ethnic households, much of this is framed in terms of financial exclusion concerns and lower rates of homeownership, relative to White households, which impact on the level and value of intergenerational transmissions (FSA, 2000; Rowlingson and McKay, 2005). There is very little attention given to the background of international migration of many minority ethnic communities or the global nature of kinship ties. Moreover, even less attention is given to land assets minority ethnic households might have access to in the country of origin. These discourses are particularly relevant to the Black Caribbean population in Britain because of the transnational nature of this community and the system of landholding that has existed since the abolition of slavery in the 1800s in large parts of the Caribbean region. This is widely referred to as family land. There is evidence in the Caribbean social anthropological literature that the process of outward migration from the region has widened inheritance claims to family land among the postwar wave of labour migrants (many of whom are now in their retirement), and by implication families established in the UK. Moreover, this literature suggests that the availability of family land is increasingly featuring within return migration plans and investments in second homes in the island of origin (Byron, 1994, 1999).

Family land is referred to fairly extensively within Caribbean academic and policy literatures. It is viewed as an important economic and symbolic resource for Caribbean families (Clarke, 1953; Besson and Momsen, 2007). The long tradition of family land in Caribbean society, and the process of outward migration to the UK, might even suggest there is a much longer tradition of land/homeownership among some Caribbean families than is acknowledged in the housing literature, even predating their arrival in the UK. The institution of family land can be traced to the collapse of the plantation system following Emancipation in the 1830s. Landless African and Creole peasantry were able to secure claims on plots of land formerly controlled by plantation owners from which they were able to establish collective rights. This was encouraged by state backing and against growing opposition from ex-plantation owners eager to re-establish their former rights (Marshall and Beckford, 1972; Stanfield et al, 2003). Under this system, land belonged to the 'community' and could take the form of a tribe, clan or confederation of villages (Clarke, 1966; Craton, 1987). This action among the peasantry to establish claims on land had clear economic implications. It is the unrestricted nature of cognate descent that land can be inherited undivided bilaterally by all descendents of the original portion of land. This means that inheritance could take place through both parents (Barrow, 1992). The scarcity of land, and the lack of opportunities to secure alternative employment, meant that it enabled families to achieve economic independence through subsistence farming. This development took on a symbolic importance as a former landless peasantry had acquired land rights and economic independence flowing from it (Besson and Momsen, 1987; Barrow, 1992). A recurrent theme in this literature is the way that family land is intimately linked to the creation and reproduction of kinship ties. This contrasted profoundly with what Besson and Momsen (1987, p 18) described as the 'kinless of the enslaved'. Land ownership enhanced the social status of newly freed slaves by providing a degree of economic independence, but was embedded within strong religious associations as a sacred burial place for family members, and the necessity that these sites remain in the control of their ancestors (Clarke, 1953). Taken collectively, family land is intimately linked to family well-being and as a symbol of financial security. The unrestricted nature that family land is inherited meant that there is a perception that it can act as a permanent economic resource for families. Although not exclusively confined to the English-speaking Caribbean, the system of family land has been influenced by French cultural traditions within Francophile Caribbean (Horowitz, 1967; Finkel, 1971) and Dutch cultural traditions in Guyana (Despres, 1970; Smith, 1971).

Caribbean society has a long established tradition of migration from the region (Chamberlain, 1998). This has shaped the way that families and kinship relations have evolved over time to adapt to the widening network of members settled globally. The Caribbean population consists of people from African, Asian and European descent, reflecting what some academics refer to as a 'postcolonial, hybrid cultural Diaspora' (Cohen, 1998, p 22). Goulbourne and Chamberlain (2001, p 32) write that 'its social structures and institutions, the forms and expressions, the values and beliefs, which constitute the culture of the Caribbean evolved and continue to evolve through the absorption and adaptation of global influences, of those who came, of those who left, of those who returned'. Prior to Emancipation in 1834, the migratory movement was into the region and involuntary. Enslaved Africans were transported into the region to work on the sugar plantations. After Emancipation and the ending of Apprenticeships in 1838 the social and racial composition, and the motives, of Caribbean migration entered a significant period of change. The construction of the Panama Canal in the late 19th century signalled another key landmark in migration patterns for the British-controlled Caribbean. Significant numbers of labourers from the islands of Jamaica, Barbados and St Lucia re-migrated to Cuba and the US after completion of the canal.

Migration to the UK after the Second World War in response to labour shortages, particularly in the public and manufacturing sectors, and the demands of an economy undergoing a period of reconstruction, marked the next watershed. Between 1948 and 1973 approximately 550,000 people of Caribbean birth migrated to the UK. The majority of Caribbean migrants arrived before the introduction of the 1962 Immigration Act, which substantially reduced further flows affecting people from the Caribbean and New Commonwealth (Chamberlain, 1997). The 1971 Census revealed that Jamaicans comprised 171,775 of the total Caribbean-born population in Britain, followed by Barbadians (27,055), Guyanesians (21,070) and Trinidad and Tobagodians (17,135).

An immediate impact that Diaspora from the Caribbean region had on family land was that it further fragmented inheritance claims to migrants settled in the UK, North America and Europe (Solien, 1959; Rubenstein, 1975). This movement of Caribbean communities had a number of implications for the system of family. First, outward migration led to a rise of absentee ownership and the reliance on kinship and social networks remaining in the Caribbean to oversee the interests of family members who had emigrated. Second, the cohort of 'first-generation' Caribbean elders, who are the focus of this chapter, would have been the first UK-based cohort to have inherited a share of family land. Third, there is emerging evidence drawn from a number of case study accounts of return migration that access to family land has been an important resource available to returnees in reducing the costs of constructing a retirement or second home (Byron, 1994; Byron and Condon, 2008). Even within the second homes literature there is little data on the ethnic profile of UK homeowners who have a second home overseas (Centre for Future Studies, 2004; Gallent et al, 2005; ODPM, 2005).

Research design

The study included two generations of Black Caribbean homeowners from the same families based in Birmingham and London. In total, 13 Caribbean elders and their families agreed to take part in the study and were selected using a combination of purposeful and snowball sampling. The main consideration for inclusion in the sample was that first-generation informants had established homeownership careers at some stage since their arrival in Britain. The choice of these two cities was influenced by the fact that they attracted the highest number of labour migrants from the Caribbean region in the immediate postwar period. The fieldwork was conducted between 2002 and 2005, and was funded by the Economic and Social Research Council (ESRC) and the Office of the Deputy Prime Minister (ODPM) (Joseph, 2007). The interviews were undertaken using life histories methodology. There is a long tradition of life history and other biographical research methods in charting the experiences of migrant communities, family histories and understanding changes in intergenerational relations (Thomas and Znaniecki, [1918-20] 1958; Bertaux and Thompson, 1993; Chamberlain, 1997; Roberts, 2002).

Informants were interviewed over several sessions using a combination of tape recordings and handwritten notes. Within the original sample, nine Caribbean elders indicated they had considered return migration at some stage or had already established a second home in the Caribbean. There were a number of sensitive issues involved in the interview process, particularly around overseas housing investments, financial and inheritance planning. Informants were presented with a number of scenarios in the topic guides enabling the study to explore how they approached inheritance planning as well as the values and meanings informants attached to housing and land assets held in the UK and the Caribbean.

The sample of Caribbean elders and their families was not intended to be representative of the postwar Caribbean migrant population; it was hoped, however, that it would contain a wide range of experiences. The informants on the whole, although describing themselves as 'working class', exhibited many characteristics of 'middle-class' lifestyles. Many were active in their local communities, church members (in the case of the Birmingham sample) or held professional occupations in the case of second-generation family members. Each informant completed a consent agreement and a short biographical profile before the interview took place. This was used to construct basic background information on a range of issues (housing history, family background, employment, migration histories etc). All the names of informants in this chapter have been changed.

How inheritances of family land took place

There were nine Caribbean elders among the sample who indicated they had received a share of family land in the Caribbean since migrating to the UK after the death of an elderly relative. The majority of these inheritances took place during the 1960s and 1970s, a period which marked the death of a generation of elderly family members (that is, parents, aunts and uncles). A pressing issue arising from the death of the relative was the decision on 'who got what' among the potential beneficiaries in the Caribbean and overseas. The following comment was typical of the views expressed:

> "I recall receiving a call from my sister to tell me the news that Ma had died ... it wasn't a great shock because she had been ill for some time ... the land that she left we shared between us [siblings], she didn't leave a will so we had to sort things out between us ... my sister who stayed in Grenada took the biggest share, it only seemed right because she work on the land and help out." (Derrick, aged 74, London)

In the likely scenario where the ownership of land is shared between family members based overseas, it was common practice to appoint a family member already living on the land or in the close proximity to take on a 'caretaking role' to protect the interests of the absentee owner:

> "Those of we who abroad usually get someone we can trust to look after things for us...." (Sarah, aged 77, Birmingham)

> "When my aunt passed away I arranged for my cousin to look after my share ... it was quite common to arrange for a relative to be your eyes and ears for those of us living in places like ... England, Canada and America...." (Mary, aged 47, London)

Informants were asked whether other members of their immediate family in the UK were involved in discussions on any matters relating to family land once it had come into their possession. These discussions usually took place at the time of the inheritance but often only involving a spouse:

> "When I heard that I was getting a share of the land that belonged to my mother, the first person that I spoke to was my wife ... there was a lot of things to sort out and I needed advice from someone I could trust but wasn't involved in the family politics ... because I live in Birmingham I needed to decide who would look after my share we

both decided that it would be best if it was my cousin who still lives back home." (Herbert, aged 72, Birmingham)

"I always discuss these things with my wife ... we needed to sort things out because our daughter lived with my mum before she died ... we felt that it was best for her to live in the old house…." (Ben, aged 72, Birmingham)

Over the passage of time, discussions about family land tended to occur sporadically, particularly on specific family occasions such as family reunions in the Caribbean, the death of another family member who also had a share of the land in question or if informants were formulating return migration plans where the land in question would be the focus of investment of UK housing wealth or savings. The following comment was typical of the views expressed:

"I didn't talk much about it [family land] to my daughter in the beginning ... it only when I start spending time back there to meet family that I talk about it a bit ... I guess there were times when it was just sat there…." (Sarah, aged 77, Birmingham)

Family land appeared to become a forgotten inheritance within families in the UK if none of the circumstances described above applied or if it was not perceived to be a realisable economic asset:

"I have the little piece of land now for over 30 years and I haven't done much with it ... I can't afford to go back and I give up on the chance to build a place on it ... it's not really much use to me now apart from the headache it give me ... I don't talk to the kids that it there…." (Sonny, aged 75, Birmingham)

"I don't think I've talked to my daughter about the land that I got from my aunt after she died ... I guess the reason for that is that I've had a run of bad luck ever since I've had it ... there is been lots of disagreement about what we should do with it ... I suppose at some point I will need to tell her [daughter]…." (Mary, aged 47, London)

Importance of family land within return migration planning

A number of migration scholars have highlighted the role played by family land within return migration planning (Byron, 1994; Besson and Momsen, 2007). Byron and Condon (2008) drew attention to the use of family land inherited by returnees as a popular site for building a home for a permanent return or as a second home. Byron (1994, pp 172-3) noted:

Land in some cases with a building on it, had been inherited by 15 per cent of the migrants while they were in Britain and 20 per cent of the Leicester sample had purchased land but had not yet built on it.

The literature on return migration surprisingly pays very little attention to the way return migration activity is financed. Even less is known about the housing investment decisions in housing markets in the country of return or the risks and opportunities associated with this. This is a particularly pertinent issue for 'return migrants' who have established multiple residences. Byron's findings revealed the importance of housing status of returnees in the UK. Homeowners featured strongly within her sample that hinted at their use of housing wealth in investing in family land and the existence of a buoyant second home market among those domiciled in the UK. My own study showed how informants were combining housing wealth accumulated from homeownership careers with lifetime savings and lump sum redundancy payments in later life towards investing in housing in the Caribbean:

> "I spend some money to build a house back home … I'd like to move back for good, but at the moment I will spend a few months in the winter there…." (Derrick, aged 74, London)

> "When I built my home in Grenada after my wife died, I used a bit of money from this house and little money I got after I took early retirement, I thought why shouldn't I enjoy the rest of my life now that I get a chance to…." (Derrick, aged 74, London)

Informants who had no definitive plans for a permanent return or in establishing multiple residences found it problematic deciding what to do with inheritance of family land:

> "The little land I get after my Ma died is split up between me, my sister in Jamaica and my brother in Canada … it hard to do much with it because we all need to agree on these things … I wanted to build a place on it but they tell me that I can't, they want to use it to do other things, in the end I get so fed up I gave in to them…." (Sarah, aged 77, Birmingham)

Even where the possession of family land formed an integral part of a possible return, tensions within family relationships in the Caribbean could sometimes prove to be a disincentive to invest UK housing wealth into family land:

> "After I get the piece of land I planned to go back home [Jamaica] and build something on it … it all go wrong after I fall out with my

brother ... I give up on the idea of going back now so it (the land) just stay there...." (Sonny, aged 75, Birmingham)

"I originally decided to put some money into building a home in Grenada on the land that I inherited with my siblings ... I was serious about going back and at the time it made perfect sense ... in the end all of the constant bickering about who owned what became a problem ... in the end I decided to abandon my plans and looked to buy land somewhere else in the Caribbean...." (Mary, aged 47, London)

Problems of integrating family land into UK inheritance planning

The decisions about 'who got what' in relation to family land and the mechanisms for deciding this within extended kinship networks were complex and occasionally fraught with tensions (Besson and Momsen, 1987). My findings reinforced this as some informants found it problematic integrating family land with UK housing assets within the context of inheritance planning. Disputes over the use of family land for some informants tended to surface when undertaking return migration plans on retirement. In most cases, the status quo with regard to the use and management of the land meant that this responsibility fell either on an immediate family member based in the Caribbean or a trusted neighbour/relative. These individuals took on a 'caretaking role' in the absence of the UK co-owner. This mirrors some of the tensions caused by absentee owners within the Caribbean social anthropology literature on family land (Solien, 1959; Greenfield, 1960; Otterbein, 1964; Mathurin, 1967; Wilson, 1973; Besson and Momsen, 1987).

Informants tended to approach inheritance planning of family land and housing assets held in the UK separately. It was generally felt that this approach would make this task less complicated:

"My husband and I have sat down before to talk about the best way to decide how we should leave the old house back home and this one here [Birmingham] when we are both gone.... I can tell you now that it's not easy [laugh] ... if I had to be honest with you we've avoided making a decision ... sometimes we think it's easier to deal with each one separately but I know that it doesn't help matters...." (Mary, aged 73, Birmingham)

"It's not easy deciding what to do with the little land I have back home.... I don't want to go to law because I know they will want to complicate things and ask me what I plan to do with my place here in England and that I should look at the whole thing [family land and UK property] one time ... I say to myself there's no need to worry about it, it take care of itself...." (Nemiah, aged 72, London)

There were a number of specific concerns expressed that these inheritances may attract the attention of UK tax authorities or might affect state benefits claims:

> "I don't want the people [UK officials] here knowing my business, what I have overseas is nothing to do with them ... why should I have to tell them that I have a little land back home [Jamaica] ... it's not worth anything to anyone ... if you get a little money from the state they think they own everything you got...." (Sonny, aged 75, Birmingham)

> "The people [UK officials] always want to know more about your personal business ... the more you tell them the more they want to know, that's why a lot of us don't bother to do things properly through a lawyer...." (Ben, aged 72, Birmingham)

The last comment by Ben hinted at some of the legal concerns some informants faced when dealing with family land that had been inherited. A number of legal issues were identified by informants that made it difficult for them to integrate family land in the 'normal run' of inheritance planning. These ranged from a lack of paperwork setting out clear legal ownership, unclear legal processes for dealing with disputes in the Caribbean and concerns that legal advice would be expensive if action was pursued in the UK. These issues all created further uncertainties and undermined informants' abilities to take decisive action on these inheritances in the same way that they might with UK housing assets:

> "It was a real mess in the end, we couldn't agree on anything.... I thought is it worth it ... if you try to get a lawyer in the Caribbean to sort things out it's going to be complicated being hundreds of miles away in London ... if you try to get a lawyer in London it's likely to cost an arm and a leg ... in any case the law is different over here [London] and you're never sure if your lawyer knows his stuff about land law in Grenada...." (Mary, aged 47, London)

> "We had a few problems when we received a letter from a developer who wanted to put an offer for our family land in Dominica ... at one point I went to see a solicitor in Birmingham.... I don't think she had a clue about these things, they know a lot about English law but not what happens in the Caribbean ... a cousin did recommend a solicitor in Dominica but in the end I didn't have to go through with it because the family decided not to sell in the end...." (Herbert, aged 72, Birmingham)

There were two informants who had adult children who remained in the Caribbean after migrating to the UK. These adult children were living on family land. Their situation highlighted some of the dilemmas faced in balancing the needs of adult children in the Caribbean and their siblings brought up in the UK. One of the big dilemmas was deciding 'who got what' in the event of the death of both parents. There were two basic questions that informants had to decide. The first was 'should the family home be given to adult children already living on it in the Caribbean?'. The second question was 'if the UK parental home was sold how should this be shared out among surviving children?'. These decisions revolved around the dual goals of how best to ensure fairness all round and how best the financial well-being of different family members could be secured.

What seemed to emerge from this dilemma were two important principles underpinning the way that informants approached these issues. The first was the belief that family land should remain intact at all costs, and that all family members should share its benefits in the event of the death of both parents. The second was the sense that the financial resources of all potential beneficiaries should be taken into account when balancing individual needs and the fate of the UK home. The financial consideration informants felt was the most important was whether adult children in the UK had accumulated housing wealth from independent housing careers:

> "It's been hard deciding what to do with our daughter and our grandchildren in Jamaica ... we've always sent money to them regularly and we're proud that they are doing well ... she has a good job and her children are doing well in school ... they've always lived on my mother's land and we've spent a lot of money to improve it ... if her father and me are gone I feel that its important that this land is shared among all of our children ... we also feel that she should get more if our house here [Birmingham] is sold ... our other children have bought their own houses in Birmingham and have a lot more going for them financially...." (Mary, aged 73, Birmingham)

> "We started to think about these things ... we want to make sure that all of our children and grandchildren are provided for ... we are lucky that they are doing good, most of them have bought somewhere and are settled in their lives in Birmingham that makes us happy ... our eldest daughter in the Caribbean hasn't had these same opportunities as her brothers and sisters in England ... I want to make sure that any money I leave from my home here in England she get a bit more to compensate ... I don't want to break up the land we have back home [Jamaica] it should belong to everyone...." (Ben, aged 72, Birmingham)

Inheritance planning was a complex process, with different strategies used when deciding the future of family land and property held in the UK. When these issues were explored with informants who did not have adult children living in the Caribbean, there was a strong view expressed that the collective well-being of family members was the overriding concern when deciding how different assets were disposed of through the process of inheritance planning. This was often best served by releasing the full economic value of housing assets held in the UK rather than disposing of family land in the Caribbean:

> "I didn't think twice about selling my East London house to pay for my new home in Dominica no way … it means that I can give money to my sons to help them on their way in life…." (Daniel, aged 73, London)

> "If pushed I would be far happier selling my home here [London] if I felt that it was the best way to provide for my kids … I'm lucky because they are all doing well, got good homes and good jobs so there's no need for me to hang on to it for the sake of it … the kids don't want me to sell it because this is where they grew up … even if I wanted to sell the home I built in Grenada after my wife died I don't think that it would make a lot of money and it's been in the family for a long time…." (Derrick, aged 74, London)

Informants who had inherited family land tended to perceive these as symbolic assets that reinforced and further embedded family histories and cultural ties with the Caribbean.

> "My home here [London] is my castle, it's at the financial centre of everything I have achieved throughout my life … the land that I have back home is my soul…." (Daniel, aged 73, London)

> "We have been very fortunate to be where we are today … we work hard for the kids and put everything we have into our home … now that we are retired we can reap the benefits of what we have put in … our home has taken care of us because its given us a lot of financial opportunities … the land that I have back home is different, it's part of my family history and tradition…." (Herbert, aged 72, Birmingham)

This finding is consistent with the literature on family land that it should be preserved for the perpetual benefit of all family members (Besson and Momsen, 1987). The possession of family land, however, took on a deeper economic significance when individuals began to make active plans for a return. The UK home remained strongly embedded within economic rather than emotional ties. This is consistent with the UK literature on the cultural construction of the home (Allan and Crow, 1989; Saunders, 1990; Finch and Hayes, 1994; Finch and Mason, 2000). Even among second-generation informants interviewed in the study and who were aware of the existence of family land, it took on an important symbolic significance:

"I'm proud when I hear my dad talk about land we own back in Grenada ... it makes me feel a part of something big and part of my family history...." (Eddie, aged 46, son of Derrick, London)

"I love going back home to Jamaica to see my relatives ... I try to go back as much as I can ... my parents inherited land a while back, they don't talk about it much so I was really excited about seeing it for myself ... I must admit it wasn't much to look at but it was still ours and it has been in the family for many generations ... I feel proud of that...." (John, aged 48, son of Nemiah, London)

Housing wealth and overseas intergenerational transmissions: intergenerational exchanges or remittance?

Intergenerational exchanges were taking place within a transnational context among some informants. Informants made clear links between their ability to make such payments and the financial security afforded them by their homeownership status:

"Yes man I used to send a little money to my Ma when she alive, real regular ... I wanted her to know that I doing alright in England, I have my place and I settle down ... when she dead I still send money over to my nephew and niece them at school and need the little money to help with their school books and things...." (Sarah, aged 77, Birmingham)

"We've been sending money to our daughter in Jamaica for some time ... she didn't come over with us when we left but has been brought up by my mother ... it's been a lot easier to send money over because we feel financially secure now that we've paid for our house and have a bit of money saved up...." (Ben, aged 72, Birmingham)

Caribbean family literature provides many examples of the way that grandparents or senior family members take on caring responsibility for children left behind by parents who have migrated for better economic opportunities. Reynolds and Zontini (2006), who advance the notion of 'cultural remittance', capture more accurately the way that cultural and financial ties are deeply embedded within intergenerational exchanges. Moreover, the symbolic significance of such exchanges were not only perceived as a sign of financial success and security in the country of settlement, but were reinforced by the homeownership status of the sender. Informants recognised the importance of maintaining relationships with family members in the country of origin because it signified they had sustained 'successful' homeownership careers and the enhanced status this had in British society, accruing, in some cases, substantial equity in their properties.

In this context, such exchanges did not come with 'strings attached', reflecting only the desire to maintain kinship and cultural ties through the transmission of financial aid. There was a degree of confusion among some informants whether these intergenerational exchanges, that in some cases had been taking place over a number of decades, were in fact remittances or intergenerational exchanges of wealth:

> "My husband and I have always sent money back to our daughter back home [Jamaica]. She was born there and has lived there with her grandparents ... the money was used to buy her clothes and books for schooling ... when she got older she wanted a bit more space so we used some money we had to build an extension on the land that belonged to the family ... it was easier for us to help her because we had paid off our mortgage and we had some money left over after we sold our home to move here [Birmingham] ... now that we have both retired we have put some money aside for our grandchildren, they are doing really well at school...." (Mary, aged 73, Birmingham)

> "We send the money to our daughter back home [Jamaica] on a regular basis ... in some ways it's no different to the money I used to send to my mother who looked after her when she was younger...." (Ben, aged 72, Birmingham)

> "I had put a bit of money aside for her [niece] for when I dead, but I thought why not give the child a bit of money now so that she could make something of she self back home [Jamaica]...." (Sarah, aged 77, Birmingham)

The boundaries between intergenerational exchanges and remittance are often blurred within the inheritance literature, which tends to view such exchanges within a national context (see for example Finch and Mason, 2000; Rowlingson and McKay, 2005) and the remittance literature (Manners, 1965; Poirine, 1997; Ratha, 2003), which takes on a more transnational perspective. However, there is emerging literature that seeks to provide insights to these perspectives (Reynolds and Zontini, 2006). Interestingly, the source of remittances within the household budget of sending households is an area that is not very well understood within the remittance literature (Adams, 2005). My findings suggest there is scope for convergence of literatures on intergenerational financial transmission as they relate to minority ethnic homeowners from a migration background.

Conclusions

There is little understanding within the literature of intergenerational transmissions of wealth within transnational communities who retain kinship ties in the receiving and sending countries. These issues are further complicated by the fact that minority ethnic households from a migration background who have accumulated housing assets in the country of settlement through homeownership careers might also have access to assets in the country of origin. These issues have been explored by using the example of Caribbean elders who have forged successful homeownership careers in the UK while inheriting a stake in land assets in the Caribbean. The evidence in the literature, pointing to the importance of family land within the process of re-migration, is supported by my study of return migration and housing wealth. The transnational nature of familial relationships, kinship and asset networks of this group provide further challenges for the inheritance literature. Obligations to families separated by migration remained intact due to patterns of 'cultural remittance' that emphasised the importance of emotional attachments, identity and the way family ties in the country of origin are utilised. This broad notion of transnational relationships is useful in describing the way that cultural and financial transmissions are able to evolve and adapt over time to reflect the shifting nature of intergenerational relationships that span international borders.

To date, the inheritance literature has struggled to incorporate these perspectives into its understanding of inheritance and intergenerational exchanges within this cohort of UK homeowners. For the families themselves, the findings suggest there are 'hidden pockets' of inheritances that over the course of time will feed into inheritance portfolios of future generations of households from a Caribbean background. These findings suggest a new research agenda for the UK inheritance literature.

Note
[1] The movement of migrants from the New Commonwealth including territories such as the Caribbean, the Indian subcontinent and Africa began after 1945 to meet the labour demands of reconstruction. The numbers of New Commonwealth migrants in 1951 was 218,000, peaking to 1.2 million in 1971 and 1.5 million in 1981 (Castles and Miller, 2009).

References
Adams, R. (2005) *Using household surveys to study remittance flows in developing countries*, International Technical Meeting on Measuring Remittance, Development Research Group, Washington DC: World Bank.

Allan, G. and Crow, G. (1989) 'Introduction', in G. Allan and G. Crow (eds) *Home and family: Creating the Domestic Sphere*, London, Macmillan.

Barrow, J. (1992) *Family land and development in St Lucia*, Barbados: Institute of Social and Economic Research.

Bertaux, D. and Thompson, P. (1993) *Between generations: Family models, myths and memories: International yearbook of oral history and life stories, II*, Oxford: Oxford University Press.

Besson, J. and Momsen, J. (1987) *Land and development in the Caribbean*, London: Macmillan.

Besson, J. and Momsen, J. (2007) *Caribbean land and development revisited*, Basingstoke: Palgrave Macmillan.

Bhat, A., Carr-Hill, R. and Ohri, S. (1988) *Britain's black population: A new perspective*, Aldershot: Ashgate.

Burman, J. (2002) 'Remittance: or diasporic economies of yearning', *Small Axe*, vol 12, no 2, pp 49-71.

Byron, M. (1993) *The housing question: Caribbean migrants and the British housing market*, Research Paper 49, Oxford: School of Geography, University of Oxford.

Byron, M. (1994) *Post-war Caribbean migration to Britain: The unfinished cycle*, Aldershot: Avebury.

Byron, M. (1999) 'The Caribbean born population in 1990s Britain: who will return', *Journal of Ethnic and Migration Studies*, vol 25, no 2, pp 285-301.

Byron, M. and Condon, S. (1996) 'A comparative study of Caribbean return migration from Britain and France: towards a context-dependent explanation', *Transactions, Institute of British Geographers*, vol 21, no 1, pp 91-104.

Byron, M. and Condon, S. (2008) *Migration in comparative perspective: Caribbean communities in Britain and France*, Abingdon: Routledge.

Castles, S. and Miller, J. (2009) *The age of migration: International population movements in the modern world* (4th edn), Basingstoke: Palgrave Macmillan.

Centre for Future Studies (2004) *Direct Line report: Second homes in the UK*, Direct Line.

Chamberlain, M. (1997) *Narratives of exile and return*, London: Macmillan.

Chamberlain, M. (ed) (1998) *Caribbean migration: Globalised identities*, London: Routledge.

Clarke, E. (1953) 'Land tenure and the family in four communities in Jamaica', *Social and Economic Studies*, vol 1, no 4, pp 81-118.

Clarke, E. (1966) *My mother who fathered me: A study of the family in three selected communities in Jamaica and St Lucia*, London: Unwin and Allen.

Cohen, R. (1998) 'Cultural diaspora: the Caribbean dase', in M. Chamberlain (ed) *Caribbean migration: Globalised identities*, London: Routledge, pp 21-35

Craton, M. (1987) 'White law and black custom: the evolution of Bahamian land tenures', in J. Besson and J. Momsen (eds) *Land development in the Caribbean*, London: Palgrave Macmillan, pp 88-114.

Davison, R. (1966) *Black British: Immigrants to England*, London: Oxford University Press for the Institute of Race Relations.

Despres, L. (1970) 'Differential adaptations and micro-cultural evolution in Guyana', in N. Whitten. and J. Szwed (eds) *Afro American anthropology*, New York, NY: Free Press.

Finch, J. and Hayes, L. (1994) 'Inheritance, death and the concept of the home', *Sociology*, vol 28, no 2, pp 417-34.

Finch, J. and Mason, J. (2000) *Passing on: Kinship and inheritance in England*, London: Routledge.

Finkel, H. (1971) 'Patterns of land tenure in the Leeward and Windward Islands', in M. Horowitz (ed) *Peoples and cultures of the Caribbean: An anthropological reader*, Garden City, NY: Natural History Press.

FSA (Financial Services Authority) (2000) *In or out? Financial exclusion: A literature and research review*, London: FSA.

Gallent, N., Mace, A. and Tewdwr-Jones, M. (2005) *Second homes: European perspectives and UK policies*, Aldershot: Ashgate.

Goulbourne, H. and Chamberlain, M. (2001) *Caribbean families and the trans-Atlantic world*, London: Macmillan Education.

Greenfield, S. (1960) 'Land tenure and transmission in Rural Barbados', *Anthropological Quarterly*, vol 33, pp 165-76.

Hamnett, C. (2009) *The madness of mortgage lenders: Housing finance and the financial crisis*, London: IPPR/Friends Provident Foundation.

Horowitz, M. (ed) (1967) *Peoples and cultures of the Caribbean: An anthropological reader*, Garden City, NY: Natural History Press.

Joseph, R. (2007) 'Housing wealth and accumulation: home ownership experiences of African Caribbean families migrating to Birmingham and London in the period 1950-1970', Unpublished PhD, Birmingham: Centre for Urban and Regional Studies, University of Birmingham.

Karn, V., Kemeny, J. and Williams, P. (1985) *Home ownership in the inner city: Salvation or despair*, Aldershot: Gower.

Levitt, P. (2001) *The transnational villagers*, Berkeley, CA: University of California Press.

Manners, R. (1965) 'Remittances and the unit of analysis in anthropological research', *Southwestern Journal of Anthropology*, vol 21, pp 179-95.

Marshall, W. and Beckford, G. (1972) 'Peasant movements and agrarian problems in the West Indies', *Caribbean Quarterly*, vol 18, no 1, pp 31-58.

Mathurin, D. (1967) 'An Unfavourable System of Land Tenure: The Case of St. Lucia', Paper read at the Second West Indian Agricultural Economics Conference, St Augustine, Trinidad, April 1967.

Modood, T. and Berthoud, R. with Lakey, J., Nazroo, J., Smith, P., Virdee, S. and Beishon, S. (1997) *Ethnic minorities in Britain: Diversity and disadvantage*, London: Policy Studies Institute.

National Statistics (2009) *Focus on ethnicity and identity* (www.statistics.gov.uk/cci/nugget.asp?id=456).

Office of the Deputy Prime Minister (2005) *Housing in England: Part 2 Owner occupiers and second homes*, London, HMSO.

Otterbein, K. (1964) 'A comparison of the land tenure systems of the Bahamas, Jamaica and Barbados: The implications it has for the study of social systems shifting from bilateral to ambilineal descent', *International Archives of Ethnography*, vol 50, no 1, pp 31-42.

Phillips, D. (1987) 'Searching for a decent home: ethnic minority progress in the post war housing market', *New Community*, vol 14, nos 1/2, pp 105-17.

Plaza, D. (2001) 'Aging in Babylon: elderly Caribbeans living in Great Britain', in H. Goulbourne and M. Chamberlain (eds) *Caribbean families in Britain and the transatlantic world*, University of Warwick Caribbean Studies Series, London: Macmillan, pp 219-31.

Poirine, B. (1997) 'A theory of remittance as an implicit family loan theory', *World Development*, vol 25, no 4, pp 583-611.

Ratha, D. (2003) 'Workers remittances: An important and stable source of external development finance' in *Global Development Finance*, Washington, World Bank, pp 157-75.

Rex, J. and Moore, R. (1967) *Race, community and conflict: A study of Sparkbrook*, London: Oxford University Press.

Reynolds, T. and Zontini, E. (2006) *A comparative study of care and provision across Caribbean and Italian transnational families*, Families and Social Capital ESRC Research Group, Working Paper Series No 16, London: South Bank University.

Roberts, B. (2002) *Biographical research*, Buckingham: Open University Press.

Rowlingson, K. and McKay, S. (2005) *Attitudes to inheritance in Britain*, Bristol: The Policy Press for the Joseph Rowntree Foundation.

Rubenstein, H. (1975) 'The utilization of arable land in an eastern Caribbean valley', *Canadian Journal of Sociology*, vol 1, no 2, pp 157-67.

Sarre, P., Phillips, D. and Skellington, R. (1989) *Ethnic minority housing: Explanations and policies*, Aldershot: Avebury.

Saunders, P. (1990) *A nation of home owners,* London, Unwin Hyman.

Smith, R. (1971) 'Land tenure in three negro villages in British Guiana', in M. Horowitz (ed) *Peoples and cultures of the Caribbean: An anthropological reader*, New York, NY: Natural History Press, pp 243-66.

Smith, S. (2005) 'Banking on housing? Speculating on the role and relevance of housing wealth in Britain', Inquiry into Home Ownership 2010 and Beyond, Paper prepared for the Joseph Rowntree Foundation.

Solien, N. (1959) 'The nonunilineal descent group in the Caribbean and Central America', *American Anthropologist*, vol 61, no 4, pp 578-83.

Stanfield, J., Barthel, K. and Williams, A. (2003) *Framework paper for land policy, Administration and management in the English speaking Caribbean*, Port of Spain: Land Tenure Centre.

Sterling, L. (1995) 'Partners: the social organisation of rotating savings and credit societies among exile Jamaicans', *Sociology*, vol 29, pp 653-66.

Thomas, W. and Znaniecki, F. ([1918-20] 1958) *The Polish peasant in Europe and America*, 2 vols, New York, NY: Dover Press.

UKHLS (2008) Update on the Ethnicity Strand of the UKHLS: March 2008, (www. iser.essex.ac.uk/files/ukhls/consultation/ethnicity/docs/Mar08_update.pdf).

Wilson, P. (1973) *Crab Antics: The Social Anthropology of English-Speaking Negro Societies of the Caribbean*, New Haven, Yale University Press.

FIVE

Housing wealth and family reciprocity in East Asia

Misa Izuhara

Introduction

There has long been debate about whether East Asia has a welfare model distinct from Western or Anglo-Saxon welfare states (see for example Goodman et al, 1998; Walker and Wong, 2005; Takegawa and Lee, 2006). While welfare provision shapes societies in particular ways, it is also often shaped by existing power structures and cultural norms. The balance of state, family and market responsibilities differ in each society, however, and small states and the significant role played by families are often highlighted as the characteristics of the East Asian model. We can then ask whether the East Asian economic miracle was at the sacrifice of welfare policy, while families bore a heavy burden of welfare provision.

Despite a variation in their size, political structures and economic developments, East Asian societies share cultural norms. This chapter highlights particular East Asian practices of family support by examining types, flows and volumes of support provided or exchanged between and over generations. It also investigates how the nature and patterns of such support exchanges have shifted as a result of more recent demographic changes, economic reforms and shifting cultural norms within and across societies. The housing dimension is used in particular to examine changing family reciprocity in contemporary East Asia. For example, there has been a shift away from co-residency and it was this living arrangement that traditionally made sharing other resources easier among family households.

The analysis of the empirical data for this chapter is focused on a comparison of two major cities in East Asia – Tokyo, Japan, and Shanghai, the People's Republic of China. In many ways these cities do not represent (the structure and composition of) their own society. Rather, they are at the forefront of socioeconomic change and such dynamism makes the cases more interesting to analyse. Being the largest and perhaps most developed cities in their own countries, these cities are likely to capture the accentuated processes of social change including shifting intergenerational relations within families. The case studies present the strategies and practices of family relations that are changing to cope with wider structural shifts taking place in these societies. Comparing these two cities (and thus the two societies) will illustrate striking differences as well as similarities.

'Filial piety' and family relations

Families have been the key institution for the provision of welfare in East Asian societies despite the varying developmental stages of their own state and market sectors. Either in the socialist welfare state of China or the corporate paternalism found in Japan, families have provided, and still provide, the main source of support in many spheres of welfare. Intergenerational relations in the region, especially those involving older people, are often bound by the norm of 'filial piety' that traditionally defined family responsibilities and governed family practice (Izuhara, 2009). Some scholars state that the traditional agricultural economy and a patriarchal–feudal social system provided the conditions for the origin and development of such family ethics in those societies (see for example Sheng and Settles, 2006).

East Asian cultures have indeed valued dependence, obligation and reciprocity in family relations. Debt and obligations often cemented their generational bonds. The Confucian-based idea is that the debt children feel towards sacrifices their parents make throughout their upbringing must be reciprocated by caring for their parents in old age. In other words, for parents, having raised children earlier in their lifecourse can serve as a credit for the receipt of support from their children in their old age (Hashimoto and Kendig, 1992). In this context, children, and sons in particular, have been considered to be great 'assets' to parents. Adult children thus traditionally demonstrated their respect towards their parents through financial and material provision as well as providing physical nursing care in later life, often in co-residency. Given the traditional patrilineal succession system often found in East Asian societies, there was an inevitable gender element in practice.

Postwar social, economic and legal changes, however, brought new ideology, functions and relations to families in the region, although traditional practices remained strong in the social structure. Although they occurred in different postwar periods with different impacts, constitutional and legal reforms in East Asian societies dissolved the pre-war patriarchal family system and introduced family democracy into areas such as living arrangements, marriage partnering and inheritance practices. The Communist revolution in China in 1949, for example, criticised many Confucian ideologies including filial piety, and elements such as a child's absolute obedience to parents in particular. However, a child's (son's) duty to care for their ageing parents remained strong, and was even legalised and reinforced under both the 1979 Criminal Law and 1980 Marriage Law (see for example Chen, 1985; Palmer, 1995). Family reciprocity throughout the lifecourse was also written into the 1982 Constitution (Palmer, 1995). In this context, only childless elders were allowed into state welfare institutions (Zhan et al, 2008). In Japan, children's financial support towards parents was also expected under the 'practice' of public assistance allocation by various local government offices. However, with the introduction of a social insurance scheme for long-term care in 2000, the direct provision of practical and personal care for ageing parents has been significantly *socialised* and *marketised*, although the boundaries over responsibility between families and the state have been shifting back and forth since the scheme's introduction (Izuhara, 2009).

Co-residency, sharing accommodation among adult generations within the family, has been one of the significant characteristics of East Asian family support. It was part of a survival or a practical response as much as a preference when resources were scarce in the past. In both China and Japan, families are getting smaller and more nuclearised with low fertility (also in China as a result of the one-child policy). In China, the average urban household size declined from 3.89 members in 1985 to 3.04 in 2002 (National Bureau of Statistics of China, 2003) while in Japan from 5.0 in 1953, to 3.14 in 1985, it went down to 2.56 in 2005 (Management and Coordination Agency, 2005). Moreover, in Japan, three-generation extended families continue to decline while elderly-only households and also households of older people living with unmarried adult children have been on the increase, reflecting recent marriage patterns. Since the demographic location of wealth is skewed towards the older generation in Japan and more towards the middle generation in urban China (Forrest and Izuhara, 2009), when combined with the current and recent economic crisis, contemporary families are experiencing prolonged dependency of adult children, creating a new mode of 'interdependence' between single adult children and their older parents. However, family nuclearisation does not always imply a weakening of (the sense of) family obligations but it inevitably alters traditional family functions and relationships.

Until very recently it was common in both urban China and Japan for older people who needed long-term care to be looked after in their own home and by their own family members. At the beginning of the 21st century, however, both societies are facing similar socioeconomic and demographic pressures. For example, prolonged longevity is increasing demands for a prolonged length of care; and low fertility means there are fewer adult children in the family available to provide older parents with such intensive care. There are different responses to alternatives to family care within the state/market systems in the two societies. In Japan, under the new social insurance scheme, the focus has been on home-centred care, while in urban China since the welfare reform of the 1990s there has been an opening up of market opportunities for institutional care so many new developments have been taking place. People's attitudes towards long-term care have also shifted away from mere family obligations in both societies. In Japan, with competing commitments of adult children, 'care for older parents' has increasingly meant the organisation and management of available resources and the provision of emotional support (Izuhara, 2009). In urban China, attitudes about institutional care have been gradually shifting from stigma to privilege or a better demonstration of filial piety due to the high cost (and improved quality) of professional care in institutions (Zhan et al, 2008). In this context, children do not need to provide direct long-term or nursing care; filial duty can be fulfilled by emotional and financial commitment by placing their older parents in a high-quality care institution (Zhan et al, 2008).

There has always been a debate about whether the one-child policy in China undermines patrilineal norms, since society and family relations are becoming more egalitarian (Deutsch, 2006). Low fertility (as a result of the policy) is not the only reason why the notion of filial piety may be diminishing, but there is a combination of factors including marketisation, consumerism and wealth created by older parents influencing the transformation of such family practice. Is there a role reversal happening? In the past, investing in children may have been for the expectation of receiving filial piety later in a parent's own lifecourse. However, today a child's investment may be made for their own future and independence in increasingly competitive societies.

Research methodology and approach

This chapter's empirical data were collected using a qualitative approach in Tokyo and Shanghai in 2007 and 2008. The Tokyo and Shanghai fieldwork formed part of a wider comparative study designed to explore housing asset accumulation and intergenerational interaction over three generations in three East Asian cities including Hong Kong. Semi-structured, in-depth interviews were carried out with adult members of three generations – one member each from grandparents, parents and adult children (grandchildren), from 12 'families' in Tokyo and 13 'families' in Shanghai. The total number of interviews was 35 in Tokyo and 38 in Shanghai, although only 11 in Tokyo and 10 in Shanghai were complete three-generation families. The overall aims of the research were to examine how work, entry to homeownership and asset accumulation played out over the lifecourse, as well as to understand the dynamics of intergenerational relations within families in order to facilitate the processes cross-nationally. After gathering a basic profile of each informant such as age, occupation and family composition, the main questions were clustered in four areas: (1) housing history; (2) current housing; (3) support and assistance to and from their parents/adult children; and (4) attitudes and aspirations regarding work, housing and lifestyles.

Purposive sampling was used to select potential informants. As a sampling strategy, the age band of the *pivot* generation was set as 50–59 years old (born between 1948 and 1957). This age band included the postwar baby boomers – they were young enough to have living older parent(s) but old enough to have grown-up children in their late 20s and early 30s. The age of grandparents was flexible, but only adult children (those over 20 years) were included for this research. The sampling frame for the pivot generation included both men and women as long as they were themselves homeowners. Only nine out of 35 respondents in Tokyo were male, while in Shanghai 18 out of 38 were male. In order to reflect a variation in income and asset levels, we attempted to sample informants with housing assets/types falling into different price ranges from, for example, different neighbourhoods, different housing types such as detached houses, flats and condominiums and different periods of developments (for example new commercial built, ex-work unit housing).

In principle, only families from which three generations agreed to participate were interviewed, apart from a few extra interviews to make up the total number. Family members were interviewed individually without the presence of other family members using a topic guide that was developed based on the analysis of secondary data. We recruited families through a variety of means including advertising locally, personal contacts and contacting employers, local institutions and resident committees. Interviews took 60–90 minutes on average and were recorded with the informants' consent, transcribed fully in the original languages and then translated into English.

Most studies in this area have been limited to examining the linkages between two generations or have focused only on the experiences and circumstances of nuclear families. Face-to-face interviews with members of three interconnected generations offer greater scope for understanding intergenerational dynamics and changing attitudes and practices in relation to shaping family reciprocity and family wealth creation in contemporary East Asian societies. In this chapter, where empirical evidence is presented, individual informants are referred to by pseudonyms with 'older', 'middle' and 'younger' indicating their generational position in the family, plus age, gender and fieldwork locations.

Generations and the housing contexts in Tokyo and Shanghai

This section introduces our three generations against the housing contexts in Tokyo and Shanghai, reflecting the socioeconomic conditions of the postwar periods. There have been sharp contrasts in the fortunes of different generations across the two societies (Forrest, 2008; Forrest and Izuhara, 2009).

Tokyo

Tokyo, the capital of Japan, is both a global city and a megacity, with over a quarter of the nation's 127 million population residing in the metropolitan area. It is a prime example of 'metropolitan dominance' politically, economically and culturally (Rohlen, 2002). It is a major financial centre but unlike many other global cities, it continues to have a significant manufacturing base. In terms of urban landscape, Tokyo has transformed dramatically from the severe housing shortages immediately after the Second World War to an urban sprawl driven by the salaried workers' desire for small, detached houses, to the more recent popularity in high-rise condominium developments (Hirayama, 2006; Izuhara and Forrest, 2008). Tokyo does not represent Japan well in its tenure patterns, existing/available housing stock and dramatic price rises and falls. For example, in response to Japan's postwar economic growth, Tokyo has constantly attracted a flow of domestic migration that has resulted in a continuous expansion of the urban rental market. Since 1968, the rates of homeownership in Greater Tokyo have been ten percentage points lower than the national average, at 50 per cent. This is largely due to exceptionally high property prices and the high concentration of single-person households. In Japan there is still a strong correlation between family formation and housing tenure – homeownership often comes after marriage (Hirayama and Izuhara, 2008). Considering a steady increase in housing prices and the more recent property bubble and bust, the timing of entry to homeownership has been crucial for postwar Tokyo residents.

The older generation in the Tokyo study were aged between 77 and 89, but the majority were in their early to mid-80s at the time of interview. At the end of the Second World War they were of marriageable age and many came to Tokyo from neighbouring prefectures and beyond in the process of urbanisation. They typically started off lodging or renting a unit in a wooden-built apartment. Interestingly, some of our sample owned small businesses such as furniture making, a wholesale business and a newspaper agency tied to their housing. This cohort was often the first generation of homeowners in Tokyo who took advantage of, for example, rising real income and government land sales in the suburbs. This generation may have eventually acquired considerable wealth during the postwar period of rapid economic growth and high price inflation in the residential sector.

The middle generation were in their 50s (born between 1948 and 1957) which included the baby boomers. This generation was the beneficiary of improved postwar public policy and socioeconomic systems, including established occupational welfare. The majority have climbed up the housing ladder with their own income, typically from renting a wooden private apartment, through small 2DK (two rooms with a dining kitchen) Housing Corporation housing, to owning a single-family home or a condominium unit. Condominium ownership has gained popularity since the Government Housing Loan Corporation (GHLC) began offering loans to purchase condominiums in 1970. This generation took advantage of company housing schemes as well as the low interest loans provided by the GHLC. This cohort, however, includes both winners and losers of the property bubble in the 1980s (Hirayama, 2006). Due to the extreme property inflation experienced in Tokyo, some families combined their resources to achieve shared housing arrangements between two adult generations (Izuhara and Forrest, 2008).

The ages of our younger sample spread from 21 to 34 – five were in their late 20s and four in the early 30s. The sample group was well educated and often had siblings. Although well supported by their parents financially, the younger generation tended to have only experienced the prolonged economic recession since the burst of the economic bubble in the early 1990s. The research found diversified paths compared with the much more linear, upward social mobility of their parents' generation. There is increased dependence of adult children on their parents, which is evident in declining marriage rates and high rates of adult co-resident children, while some double-income couples have accessed homeownership earlier due to the price fall and financial deregulation.

Shanghai

Shanghai is the largest city (with an official registered population of 13 million) located on the central eastern coast of the People's Republic of China – a strategic port location. Since the mid-19th century, modern Shanghai has been a colonial enclave in which capitalism prospered while the rest of the country remained under feudal control (Fu, 2002). By the 1930s, it had become a world-class city with an international hub of business and finance until the Chinese Communist Party took power in 1949. During the Mao period (1949-78) there was no housing market in Shanghai or China as a whole, but housing was provided by government agencies, work units and state-owned enterprises. However, since its opening up to the world economy in 1978, housing provision has been 'commodified' and 'decentralised' (Wu, 2001). Since 1991, there has been a dramatic shift in Shanghai from state-planned housing provision to the market-oriented housing system with established housing funds, rent increases and privatisation of housing ownership. Consequently, living space per capita has risen from 6.4m² in 1991 to 21.3m² in 2006, and around 80 per cent of Shanghai families now own private residential properties (Shanghai Bureau of Housing, Land and Resources Administration, 1999; Zengwei, 2006).

The older generation in our research in Shanghai were aged between 72 and 89, with the majority in their late 70s and early 80s. They had experienced significant regime shifts from Japanese occupation, the civil war, the Communist regime, to the market economy, but mostly worked through the Communist system. When the Communist Party came into power in 1949 most were around 20 years old. They were often from Shanghai and due to the rigid registration system both social and spatial movements were restricted. They all had two to five children. The older generation were typically employed by a work unit, so access to welfare, including housing, education and food, was usually sought through the work unit (Chan et al, 2008). Since the housing reform, as sitting tenants the majority had become homeowners of often privatised ex-work unit housing. Sometimes, it meant owning a single-room flat (20m²). At the time of interview, only four out of 12 older informants lived with their adult children.

The middle generation were in their 50s and all had only one child, reflecting the one-child policy enforced since the 1980s. Being the first or second child in the family, some were sent to the countryside for farming under the *Shang shan, xia xiang* (up to the mountain, down to the village)[1] programme and some struggled to come back to Shanghai. For this generation, employment was less gendered and it was common for both husband and wife to work; they usually retired at the age of 50. There was a dramatic shift on the housing front – from single-room work unit housing shared by multiple family households to newly built commercial high-rises. There were more diversified housing experiences among this age group since some still lived in privatised ex-state apartments while others purchased large commercial flats (over 100m²) with a combination of their own income, investment returns and compensation money from the neighbourhood redevelopment taking place in many parts of central Shanghai.

Our younger cohort in Shanghai were all in their 20s (mostly late 20s), reflecting the government encouragement of delayed marriage and childbirth. They were the only child in the family and they were highly educated. Renting independently away from parents was rare prior to their marriage but all four married informants lived in their own owner-occupied, commercial flat. Compared to their parents' generation, many worked in the new 'trendy' service sector, for example a private art company, marketing or running a Japanese language training school. They were very much the consumption-oriented generation, putting an importance on material ownership of housing, cars, computers and other consumer goods.

Changing patterns of family support and reciprocity

Families in East Asia have always provided a range of support to their members from sharing accommodation, personal care provision to financial support. However, the fieldwork in the two cities revealed that the types, ideologies and levels of family support appear to have shifted from extensive direct provision of both practical and personal support, such as grandparents providing childcare in co-residency, to more indirect or material types of support, including financial and emotional support.

Providing direct care to their family members was definitely a shared oriental characteristic regarding family support. Compared to other welfare areas such as healthcare and pensions, the provision of such practical and personal support was sometimes quite extensive, especially in those societies in which alternative services were limited. The role of grandparents was highlighted in many Shanghai interviews; it was not uncommon for the older generation to look after their only grandchild, sometimes extensively as substitute parents, until the child reached school age, while both parents worked:

> "[My daughter's (50)] work place was quite near our house so we took care of her son after she had a baby. Her son was brought up by us. He stayed with us during weekdays and his parents took him back on weekends. Sometimes, his parents even stayed and slept at our home over the weekends [for seven or eight years]." (older, Lau, 81, male, Shanghai)

> "My son was taken care of by his grandmother [my mother] since he was young. He spent most of his time in his grandmother's home and kindergarten. Teachers in his kindergarten had never seen me around and they thought that I was away in a different city. I seldom looked after him." (middle, Chen, 58, male, Shanghai)

There are distinctive differences here between the two cities regarding childcare arrangements. Among the baby-boomer generation in Japan, the role of housewife had high status in the early postwar economic growth period. Most children in suburban Tokyo, for example, unlike those in traditional farming families, were raised by full-time housewife mothers within a nuclear family (Sasagawa, 2006). Apart from an early divorcee informant (male aged 57), whose sons were looked after by his older mother in co-residency, it was common for our Tokyo middle informants to have looked after their children themselves. In China, the socialist system presented more equal work opportunities for husbands and wives of the current middle generation which characterises one of Mao Zedong's slogans 'Women hold up half the sky' (Tang and Parish, 2000). In Tokyo, attitudes to and practices in childcare provision for younger working couples by their parents are more irregular and consist of 'helping' in emergencies rather than providing substitute care to parents:

> "When I was raising our children, my mother lived far away so she did not help me so much. She helped me when we were moving house or when I had to attend a wedding, for instance, but she did not help me in daily life." (middle, Tanaka, 56, female, Tokyo)

However, among the current generations with dependent children, the idea of grandparents being full-time childminders seems to be quickly disappearing not only in Tokyo but also in Shanghai:

> "If he has one [child], we will definitely offer him some help. But they cannot ask us to be the babysitter or entirely count on us. To be honest, younger people today think that parents are their child's babysitters, including my son's wife. But her parents and we disagree with it. If they want a family for themselves, they ought to take care of it on their own." (middle, Tang, 58, male, Shanghai)

The levels or volume of support flow have also been changing in both societies. As societies become more affluent, while extensiveness of such direct physical care provision has been diminishing, the volume of cash flow between family generations has increased. Under the socialist system in which everything was allocated by work units, parents were unable to offer any help other than practical and physical. In Shanghai, some parents used to send small sums of money to their children who were sent to the countryside in the 1970s enabling them to buy food or a travel ticket. Now it is common in both societies for parents to invest heavily in their child's education, such as paying for extra-curricular activities, full higher education fees and accompanying expenses. Also, in contemporary Shanghai, it is fashionable for parents to save money to send their child to study abroad:

"My parents do not give me too much cash, only 800 RMB a month, but would buy me top-up phone cards, travel cards, supermarket purchase cards, so it would be pretty much enough to cover my basic living cost. My tuition fees are expensive majoring in Cyber Art. Generally it charged 5,000 RMB annually for other students, but we have to pay 10,000 RMB. To complete the whole undergraduate programme, 40,000 RMB is needed. Other fees for textbooks, reading materials, accommodation (1,500 RMB per annum), it gets even higher. Moreover, to fulfil the course work, we have to buy digital camera and a PC, otherwise coursework could not be done. It is horribly expensive. Everything needed to fulfil the course requirements, my father would buy for me. Besides, my father has reserved a sum for me in case I would like to pursue further study overseas." (younger, Huang, 20, female, Shanghai)

"Competition in the society is rather intense nowadays, if you do not have a better degree, you cannot stand on your own." (middle, Huang, 51, female, Shanghai)

Housing is another worthwhile investment for parents to make for their children. And this is one of the social policy areas in which people's expectations of the state are low in general (Hirayama, 2003). Even in Shanghai an ideological shift appears to have been made for housing provision in line with the market system (but not necessarily for healthcare and pensions) (Wong and Lee, 2001). In the Tokyo study, younger married (and divorced) homeowners, although small in number, received a substantial amount of money (¥3-5 million) to put towards their down payment. In Shanghai, it is not uncommon for parents with a son to prepare a marriage home. In one family, parents (female aged 55) even made a great sacrifice of selling their own larger apartment to fund their son's (aged 28) commercial apartment purchase which was used to run his foreign language training centre. As a result, the parents now live in an ex-state-owned single-room housing unit with a private kitchen and a toilet (approximately 18m^2 floor space).

There are various driving forces for change, including economic growth, real income growth, the development of the welfare state and marketisation which brought about, for example, increased affordability, more options and availability of services in the care industry, and financial independence of each generation's household due to savings and social security. Stages and paces of development differ between the societies, which exhibit different patterns and outcomes. Increased social and geographic mobility may be creating a barrier to conventional intergenerational practices in those rapidly modernised and modernising societies. One strong drive found in Shanghai, in particular, for reasons behind investing in their children was the experiences (and lack of aspirations) of the middle generation in their previous socio-political system:

"At that time [the Cultural Revolution], I had one simple thought – if I have any children in the future, I would try my best to support him or her for better education. The same things could not happen to my children again; they should have clear thoughts about their own future, not like my generation." (middle, Zhong, 54, male, Shanghai)

In terms of old-age care, wider 'socialisation' of care is a new trend in both societies, reflecting recent marketisation and policy developments, but location and funding of care differ. In Japan, under the new social insurance scheme on long-term care, the role of the family has been shifting from the direct provision of care to more organisational and management roles of available resources as well as emotional support (see Izuhara, 2009). In Shanghai, institutional care is becoming more acceptable or even a prestigious option for middle-income families (Zhan et al, 2008):

"Care should be provided professionally and the family can just visit and support emotionally. Some people complain 'why does his family not come and do washing in the hospital?' but you can even out-source such services nowadays. Nurses can do nursing because it is not 24 hours but only 8 hours a day." (middle, Fujii, 51, female, Tokyo)

"Now it is different from the traditional family when three generations lived together and each had a role to play within the household. Now all three generations have our own separate household. We visit one another but I think we would better not depend on one another." (middle, Miyata, 51, female, Tokyo)

"We never expect to have our child look after us, we have residential homes for older people now, and we can live there if we have money. To be honest, thinking of relying on children when we get older is very unrealistic, he has his own job and family to cope with. If I have some money, I can hire a domestic nurse or move to elderly residential home for better care. It only cost 70-80,000 RMB per year now." (middle, Tang, 58, male, Shanghai)

In socialist China, the family also played a unique role in their children's career and thus residential location. Networks are important in both societies but in particular in China – passing down a parent's work unit position to children provided an important means for those who were sent to the countryside to return to Shanghai. Family connections and support helped many in returning to Shanghai and obtaining a stable position there, and such timing eventually put those in the middle generation in an advantageous position for asset accumulation when the economic reform started:

"My mother took an early retirement. The regulation was that younger people were allowed to return to their home town as long as certain work unit was willing to accept us and therefore our *Hu Kou* [residence permit] could be transferred back. And according to regulations in the old days, children were allowed to replace their parents' post after their retirement." (middle, Zhao, 54, male, Shanghai)

Sharing accommodation and thus sharing household resources was a shared characteristic of family support in both Tokyo and Shanghai as a response to family 'survival' (in response to poverty or housing shortages). There was a lack of adequate housing or 'crowdedness' in the past that was largely experienced by the older generation in Tokyo after the Second World War, but also in Shanghai by the middle generation in the 1970s. With social change and wealth created by economic growth and reform, family nuclearisation has been taking place in both societies in different times and at a different pace:

"[Nine people lived in a small house.] I had no free time. I have four in-laws above me [parents-in-law, brother-in-law and his wife]. Wherever I looked, there was always someone there. I was never able to be alone. I woke up 5am, fed and changed my children, and cooked for the family – a cooking area and toilet were outside." (older, Yamashita, 77, female, Tokyo)

"I lived in Hong Kou district. It was a small *Ting Zi Jian* [a small room facing north which feels cold in winter] … could accommodate only one bed, one desk and a chest of drawers. We installed an attic in the cavity between the upper and lower staircases. My mother, grandmother, my siblings and I lived together." (middle, Li, 59, male, Shanghai)

"My father passed away one year before my marriage. Both sisters had to live with their husbands' families, my elder brother was still in another province not yet back in Shanghai, while my eldest brother lived with his wife's family. In those circumstances, I felt that I had to stay with my mother as one of her sons to share the burdens of the family. In addition, during that period, most people at their marriage age were desperate to get a living place as it was too difficult to achieve. But we had the attic, completely for us, about 20m^2 and downstairs was used as a sitting room nearly 11m^2. I felt very pleased and did not expect more." (middle, Xu, 51, male, Shanghai)

Family strategies were evident in both societies to maximise resources and benefits regarding housing in the two different systems and the housing markets of Tokyo and Shanghai. In Shanghai not only passing down a job position but also swapping work unit houses was used as part of family reciprocity:

> "We used to live in Cao Jia Du and received one housing unit during the relocation scheme in Lu Wan district. We gave our new housing to my daughter's husband's work unit so that her family could be distributed another bigger apartment … my daughter bought it before the distribution and could not return it. So we gave ours to the work unit to make sure they could be allocated a bigger apartment. And then we moved in here. Here is a small living space, smaller than the previous one but it is enough for us. My daughter's family live in the bigger one from the distribution." (older, Lau, 81, male, Shanghai)

In Tokyo, on the other hand, during the buoyant housing market (especially during the bubble economy of the 1980s and early 1990s), some families combined their resources to maximise their housing opportunities. Contemporary co-residency has indeed become a strategy to overcome the affordability problem in urban areas:

> "My father wanted to share everything but I did not." (middle, Kariya, 53, female, Tokyo) [Older (80) and middle Kariya built two-household housing. Middle Kariya lives upstairs and her parents downstairs with separate entrances, kitchens and bathrooms. Her father's retirement allowances and her own savings from the period she lived in her parents home rent-free were put in for the land purchase.]

> "Quite a lot of people around here live together. Land is expensive here because of the easy access to central Tokyo. Many of my school friends came back and rebuilt their parents' houses to live with them – the ground floor for parents and the first floor for their living space, for example." (middle, Asano, 55, female, Tokyo) [Middle Asano and her family occupied the top floors of a small five-storey concrete building]

Family nuclearisation occurred earlier in Japanese society in the process of postwar modernisation and economic growth. Patriarchal authority and family tradition over marriage have been lessened considerably. In Shanghai, when families talked about parental obligations, specific financial and material provision, including preparation of a 'marriage home' for the groom's family (rather than authority over partnering), were frequently mentioned. In Shanghai, common marriage housing for the middle generation was either creating space within the already small parental home (for example installing an attic) or receiving a housing allocation by their work unit. Over just one generation it has increasingly become 'purchasing a commercial apartment'. In Tokyo, on the other hand, parental responsibility appeared not to extend to the provision of a marital home, but young couples often made their own arrangements. The first house after the marriage of the middle generation in Tokyo was often a separate small rental apartment:

> "Some of my boy classmates, their parents have recently started to buy apartments for them. I asked them, why? They told me it is for marriage use. Most expect the housing price to rise continuously, so it is for their own interest to purchase it NOW. As you know, in Shanghai or in China, it is boy families' responsibility to prepare the marriage home for the new couples. Of course, it would be perfect if both cars and housing are prepared." (younger, Huang, 20, female, Shanghai)

> "Parental responsibility ends when our children graduate from a university. If they want to get married or buy a house, they should do it themselves." (middle, Tokyo)

Parents continue to support their adult children and perhaps even more so now due to the wealth created by the middle generation and the risk society in which the younger generation lives. Prolonged dependency of young adults regarding co-residency and financial support has been increasingly discussed in both societies. This new phenomenon adds a different dimension to intergenerational relations in contemporary societies. While a new middle class with greater financial independence has emerged in the new market economy, many are still supported substantially by their parents' newly created wealth through inflation, investment and compensation:

> "I would not move out. I am not the renting type. My home is right here in Shanghai. What's the point in living outside? What's more, I feel it is more comfortable to live at home [with parents]. You have got your parents' company and they can take care of many things for you. Sometimes I hang out with friends, I would come home late – but that is it. I do not think I have to move out to earn the freedom or convenience." (younger, Zhong, 25, female, Shanghai)

> "The situation is the other way round – we are taken care of by our parents. My parents come here nearly every day or every other day to prepare all our dinner.... We also give them some money but we do not feel good. They as our parents might think it is their responsibility to help children and we are their only child. But, as their children, we feel guilty and try to find a way to compensate them a bit, to give them some money is simply what we can do now. What they have done for us is far more than this." (younger, Zhao, 27, female, married, Shanghai)

"I want to leave my parents home by 30. I do not give my parents any money. I do not receive pocket money from them but my mother cooks for me and does everything. I would like to repay the debts." (younger, Yamashita, 27, female, Tokyo)

The middle generation in the lifecourse is often called the 'sandwich' generation that is expected to support both older parents as well as their own children. However, the 'sandwich' generation also applies to the generation 'having experienced a 180 degree change in family systems, values and relations' (Izuhara, 2000). In Japan, the older generation raised their baby-boomer generation in a rapidly democratising society with new family ideologies. The same process could be viewed and experienced very differently for the older generation that was brought up with traditional values under severe economic conditions. They are the last generation who obeyed their parents(-in-law) and looked after them single-handedly at home; they are also the first generation who are not looked after by their adult children under the new social insurance for long-term care scheme. However, in the case of Shanghai the generation that is experiencing such compressed social change and value shift may be the middle generation. For the current middle generation, family relations with their only child who was born and raised in the new market system will be very different from their previous norms.

In the low fertility society, the middle generation are supposed to have more time and resources to help the generations both above and below, but children are increasingly becoming burdens as opposed to assets for contemporary Shanghai families. This can be seen as a reversal of the Confucian notion of filial piety:

"People in my generation [those in their 50s] were like backbones. We took care of older parents and looked after our children. From now on, when my generation passes, China will no longer have a generation like us. Nonetheless, raising my own child is a personal thing – I should not complain." (middle, Tang, 58, male, Shanghai)

"It is impossible [for our children to buy better housing for us]. Their children will sooner or later get married and they have to reserve money to prepare for their own children's marriage housing and other relevant arrangements. They could not support two sides – older parents and their own children. We have to take care of ourselves." (older, Lau, 81, male, Shanghai)

"The traditional sense of family does not exist through entire social change. Neither I nor my son has traditional concepts of the family any more. Our next generation becomes interest-oriented, selfish. But is it good or bad? I have thought of this question for a long time, and I did admit it is good because they have to be interest-oriented in order to survive in this competitive market. But people in my generation were more concerned about public good – we shared with people thus it causes disharmony for two generations living together. I refused to be a servant to my son and his wife. And I certainly will not let my wife become one." (middle, Tang, 58, male, Shanghai)

Conclusions

As society develops, the nature, type and level of family support changes adjusting to withdraw, fill the gap or complement existing resources provided by other sectors. In general, a shift has been made from the provision of more practical help, such as the direct provision of care and sharing limited resources such as living space, to less physical support – emotional support, helping with decision making and financial support, including housing purchase and paying for children's higher education. Family relations may be simply changing from material reciprocity to more psychological interdependency (Wang and Hsieh, 2000). This shift is in line with the increasing affluence among the parents' generation in the market economy as well as competing commitments of younger generations. With increased or available funds, investing in (a small number of) children is considered to be the best strategy to improve their social capital and thus help children eventually achieve greater financial independence from their parents. In the past, family interdependence was part of East Asian cultural values but today both 'independence' and 'dependence' has increased from other generations up and down in different capacities. Older parents have become more independent from their adult children in terms of residency and retirement resources. Conversely, prolonged dependence has been witnessed among the younger generation and is likely to increase in the current economic climate.

On the one hand, urban China is following Japan's path regarding shifting intergenerational relations. The patterns of family reciprocity may be converging, but with a time lag. Younger Shanghainese and younger Tokyoites now both live in consumer-oriented modern societies. While social change has taken place over two generations in Tokyo through the postwar period, the change has been more compressed in Shanghai and has occurred within one generation. It was indeed evident that with social change and now more opportunities available in the market economy, the generations in both societies are growing away from the previously found intensive and exclusive self-help approaches. On the other hand, the shifts may be taking different routes with different implications in the two societies given their different policy regimes and social structures. Existing housing markets and labour markets, as well as welfare states, manipulate such processes and produce different family attitudes and practices. Many families, extended or nuclear, adopt the local contexts and use certain strategies to maximise their collective benefits over income streams and thus wealth accumulation over generations.

Acknowledgement

This chapter draws on a research project 'Housing assets and intergenerational dynamics in East Asian societies' funded by the Economic and Social Research Council (ESRC), UK, in 2007-08 (RES-062-23-0187).

Note

[1] Around 17 million school students and young adults were mobilised to the countryside to address youth unemployment in cities from 1968 to the 1970s. They were required to experience peasants' life there. Some of them left home and settled down there for good while others returned home later.

References

Chan, C.K., Ngok, K.L. and Phillips, D. (2008) *Social policy in China: Development and well-being*, Bristol: The Policy Press.

Chen, X. (1985) 'The one-child population policy, modernization, and the extended Chinese family', *Journal of Marriage and the Family*, vol 47, pp 193-202.

Deutsch, F.M. (2006) 'Filial piety, patrilineality, and China's one-child policy', *Journal of Family Issues*, vol 27, pp 366-89.

Forrest, R. (2008) 'Globalisation and the housing asset rich: geographies, demographies and policy convoys', *Global Social Policy*, vol 8, no 2, pp 167-87.

Forrest, R. and Izuhara, M. (2009) 'Exploring the demographic location of housing wealth in East Asia', *Journal of Asian Public Policy*, vol 2, no 2, pp 209-21.

Fu, Z. (2002) 'The state, capital, and urban restructuring in post-reform Shanghai', in J.R. Logan (ed) *The new Chinese city: Globalization and market reform*, Oxford: Blackwell, pp 106-20.

Goodman, R., White, G. and Kwon, H.-J. (eds) (1998) *The East Asian welfare model: Welfare Orientalism and the state*, London: Routledge.

Hashimoto, A. and Kendig, H.L. (1992) 'Aging in intergenerational perspective', in H.L. Kendig, A. Hashimoto and L.C. Coppard (eds) *Family support for the elderly: The international experience*, Oxford: Oxford University Press.

Hirayama, Y. (2003) 'Housing policy and social inequality in Japan', in M. Izuhara (ed) *Comparing social policies: Exploring new perspectives in Britain and Japan*, Bristol: The Policy Press.

Hirayama, Y. (2006) *Tokyo no Hate ni [Beyond Tokyo]*, Tokyo: NTT shuppan.

Hirayama, Y. and Izuhara, M. (2008) 'Women and housing assets in the context of Japan's home-owning democracy', *Journal of Social Policy*, vol 37, no 4, pp 641-60.

Izuhara, M. (2000) *Family change and housing in post-war Japanese society: The experiences of older women*, Aldershot: Ashgate.

Izuhara, M. (2009) *Housing, care and inheritance*, London: Routledge.

Izuhara, M. and Forrest, R. (2008) 'Housing strategies and intergenerational dynamics in Tokyo', Paper presented at the ISA RC21 Tokyo Conference, 17–20 December.

Management and Coordination Agency, Japan (2005) *Kokusei Chosa [Population Census of Japan]*, Tokyo: Statistics Bureau.

National Bureau of Statistics of China (ed) (2003) *China statistical yearbook: 2003*, Beijing: China Statistics Press.

Palmer, M. (1995) 'The re-emergence of family law in post-Mao China: marriage, divorce and reproduction', *The China Quarterly*, no 141, pp 110–34.

Rohlen, T. (2002) *Cosmopolitan cities and nation states: Open economies, urban dynamics and government in East Asia*, Stanford, CA: Asia/Pacific Research Center.

Sasagawa, A. (2006) 'Mother-rearing: the social world of mothers in a Japanese suburb', in M. Rebick and A. Takenaka (eds) *The changing Japanese family*, London: Routledge, pp 129–46.

Shanghai Bureau of Housing, Land and Resources Administration (1999) *Reform of Shanghai Real Estate Industry and Review of its Development*, vol 9.

Sheng, X. and Settles, B.H. (2006) 'Intergenerational relationships and elderly care in China: a global perspective', *Current Sociology*, vol 54, no 2, pp 293–313.

Takegawa, S. and Lee, H.-K. (eds) (2006) *Fukushi Regime no Nikkan Hikaku [Welfare regimes in Japan and Korea: Social security, gender and labour markets]*, Tokyo: University of Tokyo Press.

Tang, W. and Parish, W. (2000) *Chinese urban life under reform: The changing social contract*, Cambridge: Cambridge University Press.

Walker, A. and Wong, C.-K. (eds) (2005) *East Asian welfare regimes in transition: From Confucianism to globalisation*, Bristol: The Policy Press.

Wang, Q. and Hsieh, Y. (2000) 'Parent–child interdependence in Chinese families: change and continuity', in C. Violate, E. Oddone-Paolucci and M. Genuis (eds) *The changing family and child development*, Burlington, VT: Ashgate, pp 60–9.

Wong, C.-K. and Lee, P.N.-S. (2001) 'Economic reform and social welfare: the Chinese perspective portrayed through a social survey in Shanghai', *Journal of Contemporary China*, vol 10, no 28, pp 517–32.

Wu, F. (2001) 'Housing provision under globalisation: a case study of Shanghai', *Environment and Planning A*, vol 33, pp 1741–64.

Zengwei, W. (2006) 'Review of Shanghai housing funds', *Shanghai Real Estate*, July.

Zhan, H.J., Feng, X. and Luo, B. (2008) 'Placing elderly parents in institutions in urban China: a reinterpretation of filial piety', *Research on Aging*, vol 30, pp 543–71.

SIX

Grandparents and HIV and AIDS in Sub-Saharan Africa

Akpovire Oduaran and Choja Oduaran

Introduction

This chapter explores reciprocal dimensions of intergenerational relations and examines current exchange practices and rationales in the context of the severe environments found in Sub-Saharan Africa. In particular it examines the role of grandparents in family support practices, and the challenges presented to them by the rapid disappearance of the middle generation due to the epidemic of HIV and AIDS in the region.

Confronted by the pandemic problem of HIV and AIDS, Africa is beginning to rediscover and apply things that have worked in the past in terms of building tacit intergenerational relationships in an era of globalisation. Grandparenting has become even more salient today since many Sub-Saharan nations lack viable, well-monitored social policies that could provide better modern alternatives to the challenges presented by the large numbers of orphans created by the HIV and AIDS crisis. Despite rich natural resources, the wealth of Sub-Saharan Africa has not translated sufficiently into development, largely due to endless civil wars, border conflicts and weak structures for democratic governance (Oduaran, 2008). For example, the healthcare systems in many countries of the region have not been able to meet with existing expectations. Even if medical care is available, people need to travel long distances to receive it. While HIV and AIDS are decimating their human capital, the nations of Sub-Saharan Africa have witnessed new trends in and new importance of grandparenting, which is the main focus of this chapter.

Sub-Saharan Africa consists of the nations located below the Saharan desert[1]. In recent times, these nations have undergone tremendous socioeconomic and demographic changes. These changes have tacitly affected relationships among generations, which have moved away from conventional ideologies and practices. The Western monolithic system that largely conceptualises the ideal family as one consisting of a man, his wife and their children has been attractive to the educated African elites for a very long time. Under the nuclear family model it was becoming very difficult for any educated person to embrace the extended family system by virtue of the fact that the much needed resources may not be available for the judicious care of immediate family. Yet it is the extended family system that has kept many 'traditional' African families going during a period of tremendous social pressure. At the same time, however, the traditional African family system has also undergone some measure of transformation mainly due to new challenges the nations were facing. These challenges have become so intense that it is difficult for anyone to underestimate the impacts they have had on the countries' social equilibrium. Indeed, new patterns of family relations are emerging in response to the HIV and AIDS epidemic and also in response to globalisation, although the emphasis of this chapter is on the impact of the HIV and AIDS pandemic. The pandemic has induced significant family changes, value shifts and socioeconomic transfers that have not been properly documented in the Sub-Saharan Africa context to date. Moreover, the flow of support among generations is often determined by the absence or near absence of visible public policies in the domain of the lifecourse. The analysis of interpersonal relations between grandchildren and grandparents is located in the context of macro-level national and sub-continental political economy and public policy.

The issues explored in this chapter have become more salient in recent years because the population of Africa is ageing at a fast pace. Although Sub-Saharan Africa is home to about 635 million people out of a worldwide population of 6,134 billion, about 45.7 million of Sub-Saharan Africans (7.5 per cent) are aged 60 years and older (Africa 25, 2004). Due to the fact that a good number of the population have access to modern medical practice and improved well-being, it is expected that Sub-Saharan Africa will witness an exponential increase in the number of older people aged 60 years and over from the current figure of 45.7 million to about 183 million in 2050.

Sub-Saharan Africa in context

Sub-Saharan Africa is home to 10 per cent of the world's population. Its culture is very diverse due to the heterogeneous populations and geographical spread. Whereas people of Arab descent and desert nomads dominate the North, people of black ethnicity can be found largely within the tropics, and especially around the Equatorial region. There are the Yoruba in the South West, the Ibos and Efiks in South Eastern regions of Nigeria and a number of people of black ethnicity in the southern regions of the Republics of Cameroon, Gabon and the Democratic Republic of Congo, to mention just a few. The diversity highlighted here has implications for our discussion: for example it implies that we could not possibly cover grandparenting practices in all of Sub-Saharan Africa. And it is indeed not wise to try to generalise their practices. In other words, only selected practices have been identified for the purpose of our discussion. Nevertheless, there may be more commonalities than disparities among the populations when it comes to issues of family support and systems.

HIV and AIDS and the 'missing generation'

First of all, by the term 'missing generation' we refer to the young adults and the middle age group (approximately, those aged between 18 and 45) who are probably the worst affected by the HIV and AIDS pandemic in the sub-continent. They are regarded as the 'missing generation' because their resources (in terms of contributing to the economic growth of Sub-Saharan Africa) are lost during their illness and eventually due to their early death. This 'missing generation' has been a phenomenon caused by the HIV and AIDS pandemic that has had a devastating effect on the populace. The 'missing generation' has been increasing in size over the years as is demonstrated in the statistics presented below. An estimated 3.4 million adults and children were infected with HIV in Sub-Saharan Africa in 2001 alone, and by the end of that year, the sub-continent was said to be harbouring an estimated 28.1 million adults and children living with HIV/AIDS (Kelly, 2005, quoting UNAIDS, 2002). The HIV epidemic is far from being under control in Sub-Saharan Africa.

Bennell (2004, pp 1-2) points out that, although it is impossible to generalise about the epidemic across the continent, advocacy is reportedly getting in the way of objective assessment of the levels and trends of the HIV epidemic. Bennell unequivocally argues that the HIV prevalence rates are not increasing in most Sub-Saharan countries as is usually stated or implied. While that might appear to be 'good' news, it is also true that highly accurate statistics on mortality in Sub-Saharan Africa are still lacking, and we can only rely on estimates of HIV prevalence and sentinel population surveys.

By 2003, Sub-Saharan Africa's HIV and AIDS pandemic had assumed such a posture that the BBC News (2004) tagged the situation as 'grim' when viewed against the backdrop of the global spread and effects of HIV and AIDS.

Table 6.1 shows that in 2003 between 25 million and 28.2 million people were living with HIV in Sub-Saharan Africa alone, compared with 1.3 million recorded for Latin America, 350,000–590,000 for the Caribbean, 1.2 million–1.8 million for Eastern Europe and Central Asia, 0.7 million–1.3 million for East Asia and the Pacific and 4.6 million–8.2 million for South and South East Asia. In effect, while Sub-Saharan Africa harboured 61 per cent of the world's HIV cases, with 2.2 million–2.4 million deaths as of 2003, Latin America accounted for only 4.1 per cent of the total global HIV cases. Comparatively put, Australia and New Zealand accounted for 0.04 per cent with less than 100 AIDS deaths in 2003. However, for both Australia and New Zealand the occurrence of HIV and AIDS incidents alone have been meaningful in that it shows how easily the disease can be spread. Sub-Saharan African nations thought they could have some respite in view of all of the protracted efforts that have been made, but recent figures about the status of the problem have not been encouraging. AVERT (2007) released figures that give us some idea about the challenges the nations are facing.

Table 6.1: Global spread of HIV and AIDS in 2003

Regions	People living with HIV	% of world's HIV cases (approx)	New cases in 2003	AIDS deaths in 2003
Sub-Saharan Africa	25–28.2 million	61	3–3.4 million	2.2.–2.4 million
North Africa and Middle East	470,000–730,000	1.6	43,000–67,000	35,000–50,000
Latin America	1.3 million	4.1	120,000–180,000	49,000–70,000
Caribbean	350,000–590,000	1.3	45,000–80,000	30,000–50,000
North America	0.79–1.2 million	2.6	36,000–54,000	12,000–18,000
West Europe	520,000–680,000	1.5	30,000–40,000	2,600–37,000
Eastern Europe and Central Asia	1.2–1.8 million	3.9	180,000–280,000	23,000–37,000
East Asia and Pacific	0.7–1.3 million	2.8	150,000–270,000	32,000–58,000
South and South East Asia	4.6–8.2 million	17.8	0.61–1.1 million	330,000–590,000
Australia and New Zealand	12,000–18,000	0.04	700–1,000	Less than 100

Source: Adapted from BBC News (2004)

AVERT (2007) reports that an estimated 22 million adults and children were living with HIV in Sub-Saharan Africa as of the end of 2007 (see Table 6.2). During 2007, an estimated 1.5 million Africans died from AIDS. As a result, the epidemic has left behind some 11.6 million orphaned children in Africa, and it is now feared that some 30,000 Sub-Saharan children die every day from HIV. It is hardly encouraging news that the nations have not made significant progress in dealing with the challenges posed by the disease.

Table 6.2 provides a clear picture of orphan prevalence in Sub-Saharan Africa, and also clearly indicates the extent and continuity of the challenge to Africa's older people, especially grandparents, with an estimated 22 million people living with HIV.

Bicego et al (2002) have drawn attention to the fact that until recently the principle sources of orphan prevalence estimates for Sub-Saharan Africa have come from the US Census Bureau and the UN Population Division. The estimates have used the same general approach to produce projections of maternal orphan prevalence (which includes double orphans). According to Bicego and his colleagues (2002), as a first crucial step in these models, pre-AIDS and then AIDS-impacted female adult mortality rates are estimated and projected using HIV prevalence estimates and assumptions regarding the trajectory of the epidemic in adults, incubation times and survival times. They also observe that orphan 'incidence' is estimated based on adult female mortality function and adopted

Table 6.2: Sub-Saharan Africa HIV and AIDS statistics in 2007

Country	People living with HIV/AIDS	Adult (15-49) rate (%)	Women with HIV/AIDS	Children with HIV/AIDS	AIDS deaths	Orphans due to AIDS
Angola	190,000	2.1	110,000	17,000	11,000	50,000
Benin	64,000	1.2	37,000	5,400	3,300	29,000
Botswana	300,000	23.9	170,000	15,000	11,000	95,000
Burkina Faso	130,000	1.6	61,000	10,000	9,200	100,000
Burundi	110,000	2.0	53,000	15,000	11,000	120,000
Cameroon	540,000	5.1	300,000	45,000	39,000	300,000
Central African Republic	160,000	6.3	91,000	14,000	11,000	72,000
Chad	200,000	3.5	110,000	19,000	14,000	85,000
Comoros	<200	<0.1	<100	<100	<100	<100
Congo	120,000	3.5	43,000	6,600	6,400	69,000
Côte d'Ivoire	480,000	3.9	250,000	52,000	38,000	420,000
Democratic Republic of Congo	400,000-500,000	1.2-1.5	210,000-270,000	37,000-52,000	24,000-34,000	270,000-380,000
Djibouti	16,000	3.1	8,700	1,100	1,100	5,200
Equatorial Guinea	11,000	3.4	5,900	<1,000	<1,000	4,800
Eritrea	38,000	1.3	21,000	3,100	2,600	18,000
Ethiopia	980,000	2.1	530,000	92,000	67,000	650,000
Gabon	49,000	5.9	27,000	2,300	2,300	18,000
Gambia	8,200	0.9	4,500	<1,000	<1,000	2,700
Ghana	260,000	1.9	150,000	17,000	21,000	160,000
Guinea	87,000	1.6	48,000	6,300	4,500	25,000
Guinea-Bissau	16,000	1.8	8,700	1,500	1,100	6,200
Kenya	1,500,000-2,000,000	7.1-8.5	800,000-1,100,000	130,000 180,000	85,000-130,000	990,000-1,400,000
Lesotho	270,000	23.2	150,000	12,000	18,000	110,000
Liberia	35,000	1.7	19,000	3,100	2,300	15,000
Madagascar	14,000	0.1	3,400	<500	<1,000	3,400
Malawi	930,000	11.9	490,000	91,000	68,000	560,000
Mali	100,000	1.5	56,000	9,400	5,800	44,000
Mauritania	14,000	0.8	3,900	<500	<1,000	3,000
Mauritius	13,000	1.7	3,800	<100	<1,000	<500
Mozambique	1,500,000	12.5	810,000	100,000	81,000	400,000
Namibia	200,000	15.3	110,000	14,000	5,100	66,000
Niger	60,000	0.8	17,000	3,200	4,000	25,000
Nigeria	2,600,000	3.1	1,400,000	220,000	170,000	1,200,000
Rwanda	150,000	2.8	78,000	19,000	7,800	220,000
Senegal	67,000	1.0	38,000	3,100	1,800	8,400
Sierra Leone	55,000	1.7	30,000	4,000	3,300	16,000
Somalia	24,000	0.5	6,700	<1,000	1,600	8,800

Country	People living with HIV/AIDS	Adult (15-49) rate (%)	Women with HIV/AIDS	Children with HIV/AIDS	AIDS deaths	Orphans due to AIDS
South Africa	5,700,000	18.1	3,200,000	280,000	350,000	1,400,000
Swaziland	190,000	26.1	100,000	15,000	10,000	56,000
Togo	130,000	3.3	69,000	10,000	9,100	68,000
Uganda	1,000,000	6.7	520,000	110,000	91,000	1,000,000
United Republic of Tanzania	940,000	5.4	480,000	130,000	77,000	1,200,000
Zambia	1,100,000	15.2	560,000	95,000	56,000	600,000
Zimbabwe	1,300,000	15.3	680,000	120,000	140,000	1,000,000
Total Sub-Saharan Africa	22,000,000	5.0	12,000,000	1,800,000	1,500,000	11,600,000

Notes: Adults are defined as men and women aged over 15 years, unless specified otherwise. Children are defined as people under the age of 15 years, while orphans are people aged under 18 who have lost one or both parents to AIDS.

Source: AVERT (2007)

fertility rates in the reference populations (Bicego et al, 2002). What is important to us in this context is that the measures have revealed a steady increase in the number of orphans in the sub-continent, but what should be even more important is the implication of this increase on the older generation.

A body of literature on HIV and AIDS in Sub-Saharan Africa has built up rapidly over the past few decades. Almost all aspects of the pandemic have been studied, but there is still little quality information available on how HIV and AIDS have negatively impacted on the older generation in African families. To date, this dimension has been little explored (see for example HelpAge International, 2004; Oduaran, 2004, 2008). Yet grandparents are known to have become both a social and an economic resource that Sub-Saharan Africa will rely on in the face of the global economic recession, which is likely to lead to reduced national budgets for social services, and they are also becoming recognised contributors to the social capital of their grandchildren.

New trends in grandparenting

There is no doubt that the HIV and AIDS pandemic has produced public health, socioeconomic and cultural crises in many countries in Sub-Saharan Africa. Grandparenting, as a social resource that has been relied on to deal with so many familial crises, has not been spared either. The pandemic has negatively impacted on cultural values as the extended family system has been stretched beyond its limits. Elsewhere, we have demonstrated how HIV and AIDS have helped to strengthen traditional values in intergenerational relationships (see Oduaran, 2008). We quoted that there are many grandparents who would rather 'take the place of their grandchildren at the "altar" of death by HIV and AIDS' (2008, pp 56-66). This illustrates the love that grandparents show for the dying children, grandchildren who in many Sub-Saharan African cultures are regarded as priceless jewels. Also, this partly accounts for the ignorance with which they manage the children's last days. Even though the older age cohorts may not be counted among the sexually active segments of society in terms of contracting HIV by way of sexual intercourse, they have been paying the painful price for the failure of their young people to heed the clarion call for protected sexual intercourse. In Sub-Saharan Africa, the HIV and AIDS puzzle seemingly remains a myth that has not been fully comprehended because of cultural misunderstandings of the reality of the pervading destructive potential of the epidemic.

Out of empathy, older men and women in Africa have become carers for their children and grandchildren who have contracted HIV. Cohen (2003) identified that, in Africa alone, it is estimated that there are some eight million children who have lost either one or both parents to HIV-related illnesses. Indeed, when the deaths occur, the burden of caring for the orphaned children rests on the family, and older people in particular. For these older people, the burden of prolonged illnesses associated with HIV and then the consequent deaths rests heavily on their shoulders.

Culturally, older people have no choice but to help dying family members and the children that are left behind. Moreover, older people are not only affected socioeconomically, but they are also sometimes infected through such close physical contact, and may die. In a context where illiteracy, ignorance and poverty abound in damaging proportions, the multidimensional impacts of HIV and AIDS need to be better understood (Oduaran, 2008). Whether affected or infected, the realities of compassion and sorrow abound, as is illustrated by the words of the older people themselves. For example, an older woman from Botswana who cares for her adult son suffering from AIDS stated:

> "I cannot go to funerals or weddings, not even to church because I have to be with him all the time, or most of the time … I can't even go to the fields to plough." (quoted in HelpAge International, 1999a, p 1)

According to Fleshman (2001), a 70-year-old woman raising her four grandchildren in Zambia told a researcher that:

> "… ever since these children were brought to me I have been suffering. I am too old to look after them properly. I cannot cultivate … and the food does not last the whole year." (quoted in AVERT, 2005, p 11)

This is an example of how the ageing process is not considered an excuse for abandoning the traditional role of caring for grandchildren.

In Zimbabwe, a 65-year-old man who is a carer for three school-aged children said:

"Looking after orphans is like starting life all over again, because I have to work on the farm, clean the house, feed the children, buy school uniforms.... I thought I would no longer do these things again. I am not sure if I have the energy to cope." (*The Namibian* (2002) 'Older AIDS caregivers face stigma', allafrica.com, 16 December, quoted in AVERT, 2005, p 11)

The three examples featured in these quotes indicate that grappling with the HIV and AIDS pandemic in Sub-Saharan Africa leaves no one with choices to make. Both the grandparents and their grandchildren have to move beyond the traditional caring programmes built around African customs and values to understanding a phenomenon that is almost overwhelming.

Traditionally, African children and grandchildren were expected to take care of their ageing parents and grandparents. William Eagle (2007) quotes an old *Yoruba* saying (words of wisdom which are commonly passed on to the younger generations by their elders) that illustrates the traditional expectation of the care of the aged people as follows:

"The bush rat gave milk to its children when they were small. When it grows old, it then drinks from its children's breasts." (Eagle, 2007, p 1)

This saying implies the reciprocal expectations between the generations in families: you take care of your children (and grandchildren) so that they in turn will care for you when you become old. These expectations are very valid in social systems that have very weak pension schemes, as is the case in many Sub-Saharan African countries today. In Botswana, for example, retired civil servants receive pensions of about P100 (100 Pula = US$12) per month, which barely enables them to meet their most basic needs. Botswana has a system of free medical care for older people, and this provision is much better than what is available in many other countries such as Nigeria and Malawi. Unlike countries of the North, including the US and the UK, many countries in Africa are yet to have in place residential care for older people. Even where such care homes exist, their patronage would scarcely be appreciated as the age-old cultural expectactions for children and grandchildren to care for their elderly parents and grandparents are still very much valued. Unfortunately, the expectation has been weakened by the combined forces of rural–urban migrations, international emigrations, deaths from HIV and AIDS, poverty and other social trends (Eagle, 2007). The reality of the situation is that the number of orphans and vulnerable children has been dramatically increased beyond that which modern social support systems can handle on the sub-continent. While the traditional extended family system is treasured greatly by Africans, it is beginning to be revisited and reinforced by cultural systems that may be found, for example, among Batswana in the nation of Botswana and the Yoruba, Igbo, Ijaw and Urhobo ethnic groups in Nigeria.

In fact, among the Urhobo in the Niger Delta State of Nigeria, sending elderly parents or grandparents to government-run homes for older people is considered to be a sign of ingratitude. Anyone from the Urhobo ethnic group who tries to send their parents or grandparents to such homes is considered within the cultural milieu as rather 'wicked'. In Yaba, in the Lagos State of Nigeria, for example, there is a home for older people aged 60 years and over that has been running for a long time on public funds, but has of late not been receiving residents. It is not easy to explain why this is the case because literature on the subject has not revealed any possible reason. In some ways, the tradition has stood the test of time. In such ethnic groups, there are transparent and close links that are unique among the people who do everything they can to sustain their traditional systems. What has been said for the Urhobo ethnic group holds true for the larger Yoruba ethnic group and for other minority ethnic groups such as the Isokos in the same geographical location as the Urhobo.

Eagle (2007, p 1) quotes HelpAge International to the effect that there are over six million children in Sub-Saharan Africa who are being cared for by their grandparents. What this means is that the expectation expressed in the Yoruba saying has, in some ways, been rendered invalid. Rather than expecting the mother 'bush rat' to get some breast milk from the 'baby bush rat', the former has had to look elsewhere for help. That is, if there is any help available at all. In fact, the mother 'bush rat' has little hope in waiting for any future support, and must therefore continue to provide for the children.

The HIV and AIDS pandemic has brought with it a scenario in which the family structures and traditional support systems have been so negatively altered that older parents and grandparents have no one to care for them. This is the likely situation in many Sub-Saharan African countries, probably with the exception of Botswana, Lesotho and Mauritius, which have universal and reliable pension schemes and allowances for everyone over a certain age (Eagle, 2007). Even in such success cases as the countries that have already been cited, pension monies and allowances received are clearly shared by orphaned children and grandchildren. In effect, the presumed benefits may be minimal because of the extra burden added to the family and the loss of income from the 'missing generation'.

Beyond monetary considerations, grandparents in Sub-Saharan Africa are witnessing some tensions in other aspects of family support. It was previously sufficient for grandparents to fend for their grandchildren in terms of feeding, clothing, housing and security; this was their duty. Then, in addition to conventional expectations, grandparents were also expected to assist in the 'proper upbringing' of their grandchildren. In other words, moral development has become another serious duty of grandparents, in addition to other community development responsibilities.

Modern development has meant that grandparents need to be literate enough to support school attendance and the academic development of their grandchildren. Where it was once enough to just tell grandchildren moonlit stories that revolved around their cultural and historical lineages, grandparents must now go beyond that and have some knowledge of modern technologies such as computers and use of the internet. Indeed, the whole idea of 'cyber grandparents' is something that grandparents in the West are getting used to now, and this has been shifting into the sub-continent (Heyman and Gutheil, 2008). Therefore, if you are a grandparent in the African context, you not only have to provide your grandchildren with food, clothing and shelter but actually in many instances also shepherd them to school and get involved in their education (thus the child's future). HelpAge International (cited in AVERT, 2005) has reported that in the Kalomo District of Zambia school attendance rose after older people were provided with cash transfers, while in contrast, in Tanzania, only about 146,000 children orphaned by HIV and AIDS could afford school fees as their grandparents had no pensions (quoted in Eagle, 2007, p 2). (This is why the activities of an organisation such as HelpAge International, who support senior citizens without access to pension schemes, become important to Africans.) HelpAge International has also launched successful animal rearing projects for older people in Ethiopia, Kenya and Uganda to enable them to raise their own income to support younger family members (Eagle, 2007). Economic empowerment for older people in the sub-continent could go a long way towards preparing individuals for their grandparenting roles, and make an effective contribution to social capital development. However, there has been another trend in grandparenting.

As grandchildren are orphaned by AIDS deaths, grandparents have had to add a new dimension of caring. First, prior to looking after their grandchildren, grandparents cared for their adult children who were HIV positive; tremendous stress and social cost are attached to such support. However, the trauma is probably made worse when these same grandparents are then asked to care at another stage for the orphaned grandchildren. These grandparents do not always consider the risk factors, initially. In many instances they have no choice, even when there are public care services, as there are in some countries. The tradition of the African population tends to place the burden of taking over the care of orphaned grandchildren on the grandparents within the family. There is often no debate about it and no alternative is sought – refusal to care would lead to stigma for the family.

Caring for orphaned children with HIV and AIDS has meant that grandparents have had to learn some medical/health treatments in order to deal with HIV infections. In some cases, they are completely ignorant about the disease and, because of their ignorance, some grandparents become infected themselves from careless handling of waste materials and the administration of drugs to infected children.

Yet research and education on HIV and AIDS in Sub-Saharan Africa has hardly considered the important role played by grandparents in terms of dealing with the pandemic. They are often treated as an unknown quantity in the statistical data that are generated and policies pay hardly any attention to the significant contributions that they are making. Whereas the African Union has always expressed interest in developing policies that protect older people in the sub-continent, the reality of the situation on the ground is that there is little to report about social security systems that adequately care for the older population in Africa. Our general observation has revealed that, in Nigeria for example, public pension schemes have not yielded evidence of considerate and adequate provisions for older people. In Nigeria older people who served the Federal Government of Nigeria have to travel several hundreds of kilometres to Abuja, the capital, to collect somewhat miserable pension allowances. Many of those travelling to Abuja do not have enough money to stay in decent hotels, and it has even been alleged that some of them do not get back home alive.

Reciprocal dimensions of intergenerational relationships

The new trend being witnessed in grandparenting in Sub-Saharan Africa has clear implications for intergenerational relationships. HIV and AIDS have seriously altered the focus and direction of the flow of intergenerational support in Sub-Saharan Africa. The focus and direction for grandparents has moved away very subtly from engagement with transmitting cultural values and the raising of grandchildren under conditions of peace and economic and social stability to confronting death with so much compassion and bravery, and thereby causing sorrow and untold hardships. Certainly, it is necessary to highlight how the current trend is being altered in Sub-Saharan Africa because of the HIV and AIDS epidemic.

First, as Schneider and Moodie (2002, p 5) argued, HIV and AIDS in Sub-Saharan Africa has already resulted in increased numbers of rootless, uneducated and unnurtured young people living on the streets who are at risk of becoming 'a lost generation of potential recruits for crime, military warlords, and terrorists'. If, as Schneider and Moodie (2002) suspect, orphaned children do in reality become 'rootless, uneducated and unnurtured', the intergenerational practices in Sub-Saharan Africa will have to grapple with becoming more involved in:

- strengthening and transmitting to the orphaned children those strong traditional values that continue to unite people under the extended family system;
- ensuring that the orphaned children are enrolled in schools, helping them with their studies and ensuring that the grandparents themselves have a minimum level of literacy and education;
- exploring ways and means of reversing the vicious cycle of poverty by forming small business enterprises aimed at empowering people financially so that they can meet the basic nutritional needs of the orphaned children.

These may be some of the ways of dealing with the downstream consequences of HIV and AIDS, but by far the most important challenge that faces intergenerational practice in Sub-Saharan Africa is how (as a matter of urgency) generations can unite to reverse the spread of HIV and AIDS.

Belsey (2005) rightly pointed out that one dimension of the impact of HIV and AIDS for intergenerational relationships and families of individuals who are infected with the virus is that there would be increased pressure to undergo the process of adaptation and support. In particular, families would have to undergo the redefinition of relationships within the larger social environment and would then need to address AIDS-associated stigmatisation, which has apparently hindered the effectiveness of the public campaign aimed at resolving the challenges posed by the epidemic, and how to care for infected relations. That has already happened in Sub-Saharan Africa. Grandparents have become the main carers or 'substitute parents'; as the extent of the 'missing generation in the middle' becomes greater, intergenerational relationships have taken on a new dimension of reciprocal actions. While the grandchildren still expect their grandparents to administer traditional care functions, they are themselves now educating their grandparents about stigmatisation.

Belsey (2005, p 85) also reported another new development described as 'parentification' that has evolved as a result of the pandemic. The new term describes the situation in which Sub-Saharan African countries have been thrown into systems and circumstances that have increased the risk of inappropriate and premature assumption of adult roles by children or adolescents who have to look after their younger siblings. In most cases, we are talking about children or adolescents who are assuming parenting roles before they have a chance to become emotionally and spiritually developed enough to carry out those roles. They are forced into roles for which they have no skills, resources or preparation. The implication here is that grandparents may be asked to mentor the children and adolescents who have found themselves in this predicament. Finally, the pandemic has produced a new pattern in socioeconomic transfer that is reciprocal in its nature. Rather than expecting grandchildren to transfer socioeconomic capital to parents and grandparents, the grandparents are the ones who are now increasingly engaged in transferring such capital to their grandchildren.

Challenges and mitigations

The discourse envisaged in this chapter would not be complete without an attempt to indicate the challenges and possibly the mitigations that are relevant in this context. The first challenge that anyone who is interested in exploring this topic faces is the apparent lack of valid data and literature (Aboderin, 2004; Oduaran, 2004, Ferreira, 2008). A search of the web would testify to this fact. A possible explanation proposed here is that anything that might have been written by African scholars on the subject in sources within the continent is rarely included on the World Wide Web. This means that anyone relying on information from that kind of source would almost automatically be under-informed. In fact, very few journals and books published within Africa ever find their way into the international academic or popular circle. So hard data on socioeconomic transfers between grandparents and grandchildren are very hard to come by, and this is indeed the case for many African countries including south of the Sahara, with the exception of South Africa. This can only be reversed if African scholars are perhaps encouraged and assisted to upload whatever information they have on the subject onto the web. For example, the beautiful picture that Hagestad (2006) painted of the continued parenting of the middle generation and the ties between grandparents and grandchildren in three-dimensional perspectives in Norway also exists in Africa. The problem is that studies of intergenerational relationships within Africa are still very scarce and only a few gerontologists have actually paid attention to this relatively new field in the African context.

It is also very difficult for anyone who is interested in describing the micro and macro perspective of intergenerational relations and transfers in Africa to get much further than piecing together some anecdotal verbal accounts that had been in existence and how that might have changed little in recent times. In fact, if we were to describe quantitative data such as the simultaneous care of parents and children or family transfers involving three generations studied in a longititudinal way, or even the redistributive effects of generational transfers in such detail along the lines suggested by Attias-Donfut and Wolff (1999), Arrondel and Masson (2001) and Agree et al (2003), there would hardly be any space to highlight other salient aspects of the problem. Nevertheless, we know that all of the features and concerns indicated by scholars in the West do exist and have transpired on the continent of Africa for centuries.

And then, the last major challenge that Sub-Saharan Africa would have to address is how best to respond to the obvious emergence and prevalence of the 'lost generation'. If the young people orphaned by HIV and AIDS are left alone to fend for themselves in the way they are right now, we will soon have an even more difficult problem to deal with. First, the category of young Africans implied here may not have been adequately identified as such by the statistical returns – very few Sub-Saharan African nations report to UNICEF and UNESCO. To the best of our knowledge, no one has taken the time and space to scientifically study the effect of the 'lost generation' for current cohorts of grandparents. We saw earlier in this chapter that grandparents do in fact become 'parents' again in the midst of dwindling resources as they grow older. When the children who were expected to care for them in their old age become helpless, it then means that there can be no social transfer on the scale reported in the Western world. In effect, the so-called 'lost generation' are not in any reasonable position to support the very grandparents who had stood in the gap for them. This reality becomes even more disturbing as most of the governments in Sub-Saharan Africa are yet to make the least provision for social security systems that can effectively deal with the issue. In that case, we would have a double tragedy on our hands in not only having failed to help the 'lost generation' and their grandparents but, even more painfully, 'ignorantly' creating a pool of miscreants from where warlords in the continent can enlist recruits for endless civil wars and crimes. One major way of averting this looming crisis is to take statistical account of the 'lost generation', and to make adequate provision for their education and general upkeep.

Judging by the nature of the challenges faced on the subject in Africa, it might be trite to make a plea for some kind of collaborative work between scholars in the North and South so as to bring on board the rich information that is available on the subject, but which unfortunately is not being reported as such to help it gain international attention. It is also lamentable that many African governments do not seem to recognise the importance of intergenerational relationships and transfers that have been occurring in the continent or it is generally assumed to be part of our culture and therefore not to need any rigid scholarship and research. If that is the assumption, this kind of attitude can hardly take Africa very far. In order to have valid data and analysis on this subject, it is time to do more in the direction of promoting collaborative research that is multidisciplinary in nature. If this call is heeded, we are almost sure that we would be cultivating an African cultural artefact which will be priceless at this time when the HIV and AIDS pandemic has drained so much of our resources, but certainly not our hope, for a better, healthier and safer Africa.

Conclusions

Sub-Saharan Africa is undergoing more dramatic changes in the roles, practices and patterns of grandparenting than it could ever have imagined before the 1980s, when a new disease with devastating effects on people's social, cultural and economic values was discovered. The HIV and AIDS pandemic has been a major concern for Sub-Saharan Africa because it has considerably altered the balance that countries had tried to maintain in terms of national income allocation among the competing sectors for national development. Almost without any preparation, the sub-continent woke up to the reality of seeing its grandparenting tradition and intergenerational relationships altered. This chapter has shed some light on this new engagement. The most challenging aspect in all the new developments is that the continent has not given up on its usual compassion and spirit of volunteerism for which grandparents are well known and for which they receive no formal appreciation or recognition. This chapter has drawn attention to some of the challenges that face any scholar who is willing to explore the subject. Mitigations reflecting the challenges have been indicated, but this is just the beginning, and should be further consolidated by way of drawing attention to the subject. There are gaps in the literature that need to be filled in a global articulation of the subject pursued in this volume. We hope that as Sub-Saharan Africa continues to grapple with these challenges, the African Union and international agencies that are keenly interested in ensuring that Africa is not left behind in the global race for rapid social and economic development in a competitive atmosphere pay closer attention to the role of older people in the different communities.

Considering the fact that grandparents have been shaping continental responses to the challenges of modern development, they justifiably deserve more research and policy attention than they are currently receiving. The positive aspect about our own experience is that there is a ray of hope on the horizon, judging from the policies and structures that are being put in place, for example in some Sub-Saharan countries including Botswana and South Africa. We hope that when other African countries come up with effective social policies that pay sufficient attention to older people, we will be in a better position to boast about what we have been able to achieve for ourselves.

Note
[1] Sub-Saharan Africa typically comprises Angola, Benin, Botswana, Burkina Faso, Burundi, Cameroon, Cape Verde, Central African Republic, Chad, Comoros, Democratic Republic of Congo, Republic of Congo, Côte d'Ivoire, Equatorial Guinea, Eritrea, Ethiopia, Gabon, the Gambia, Ghana, Guinea, Guinea-Bissau, Kenya, Lesotho, Liberia, Madagascar, Malawi, Mali, Mauritania, Mauritius, Mozambique, Namibia, Nigeria, Niger, Rwanda, São-Tomé and Principe, Senegal, Seychelles, Sierra Leone, Somalia, South Africa, Sudan, Swaziland, Tanzania, Togo, Uganda, Zambia and Zimbabwe.

References
Aboderin, I. (2004) 'Modernisation and ageing theory revisited: current explanations of recent developing world and historical Western shifts in material family support for older people', *Ageing and Society*, vol 24, no 1, pp 29-50.
Agree, E., Bissett, B. and Rendall, M.S. (2003) 'Simultaneous care for parents and care for children among mid-life British women', *Population Trends*, vol 112, pp 29-35.
Arrondel, L. and Masson, A. (2001) 'Family transfers involving three generations', *Scandinavian Journal of Economics*, vol 103, pp 415-43.
Attias-Donfut, C. and Wolff, F.C. (1999) 'The redistributive effects of generational transfers', in S. Arber and C. Attias-Donfut (eds) *The myth of generational conflict: The family and state in ageing societies*, London and New York, NY: Routledge, pp 22-46.
AVERT (2005) 'HIV/AIDS Orphans Statistics' (www.avert.org/aidsorphan.htm. pp1-11).
AVERT (2007) 'Sub-Saharan Africa: HIV and AIDS statistics' (www.avert.org/subaadults.htm).
BBC News (2004) 4 March (http.news.bbc.co.uk/1/1/shared/sp/hi/Africa/03/aidsdebate/html).
Belsey, M.A. (2005) *AIDS and the family: Policy options for a crisis in family capital*, New York, NY: United Nations Department of Economic and Social Affairs.
Bennell, P.S. (2004) 'HIV/AIDS in Sub-Saharan Africa: the growing epidemic?' (www.eldis.org/hivaids/questioningnumbers.htm), pp 1-5.
Bicego, G., Rutstein, S. and Johnson, K. (2002) 'Dimensions of the emerging orphan crisis in sub-Saharan Africa' (www.sciencedirect.com/science).

Cohen, D. (2003) 'Poverty and HIV/AIDS in Sub-Saharan Africa', HIV and Development Program (www.undp.org.hiv/publications/issues/English/issue27ehtml).

Eagle, W. (2007) 'Activists for the aged press for greater care, pensions in Africa', NewsVOAcom (www.voanews.com/englsh/africa/2007-02-19-voa35.cfm).

Ferreira, M. (2008) *Ageing policies in Africa: Regional dimensions of the ageing situation*, Economic and Social Affairs, New York, NY: United Nations, pp 63-83.

Fleshman, M. (2001) 'AIDS orphans: facing Africa's silent crisis', *Africa Recovery*, vol 15, no 3, October, p 1.

Hagestad, G.O. (2006) 'Transfers between grandparents and grandchildren: the importance of taking a three-generational perspective', *Zeitschrift für Familienforschung*, 18 Jahrg, Heft 3/2006, S 315-332 (www.zeitschrift-fuer-familienforschung.de/pdf/2006-3-hagestad.pdf).

HelpAge International (1999a) *The ageing and development report: A summary*, London: HelpAge International.

HelpAge International (1999b) *Addressing older people's rights in Africa: Good practice guidelines*, Kenya: HelpAge International Africa Regional Development Centre.

HelpAge International (2004) 'HIV/AIDS and older people: the African situation' (www.helpage.org).

Heyman, J.C. and Gutheil, I.A. (2008) 'They touch our hearts: the experience of shared site intergenerational program participants', *Journal of Intergenerational Relationships: Programs, policy and research*, vol 6, no 4, pp 397-412.

Michiels, S.I. (2001) 'Strategic approaches to HIV prevention and AIDS mitigation in rural communities and households in Sub-Saharan Africa,' *SDimensions*, Rome: Food and Agricultural Organisation.

Oduaran, A. (2004) 'Living in the valley of death: intergenerational programs, poverty and HIV/AIDS', Keynote address given at the 2004 ICIP International Conference, University of Victoria, Canada, 3-5 June.

Oduaran, A. (2008) 'Compassion and sorrow as irreducible minimum for intergenerational practice in Sub-Saharan Africa', *Journal of Social Sciences*, vol 16, no 2, March.

Schneider, M. and Moodie, M. (2002) *The destabilizing impacts of HIV/AIDS*, Washington, DC: Centre for Strategic and International Studies.

UNAIDS (Joint United Nations Programme on HIV/AIDS) (2001) *Report on the global HIV/AIDS epidemic*, New York, NY: UN.

SEVEN

Spiritual debts and gendered costs

Pascale F. Engelmajer and Misa Izuhara

Introduction

In recent decades, patterns of migration in Thailand have evolved, and have shown an increase in rural–urban female migration relatively to male migration (Arnold and Piampiti, 1984; Tangchonlatip et al, 2006), a trend that is also found in transnational migration (see for example APMRN, 1995). While the primary motivation for such an increase is certainly economic – women seek better opportunities in the capital or in tourist resorts – there are other explanations such as altruism (normative expression of gratitude) and part of the 'generational contract' (repayment or prepayment of migrants towards their household, especially in societies where formal welfare is limited) which make it more urgent for some women to migrate and, often, to even engage in hazardous work (Osaki, 2003; Vanwey, 2004; Rende Taylor, 2005). Another brief explanation that is often given concerning Thai society is related to their religious belief: children owe their parents a debt, which sons repay by joining the Buddhist *sangha*, and daughters repay by providing material support (see for example Mills, 1999).

The gender difference that underlies the motivation for migration and choice of occupation has not been researched in any great depth. Some academics have worked across disciplines to examine the link between economic choices and religious and cultural practices (Keyes 1983, 1984; Kirsch, 1985). In much Asian literature examining intergenerational relations within the family, for example, there is an inevitable discussion of 'filial piety' and filial obligations. Filial piety appears to be conceptualised and practised quite differently in the wider Asian region where social norms have different roots (that is, Confucianism, Buddhism) (see for example Sung, 2003; also see Chapter Five of this volume for East Asian practice). Moreover, while much contemporary social research has investigated, in a cross-disciplinary way, the patterns, motivations and implications of female migrations in the developmental context, exploring the origin of such ideology and discourse has rarely been considered. It is therefore worthwhile examining the cultural and religious origins of intergenerational relations to see how they have evolved from their recorded textual beginnings to contemporary societies. It seems that careful analysis of religious texts can shed some light on behaviour patterns that seem strongly entrenched in the Asian population. In this chapter, Thailand is selected as a case study society given a combination of its distinctive religious and cultural orientations and the high volumes of both intra- and international migration. The main aim of this chapter is thus to take an interdisciplinary approach, and to bring together textual analysis of ancient religious texts and social research into migration patterns by sharing our knowledge and methodology in order to understand contemporary discourse in Thai society.

The Thai idea of filial duty has ancient roots that can be traced back to the Pāli canon, the canon of Theravāda Buddhism, the largely dominant religion in Thailand. The filial obligations that are clearly set out in the ancient Indian texts were adapted in the Thai cultural landscape, and the emphasis on the son's ordination as a means of repaying his debt is found in later Northern Thai religious texts (Keyes, 1983). Nowadays, the idea that children owe a debt to their parents is deeply entrenched in Thai culture and forms the basis of parent–child relationships. It is drawn on to explain the differences between sons' and daughters' filial obligations, and it is also used as a rationale for female economic behaviours, such as migration and choice of occupation. The emphasis on daughters' obligations towards their parents can be found in a wide range of material, from academic research (for example Mills, 1999) to so-called 'true stories' relating the life of sex workers (see for example Sharron, 2006).

In this chapter, we seek to summarise the position of ancient texts on the idea of filial duty, and its implications for Thai society (in which ordination for women is impossible[1]). We also examine patterns of female migration and how they correlate with the notion of 'dutiful daughter'. While this notion that a dutiful daughter provides financial and material support for her parents is a very prominent one, the extent to which this model is accurate across social classes and across time is an area that needs further investigation. This chapter concludes with some discussion on the link between the religious texts and contemporary human behaviours.

Religious context

Many authors writing on Thai families mention the obligation faced by children to repay their parents' care (Montgomery, 2001; Esara, 2004), and the distinct ways in which sons and daughters traditionally do so (Vichit-Vadakan, 1994; Limanonda, 1995; Richter, 1996; van Esterik, 1996; Montgomery, 2001; Mee-Udon and Itarat, 2005; Rende Taylor, 2005). However, very few authors have sought to examine the origin of such gendered behaviours, and in any depth how these radically different patterns of reciprocity have emerged from the early Buddhist texts (see Keyes, 1983; Kirsch, 1985). The population of Thailand is predominantly Theravāda Buddhist, and the pervasive influence of the religion is apparent at many levels in the life of the Thai people. The scriptures of Theravāda Buddhism (often referred to as the 'Pāli canon') contain descriptions of appropriate and beneficial family relationships. While the majority of Thais would not understand or know the Pāli texts directly, most, if not all, of them would know many stories based on texts from the canon, or from post-canonical literature, such as adaptations of the *Jātakas*, the stories of the previous births of the Buddha, and Thai culture is steeped in the Buddhist tradition (Kirsch, 1985). Examining the ancient texts may allow for a deeper understanding of the present patterns of reciprocity, and of the gender differences that characterise them.

References to parents are scattered throughout the Pāli canon. The canonical texts emphasise that we owe our existence to our parents, stating that: 'one is born of father and mother' (for example D I 34, D I 76)[2], and to their benevolence, in particular that '[they] do much for children; they bring them up, nourish them and introduced them to the world' (A I 68). This is compounded, in the case of mothers, by the particular hardships of childbearing and childbirth that they go through 'with much anxiety, as a heavy burden' (M I 266). The debt incurred by offspring, then, is presented as immeasurable, and this is confirmed by a lengthy and colourful description in the *Anguttara* (A I 61). The Buddha states that there are two persons that cannot be repaid (*na suppatikāram*). He goes on to give examples of what children can do for their parents, and still not repay them. He declares that if one were to live a hundred years and carry one parent on each shoulder during that time, and meanwhile 'anoint them with balms, massaging, bathing and rubbing their limbs' (A I 61), even if one were to 'establish [one's] parents in supreme authority ... over the mighty earth abounding in the seven treasures' (A I 61) he would not repay parents for giving him life and nurturing.

The texts, in addition to describing children's obligations towards their parents, also declare the rules for proper behaviour of each towards the other, and show their reciprocal quality. In the *Sigālaka sutta* (D III 189), the ancient Indian brahmanical practices that applied to householders are adapted for Buddhist purposes, and the Buddhist householder is enjoined to perform five actions for his parents: support them as they have supported him, carry out their duties for them, 'keep up the family tradition, ... be worthy of his heritage' and then, after their deaths, give offerings to the *petas* on their behalf. Parents are expected to reciprocate in the five following ways: they 'restrain him from evil, support him in doing good, teach him some skill, find him a suitable wife and, in due time, hand over his inheritance to him' (D III 189). Some of these are themes that we still find in Thai society today.

Numerous passages in the canon underline the need for children to support, venerate and respect their parents. Mother and father always come first in lists representing social hierarchy (S I 178, S V 409, S V 467). They are equated with gods and spiritual teachers, and are worthy of offerings (A II 68). They should be worshipped and honoured (A II 68, A III 75, D II 306, Sn 404, S I 178). Supporting parents is a sign of moral superiority (S I 90), and a source of merit (S I 181, A I 88), whereas behaving wrongly towards your parents is a sign of foolishness and a source of much demerit (A I 88, A II 3), and even results in children not being successful in their lives, especially in their old age (Sn 404). In the extreme case of wrong behaviour, killing one's parents leads one to 'misery and distress in hell' (A III 146).

Parents must be supported by providing them with food and drink (including feeding them with one's own hand), clothing and housing, and even bathing and massaging their bodies, and washing their feet (A II 68), a range of obligations that appear prominently in the *Jatakas*. All these actions represent the proper behaviour of 'good' children towards their parents. However, while it reciprocates the care that parents have given their children, the texts claim that it does not repay what the parents have done for their children (A I 61).

There is nowhere, in the *Nikāyas*, a clear explanation of why parents cannot be repaid. The only explanation that the *Anguttara* passage itself gives is that parents 'do much for their children, they bring them up, nourish and introduce them to the world'[3]. While it is understandable that society would insist on the importance of parents' nurture and care and emphasise the need for 'repayment', the debt seems to have significance beyond mere social expectations. Material support is obviously not enough to repay the debt, and thus it leads us to question the nature of the debt and how it can be repaid. Fortunately, the *Anguttara* passage tells us immediately that the only way to repay your parents is to introduce them to the Buddhist path, here summarised as faith, morality, generosity and wisdom (A I 61).

Two types of debt and corresponding relationships of reciprocity are apparent from this. One (which has just been described and which the Pāli texts describe in a rather colourful way) is firmly set in the worldly realm. The other, which does not appear to be explained explicitly, needs some attention. If we consider the 'worldly' debt, it is repaid with the same currency, so to speak. Parents provide care, nurture and education at the beginning of life; children provide care, nurture and funerary rites at the end of life. Therefore the nature of the repayment is comparable to the nature of the debt. We can safely assume that the other type of debt implies a similar relationship.

A passage in which the Buddha speaks with his aunt Mahāpajāpati repeats the exact phrases found at A I 61. Mahāpajāpati is described by Ananda as one who has 'done much for the Buddha, who has taken care of him, nourished him, and given him milk, who gave him milk when his mother died'[4]. Three terms here used to describe Mahāpajāpati are the same as those used to describe parents in the *Anguttara* passage. Ananda further explains what the Buddha has done for Mahāpajāpati, that is, it is thanks to the Buddha that she has become entered on the Buddhist path and reached a certain level of attainment, and is irreversibly on the path to *nibbāna*.

The Buddha concurs, emphasising that one who has done what he has done for Mahāpajāpati cannot be repaid by 'paying homage to him, rising up for him, according him reverential salutation and polite services and by providing robes, almsfood, resting places and medicinal requisites' (M III 254).

We have here an inversion of what we had found in the *Anguttara* passage. While in the *Anguttara* it is the parents that cannot be repaid (the same phrase is used), in the *Majjhima*, it is the Buddha that cannot be repaid. While the text does not explicitly state that the Buddha repays Mahāpajāpati by teaching her the *dhamma*, the implication is made very clearly when Ananda claims that the Buddha has also done much for Mahāpajāpati. The parent–child relationship is clearly established between the Buddha and Mahāpajāpati (use of the same terms), and the 'payment' of the filial debt (proclaimed as the only repayment possibly in the *Anguttara*) is epitomised by the Buddha's teaching of the *dhamma* to his foster mother.

From this brief observation, it can be concluded that there are two aspects to the parent–child relationship as it appears in the Pāli canon. On the one hand, children must repay their parents the nurture and care they receive from conception to adulthood. On the other hand, a more subtle debt, which cannot be repaid by material support but only by teaching your parents the *dhamma*, adds a spiritual dimension to filial obligations. This spiritual dimension, while never explicitly stated, seems to be present in passages that link the role of parents with that of the Buddha as the teacher *par excellence*.

The weight of this debt has to be put in its proper religious context. According to Buddhist tradition, beings are reborn innumerable times until they escape from the round of rebirths by achieving *nibbāna*, the highest spiritual goal. Until then, beings can be reborn in a variety of states from the lower realms of the *petas* (hungry ghosts) to the highest realms of the *devas* and *brahmās* (gods), as well as human beings. The realm and the circumstances in which beings are reborn depend *grosso modo* on the spiritual merit they have accumulated during previous lives. Every *kamma* (an act that is intended, and also includes thoughts) has a consequence on the store of merit beings accumulate, and therefore on the quality of their future rebirths and, furthermore, on their relative proximity to achieving *nibbāna*. Obtaining a human life is crucial as it is the only life that has enough of sorrow and happiness to motivate beings to set on the path to *nibbāna*. However, obtaining a life as a human being is a rare event, as a simile found in the canon, and repeated in most Buddhist traditions from Sri Lanka to China, shows. The simile claims that it is less likely for a person to be reborn in a human birth than for a blind turtle who comes up to the surface of the ocean once every hundred years to put its neck through a yoke with one hole in it (M III 170)[5].

Put simply and succinctly, as the physical basis for rebirth in the human realm, and thanks to their support in early life, parents therefore provide the foundations from which it is possible to advance towards the highest spiritual goal. It is in this context that the claims that nothing that children can do for their parents can repay them need to be viewed. In fact, the passage that makes this claim goes on to present the only way in which it is possible to repay parents for their kindness, and that is to introduce them on the Buddhist path: 'incit[ing], settl[ing] and establish[ing one's parents] in the faith, ... in morality ... and in wisdom ... does more than repay what is due' (A I 61), thereby, in a way, providing them with the same opportunity to achieve *nibbāna* which they have given their children.

The implications of this 'repayment method' will be discussed later. For the moment, suffice to say that it has a major impact on the way men and women can fulfil their filial obligations in Theravāda countries, where there is no ordination for women, and this is particularly so in Thailand.

The spiritual nature of the debt that children incur towards their parents is therefore neatly established by the texts insisting on the rarity and significance of a human life to obtain *nibbāna*. It is not based on the more prosaic aspects of parents' care for children.

Contemporary Thailand

Filial obligations are still important in contemporary Thai social life and embedded firmly in education and children's upbringing. An often-quoted statement made by the Office of the Prime Minister stresses that 'children caring for their parents, especially in their old age, is still a feature of Thai life, especially in rural areas' (Limanonda, 1995, p 77). This is illustrated in research conducted by Niels Mulder (1997) on the Thai national school curriculum. At primary school level the reciprocal relationship between parents and children is established in a rather unequal way, with parents' affection and care being presented as granted and unquestionable (echoing the Buddhist canonical texts), and children's 'absolute obligation to please' their parents being expressed by 'respectful and obedient behaviour, helping in the tasks around the house ... and later, caring for the parents in sickness and old age, then making merit for them after death' (Mulder, 1997, p 35).

This obligation that children have towards their parents is expressed in Thai by the term *bun khun*, which is 'a favour or benefit bestowed and for which one is obligated to do something in return' (Panyarachund, 1996, p 186). In the parent–child relationship, it is the idea that children owe a debt to their parents because of their parents' self-sacrifice when bearing and raising them. It is noteworthy that, as is found in the canonical texts, the debt that children owe their parents is not conditional on parents actually having performed in a particular way. Parents, simply by giving life and nurture in early childhood, have fulfilled their obligations towards their children. There is further the same notion that that *bun khun* cannot be repaid no matter what children do (Panyarachund, 1996, p 186). Anthropological research in various contexts also shows the continuing significance of this bond of reciprocity that puts the children in an incontestable debtor position. One informant tells a researcher that 'children owe a debt of merit [*bun khun*] to their parents for their having endured the hardship of childbearing and child rearing' (Rende Taylor, 2005, p 413). The concept seems to remain remarkably stable through time and across social classes.

While all children incur the same debt towards their parents, it is clear that the way of repaying the debt is not the same for sons and daughters. This practice makes Thai society distinct from other Asian societies, for example those with Confucian influence (see Chapter Five for further discussion). The canonical texts emphasise that the debt can only be repaid by establishing one's parents in the *dhamma*, the teachings of the Buddha. In the canon, there are several instances of monks instructing their parents, in particular their mothers. Even the Buddha is said to have ascended to the Heaven of the Thirty-Three Gods to teach the *dhamma* to his mother (who had died seven days after his birth) (Gethin, 1998, p 203). He is also shown teaching his father (J IV 50) and, of course, he not only established his foster mother, his aunt Mahāpajāpati, on the path, but he eventually agreed to ordain women at her request, accepting her as the first nun.

The idea that children can repay their filial debt by teaching their parents the *dhamma* is one that seems to have completely disappeared from today's Thailand. However, in the case of sons, there is still a clear relationship between repaying the filial debt and religious practice. It is commonly accepted that sons repay their parents, and especially their mothers, by ordaining as monks in the *sangha* (Panyarachund, 1996, p 186). Even the King of Thailand is said to have ordained for the sake of his mother (Handley, 2006, p 132). Short-term ordination is still considered the best way for a son to repay his debt to his mother, and remains a very strong ideal in Thailand, although the actual practice has become less common (Montgomery, 2001).

The connection between teaching the *dhamma* and being ordained is rather obvious, as in traditional Buddhist societies, the *bhikkhus* would teach the laity, and still today monks are involved in a wide variety of activities during which they may also impart some teachings. However, the Thai tradition has transformed the notion found in the Pāli texts into a possibly more convincing and appealing process that connects the ordination of a son to the merit gained by his parents, especially his mother, and to his own repayment of the filial debt, without necessarily involving direct teaching from the son to the parents.

Charles Keyes (1983) has shown how the inclusion of certain post-canonical texts during ordination ceremonies in Northern Thailand emphasises the transfer of merit from sons to parents that is achieved when a son becomes ordained. The text which he examines tells the story of parents who escape from hell on dying because their son has been ordained as a monk. Neither of them has led morally exemplary lives, but *Yama*, the Lord of Hell, finds that he cannot throw the mother into hell because the son has been ordained as a novice. Similarly, the father, who is reborn as a ghost, is released from this state on account of his monk son (Keyes, 1983). As Keyes explains, this story clearly illustrates the way Thai society has resolved the tension inherent in the ordination process: giving up a son to the *sangha* (the Buddhist community) has spiritual value for parents. Indeed, it has value for sons as well, because ordination, even for a short period as is customary in Thailand, seems to have become accepted as a way for sons to entirely clear their debts towards their parents. Through the concept of transfer of merit, the act of ordination replaces the ancient texts' injunction to teach their parents the *dhamma* in order to repay their debt fully. In modern Thailand, the result is that sons are not expected to 'support their parent's families' but daughters 'must repay [the *bun khun*] by working to support' them (Panyarachund, 1996, p 186).

Being a 'dutiful' daughter

In practical terms, the obligation for Thai children to support their parents, especially in their old age, is mostly an obligation for daughters. As a result, the burden of care falls primarily on daughters' shoulders. As observed above, this notion that daughters must provide material and financial support to their parents is found in a wide range of written materials 'introducing' Thai culture and society, including popular English language literature and guidebooks destined for foreign tourists and long-term visitors. It thus seems to imply that the underlying concept of such a 'dutiful daughter' deserves further investigation and examination in Thai language material such as magazines, popular novels and TV programmes in order to ascertain how such discourse is maintained and reinforced through contemporary popular culture. For the moment, it must be noted that certain traits emerge from the different contexts in which daughters' obligations are mentioned. The 'dutiful daughter' is one who sacrifices her life for her parents. If the support that she is able to provide when staying with her parents is not enough, she is willing to move to the capital, or any other place, to find work that will allow her to provide for their financial and material needs, and even to improve their status in the village. Eventually, she is even willing to marry a foreign husband or enter hazardous occupations such as prostitution, if necessary. The shame and 'loss of face' associated with sex work is, to a certain extent, alleviated by the higher purpose of fulfilling her *bun khun* (debt of merit).

These expectations do not seem to be found towards sons: sons are not expected to remit their earnings to their families as much as daughters (see Mills, 1999; Mee-Udon and Itarat, 2005, Rende Taylor, 2005), and we can safely assume that repaying *bun khun* is not the main (if at all) motivation for male migration. Sons are expected to ordain in the Buddhist monastic community even for a very short period of time in order to repay their parents, and especially their mothers, who are barred from ordination. Even though it is becoming rarer for sons to ordain, it still remains a strong ideal (Montgomery, 2001).

Conversely, a study of Thai women who join a female monastery (without the full ordination available to men) notes that women's ordination is not perceived in the same way as that of men. In Lindberg Falk's research (2007, p 199), one informant remembered that when she joined the monastery, her mother complained that: 'When girls become ordained, there is no comfort. When boys become ordained, everybody is happy'. Full ordination for women has been rejected very strongly by the Thai monastic institution, and the few Thai women who have sought to be fully ordained have been reviled by the established *sangha* (Dhammananda, Al Jazeera).

The notion of 'dutiful daughter' remains entrenched in contemporary Thai society as women, especially single mothers with dependent children, come to Bangkok with a 'very strong commitment that as daughters [they] have to support [their] family (both children and ageing parents)'[6]. However, there is not necessarily mention of a religious aspect for their decision. The concept of 'dutiful daughter' remains entrenched, especially as the motivation behind women's obligations, but it is evident that it has just become a strong normative discourse in contemporary practice, and has lost its connection to the religious discourse. Today, both migrant women and service providers 'do not know the rules about the religious teaching'. For them, 'it is a "tradition and folklore"; and the religion has little to do with their decisions but they make their decision based on their willingness to help the family left in the rural area' (Sarochinee Anyawachsomrith, personal communication, 9 February 2009).

In traditional society, the difference of expectations from sons and daughters did not have a very deep impact on the burdens that had to be borne by daughters. It can even be speculated that this burden of care on the daughters dovetailed perfectly with the predominantly uxorilocal nature of Thai families. Sons were not expected to provide support to their family of origin, because they moved to their wife's family, or they ordained as monks (dependent on alms from the community for their livelihood). On the other hand, daughters remained with their family of origin, were expected to care for their parents and inherited their land. However, in a rapidly changing and increasingly consumer-oriented society, these arrangements have changed considerably, especially as the economy has become monetarised and integrated in the global economy. Expectations for material support have grown manifold (Montgomery, 2001). Where parents expected a younger daughter to care for them in their old age, they now often expect daughters to provide them with the means to outdo their neighbours in consumer goods (Rende Taylor, 2005). This has consequences on female patterns of migration, and also on the kind of occupations daughters are ready to take up in order to be a 'dutiful daughter'. For example, repaying *bun khun* is the dominant theme when sex workers explain their motivation to engage in sex work (Phongpaichit, 1982, cited in Montgomery, 2001, p 65).

Processes and motivations of female migration

This section moves on to explore how such family ideology and religious beliefs regarding family obligations that originated in the ancient religious texts and more modern writing and discourses translate into contemporary family practice. In particular, by looking at the recent patterns and motivations of female migration from rural areas to Bangkok, it examines how children repay the spiritual debt to their parents, and whether gender plays a significant role in family reciprocity.

Following the global trend, significant migration both nationally and internationally started taking place in Thailand in the mid-1980s. Globalisation, for example, brought an economic boom in the East Asian region that increased foreign direct investment to Thailand resulting in the shift from an agriculture-based export economy to a more manufacture-based one in this period. During the decade from the mid-1980s it is estimated that the Thai economy grew on average 10 per cent annually (Warr and Nidhiprabha, 1996). Rural migrants made significant labour contributions to the expanding manufacture-based economy in and around Bangkok and many of them were young and female (see for example Phongpaichit and Baker, 1996; Mills, 1999; Curran et al, 2005). New and expanding employment opportunities through the export-led economic development in the metropolis indeed attracted rural migrants, who also had to face difficult conditions in rural areas, such as poverty, previous high fertility and limited opportunity in the land-based economy especially in Northern Thailand.

The patterns of rural migration are distinct and certain cultural influences can be observed. According to the 1992 National Migration Survey in Thailand[7], the majority of migrants (78 per cent) lived in rural areas and rural–rural migration (rather than rural–urban) was most significant (45 per cent). The northeast was the most mobile region, with 20 per cent of men and 13 per cent of women having moved for at least a period of time during the survey period – such temporary moves to urban areas have been common in the northeast for decades (de Jong et al, 1996, p 750). The vast majority of migrants (59 per cent) were under 25, and although men still dominated migration, 44 per cent of migrants were women. The Bangkok region attracted the most single migrants and migration was more prevalent among the highly educated population.

Factors influencing people's decision-making process to migrate are often complex and multiple. Traditional migration theories have often been dominated by economic determination, dominated by male migration, and migration is often thought to be a collective action of labours in a global economy and political system (see Castles and Miller, 2003). Increasingly, however, people move globally due to social, personal, institutional or environmental reasons including family reunion, family formation and educational benefits or even for the climate. The feminisation of migration is also a recent phenomenon that highlights women's increasing role in the migratory movements (Ackers, 1999; Castles and Miller, 2003). In the Thai context, although rural–urban migration could be still largely driven by economic determinants with increasing urbanisation and the shift towards wage-earning employment, the recent evidence of increasing single female migrants challenges the male-dominated and family-as-a-unit approach to understand the patterns and processes of migration. The decision-making processes of Thai migration are indeed gendered and individuals' decisions are usually linked to family context (for example UN, 1993; de Jong et al, 1996, p 749). It is often a combination of economic and non-economic reasons – while boosting the household economy is one reason, personal aspirations for adventure, social advancement, autonomy and freedom from the family household could be another. The motivation of female Thai migration can also be 'cultural' – 'the desire to repay their parents for raising them and being in some ways equivalent to a son entering the monkhood' could be still a strong underlying factor (Lim, 1993).

In rural Thai society, migration decisions are often made in the context of households and in response to the needs, obligations and aspirations of individual family members (Mills, 1999). Families in rural Thai society are matrilineal (Curran et al, 2005, p 231): Daughters thus take the main responsibility in helping the household with domestic tasks, caring for younger and older family members as well as financial contributions. Sons are expected to leave their original family for ordination or marriage. Therefore, at marriage, the daughter's family often provides a marriage home and the husband moves into his wife's family home and stays there often until the first child is born. There are higher expectations for daughters than sons to bring material as well as financial resources to the household. In return, the family reciprocates the daughter's contribution by leaving her real estate properties (see Keyes, 1984). Migration of daughters thus means that although there are advantages in receiving money from daughters' urban employment, there is the loss of daughters' contribution to household tasks as well as the delay in obtaining a son-in-law to provide the farm labour.

There are therefore clear household expectations towards sons and daughters in the rural Thai context. The religious beliefs regarding ordination, family tradition and marriage patterns shape not only obligations and future relationships of individual family members but also boys and girls are encouraged to socialise in different ways (Mills, 1999, p 80). Sons are allowed more independence in their daily activities while young women stay closer to home and are expected to perform household tasks. Such differentiated treatments of sons and daughters have created greater trust and normative expectations around reciprocity among parents and daughters themselves and that influences how responsible they should be financially towards the original family once they migrate to the metropolis (Curran et al, 2005). Parents tend to encourage daughters to migrate partly due to their reliability in remitting back to the family. However, daughters' migration also creates tensions between generations because of the loss of parental authority over daughters' labour and sexuality in an increasingly modernised society (Mills, 1999). Migrant daughters' commitment in maintaining financial support towards their families at a distance is also closely linked to the traditional 'generational contract' – daughters' expectation and reliance on receiving inheritance in the future. In contemporary society, however, 'investing in children' may take different forms as parents nowadays may decide to give their daughters education (greater social capital) rather than land as inheritance, since higher education leading to better job opportunities could provide better economic security to the family in the long run' (Richter and Podhisita, 1992).

Moreover, family roles are determined by birth order as well as gender. Not only gender but birth positions of children, especially daughters, also differentiate their opportunities and risks in rural Thai society (Rende Taylor, 2005). In the northeast region, for example, home help and reproduction are important roles for first-born daughters. The first-born daughter is therefore responsible for younger siblings, and their roles being close to home reduces their risks associated with (hazardous) employment away from home, but at the same time may also reduce their opportunities regarding life chances. Middle-born daughters are more likely to act as financial assistants, reflecting the tradition of using children to pay family debts. The middle-born daughters thus have a higher likelihood of migration and higher chances of working in hazardous work conditions including in the commercial sex industry. Youngest daughters tend to receive greater household resources for investment, education and inheritance. Such higher investment and expectations on the youngest daughters to succeed, however, sometimes jeopardises their situations, not being able to farm but entering into hazardous labour at the youngest ages (Rende Taylor, 2005).

At their destination, young female migrants tend to take up low-skilled jobs in a factory, as a domestic servant, or even as a commercial sex worker. For example high rural–rural migration indicates that their migration destinations could be another rural region, working in a factory producing electronics goods, owned by multinationals. Some ethnographic research conducted in the northern region, for example, highlights that despite the clean and modern images promoted by the electronics industries, the reality of workers, the majority of whom are young women, is associated with a wide range of occupational health problems, with longer working hours and without organised unions (Theobald, 2002). Moreover, Mills (1999) highlights migration consequences – for those who have migrated to the capital, there is a high temptation associated with material urban living and a difficulty in remaining focused on their financial responsibility to support their family back home. Another issue is commercial sex work that is highly visible in urban areas, whether in Bangkok or in popular beach resorts, and has always had a strong link to domestic as well as international migration. Some authors point out that prostitution has a long history in Thai culture (Cohen, 1996; Hong, 1998). Hendrijani (2005) even argues that 'Buddhism does not blame women who have to work as prostitutes for a living – all people including prostitutes have an equal opportunity to reach a higher religious achievement'. In this religious context, 'supporting the family financially is considered to be a high merit-earning act' and achieving this goal is, in a way, more important than the means to achieve it. In other words, women who become prostitutes to support their family are much less stigmatised in the Thai cultural context than in other Asian societies. Women can return home after a few years of working as commercial sex workers in urban areas and can live in the village with their wealth and face little stigma from their community (Peracca et al, 1998; Rende Taylor, 2005), although there is some controversy around how much stigma former commercial sex workers have to confront (Hong, 1998).

Conclusions

In this chapter we have attempted to use an interdisciplinary approach to examine intergenerational relations and, in particular, the gendered obligations faced by Thai adult children in reciprocating the care and support they have received from their parents. We analysed the ancient Theravāda Buddhist texts to determine the role and importance of filial obligations that can be found in those texts and to determine whether they affect contemporary attitudes towards filial obligations. Despite the numerous claims that gender differences in filial obligations are rooted in the Theravāda Buddhist tradition of Thailand, close examination of the canonical texts leads to three main conclusions. First, the texts reveal a very strong emphasis on family reciprocity and insist in particular on children's obligations towards their parents, and the special spiritual debt they owe them. Second, the texts indicate that, despite the need for children to provide support and care for their parents, especially in their old age, the only way to repay the spiritual gift of a human life is to introduce one's parents to the Buddhist path, to teach them *dhamma*, the Buddha's teachings. Finally, the texts, while male–oriented as most religious and traditional texts are, make no explicit difference between sons and daughters, and thus recognise the same obligations for both male and female offspring, and consequently the same means of fulfilling these obligations. As a result, while it is easy to trace the importance of filial obligations in contemporary Thailand back to the ancient texts, even to the point of noting similar expressions between the ancient texts and contemporary discourse, it is necessary to examine how the tradition has evolved in the Thai cultural context, and how factors other than canonical Therāvada Buddhism have contributed to produce the gender differences found today.

The most obvious difference between the canonical texts and contemporary Thailand is that the Therāvada female order does not exist any more. In Thailand there never was a female *sangha*. As a result, the only way to repay the spiritual debt to one's parents is unavailable to daughters. As discussed above, Keyes (1983) has shown how some Northern Thai religious texts point to the son's ordination being the means for parents' salvation from their own evil actions. By allowing their son to ordain into the *sangha*, parents gain salvation. However, they lose their son's labour and support, as monks are not allowed to work, or to earn any income. The logical next step is to shift the whole 'worldly' burden of care and support to daughters who cannot repay the spiritual debt. This attitude, combined with the uxorilocal nature of Thai family structure that meant that daughters remained with their families of origin and sons moved to their wife's families, explains how the gender difference has arisen and become entrenched in Thai culture. This attitude that women cannot become nuns is very strong in Thailand (Dhammananda, Al Jazeera). The national *sangha* refuses to consider the possibility of establishing a female *sangha*. The predominant attitude is that women are 'lower than men' and therefore not able to be monks (Dhammananda, Al Jazeera).

While the interdisciplinary approach is not always seamless, its findings reveal ancient roots to a modern discourse, and show how that discourse has been adapted to changing historical and cultural conditions. What it may also show is that a religious discourse is being drawn on, not only as a motivation, but rather as a rationalisation of certain economic behaviour, especially in the case of sex work: women who engage in the sex services industry rationalise and legitimise their economic behaviour by drawing on the notion of filial debt, and the particular obligations faced by daughters (Archavanitkul and Guest, 2000). Furthermore, in the case of these very behaviours considered unacceptable, Thai society may use the concept of filial duty to explain away the gender difference in filial obligations, and the heavy burden imposed on daughters by resorting to an 'honourable' motivation that lessens the objectionable character of the economic activity such as commercial sex work (Hong, 1998; Archavanitkul and Guest, 2000). The notions of 'filial duty' and 'dutiful daughter' become a legitimising discourse within society that allows certain forms of economic behaviours to be practised with less stigma and rejection[8].

However, we must use caution in seeing these notions as primary motivation for migration and choice of occupation, and ensure that other causes, such as structural factors (for example poverty, lack of education, limited range of economic opportunities and state welfare provision), are not obfuscated by cultural and religious explanations, but rather seen within their context to find better ways of addressing them. It must be recognised that the discourse around filial obligations remains very strong in Thailand, especially, but not exclusively, in the rural areas of Northern Thailand and Isaan, and that it is a discourse that affects men and women differently. We then pose a question as to how much it is still applicable to families in the context of current social change. There must be an increasing contestation between the traditional values and the forces of globalisation modernising/westernising family practices in Thai society. The role that this discourse plays in Thai society, and its tenor in the Thai cultural landscape, deserves further empirical research.

Notes

[1] It should also be considered whether female ordination would be perceived as a source of merit making as fruitful as male ordination (see, for example, Lindberg Falk, 2007).

[2] The main source used for this discussion is the Sutta Pitaka (the Basket of Suttas) of the Pāli canon. The Sutta Pitaka is divided in five Nikāyas: the Dīgha Nikāya (D), the Anguttara Nikāya (A), the Majjhima Nikāya (M), the Samyutta Nikāya (S) and the Kuddakha Nikāya. The passages are customarily referred to by using the initial letter of the individual Nikāya, the volume in which the passage is found, and the page number of the Pāli Text Society edition of the Pāli texts (a Roman script edition of the Pāli canon). The volumes comprising the Khuddaka Nikāya are referred to individually; the two used here are the Sutta Nipāta (Sn) and the Jātakas (J).

[3] A I 62 *bahukārā ... mātāpitaro puttānam, āpādakā posakā imassa lokassa dassetāro.*

[4] M III 253 *bahāpakārā ... mahāpajāpatā gotamā bhagavato mātucchā āpādikā posikā khārassa dāyikā, bhagavantam janettiyā kālakatāya thaññam pāyesi.*

[5] M III 170. In the simile found in the Pāli canon, it is a man who has 'gone to perdition' who is less likely to be reborn as a human. Most traditions, including the Theravāda tradition, have expanded the meaning to every human life.

[6] Information gained through a questionnaire response from a service provider (to migrant women) in Bangkok in 2009 by the authors. The organisation provides training to 400 women mainly from the Northern region. Seventy per cent of its clients were single mothers whose dependent children were looked after by their parents.

[7] The results could be skewed including the high percentage of migrants in the northeast region because the survey was conducted in the wet agricultural season (Report of the 1992 Migration Survey, POPLINE 103173).

[8] It may also be noted that commercial sex work, especially within the context of foreign tourism, is a very large source of income for Thailand as a country.

References

Ackers, L. (1999) *Shifting spaces: Women, citizenship and migration within the European Union*, Bristol: The Policy Press.

APMRN (Asia Pacific Migration Research Network) (1995) *Migration issues in the Asia Pacific: Issues paper from Thailand* (www.unesco.org/most/apmrnw14. htm).

Archavanitkul, K. and Guest, P. (2000) 'Migration and the commercial sex sector in Thailand', Thailand: Institute for Population and Social Research, Mahidol University (www.seameo.org/vl/migrate/frame.htm).

Arnold, E. and Piampiti, S. (1984) 'Female migration in Thailand', in J.T. Fawcett, S.E. Khoo and P.C. Smith (eds) *Women in the cities of Asia: Migration and adaptation*, Boulder, CO: Westview Press, pp 143-64.

Castles, S. and Miller, M.J. (2003) *The age and migration: International population movements in the modern world* (3rd edn), Basingstoke: Palgrave Macmillan.

Curran, S.R., Garip, F., Chung, C.Y. and Tangchonlatip, K. (2005) 'Gendered migrant social capital: evidence from Thailand', *Social Forces*, vol 84, no 1, pp 225-55.

de Jong, G.F., Richter, K. and Isarabhakdi, P. (1996) 'Gender, values and intentions to move in rural Thailand', *International Migration Review*, vol 30, no 3, pp 748-70.

Venerable Bhikkhuni Dhammananda, Interview on Al Jazeera, 'Everywoman: Buddhist nuns and hijab fashion', 28 August 2007, www.youtube.com/watch?v=nMnSK8Hp-gs&feature=channel_page.

Esara, P. (2004) 'Women will keep the household', *Critical Asian Studies*, vol 36, no 2, pp 199-216.

Gethin, R. (1998) *The foundations of Buddhism*, Oxford: Oxford University Press.

Handley, P. (2006) *The King never smiles: A biography of Thailand's Bhumidol Adulyadej*, New Haven, CT: Yale University Press.

Hendrijani, A.B. (2005) 'Prostitution: in search of cultural concepts in Thai contexts', in *Economic prospects, cultural encounters and political decisions: Scenes in a moving Asia (East and Southeast)*, The Work of the 2002/2003 API Fellows, Kuala Lumpur.

Hong, L. (1998) 'Of consorts and harlots in Thai popular history', *The Journal of Asian Studies*, vol 57, no 2, pp 333-53.

Keyes, C. (1983) 'Merit-transference in the Kammic theory of popular Theravada Buddhism, in C. Keyes and E. Valentine Daniel (eds) *Karma: An anthropological inquiry*, Berkeley, CA: University of California Press.

Keyes, C. (1984) 'Mother or mistress but never a monk: Buddhist notions of female gender in rural Thailand', *American Ethnologist*, vol 11, no 2, May, pp 223-41.

Kirsch, A.T. (1985) 'Text and context: Buddhist sex roles/culture of gender revisited', *American Ethnologist*, vol 2, no 2, pp 302-20.

Lim, L.L. (1993) 'The structural determinants of female migration', in UN (United Nations), *Internal migration of women in developing countries*, New York, NY: UN, pp 207-22.

Limanonda, B. (1995) 'Families in Thailand: beliefs and realities', *Journal of Comparative Family Studies*, Spring, vol 26, no 1, pp 67-82.

Lindberg Falk, M. (2007) *Making fields of merit: Buddhist female ascetics and gendered orders in Thailand*, Copenhagen, Denmark: NIAS Press.

Mee-Udon, F. and Itarat, R. (2005) 'Women in Thailand: changing the paradigm of female well-being', in J. Mancini Billson and C. Fluehr-Lobban (eds) *Female well-being: Toward a global theory of social change*, New York, NY: Palgrave Macmillan, pp 285-308.

Mills, M.B. (1999) *Thai women in the global labor force: Consuming desires, contested selves*, Chapel Hill, NC: Rutgers University Press.

Montgomery, H. (2001) *Modern Babylon: Prostituting children in Thailand*, Oxford: Berghahn Books.

Mulder, N. (1997) *Thai images: The culture of the public world*, Chiang Mai: Silkworm Books.

Osaki, K. (2003) 'Migrant remittances in Thailand: economic necessity or social norm?', *Journal of Population Research*, vol 20, no 2, pp 203-22.

Panyarachund, A. (ed) (1996) *Thailand; King Bhumibol Adulyadej, The Golden Jubilee: 1946-1996*, Singapore: Archipelago Press.

Peracca, S., Knodel, J. and Saengtienchai, C. (1998) 'Can prostitutes marry? Thai attitudes toward female sex workers', *Social Science and Medicine*, vol 47, pp 255-67.

Phongpaichit, P. (1982) *From peasant girls to Bangkok masseuses*, Geneva: International Labour Organization.

Phongpaichit, P. and Baker, C.J. (1996) *Thailand's boom and bust!*, Sydney: Allen & Unwin.

Rende Taylor, L. (2005) 'Dangerous trade-offs: the behavioural ecology of child labor and prostitution in rural Northern Thailand', *Current Anthropology*, vol 46, no 3, pp 411-31.

Richter, K. (1996) 'Living separately as a child-care strategy: implications for women's work and family in urban Thailand', *Journal of Marriage & Family*, May, vol 58, no 2, pp 327-39.

Richter, K. and Podhisita, C. (1992) Thai family demography: a review and research prospects', *Journal of Population and Social Research*, vol 3, nos 1-2, pp 1-19.

Sharron, D. (2006) *My name is Lon, you like me? A true story*, Bangkok: Bangkok Books.

Sung, K.-T. (2003) 'Filial piety: Buddhists' way in East Asian', *Journal of Religious Gerontology*, vol 14, no 4, pp 95-111.

Tangchonlatip, K., Punpuing, S., Chamratrithirong, A., Guest, P. and Curran, S. (2006) 'Migration and gender-based occupational segregation in Bangkok', *Journal of Population and Social Studies*, vol 15, no 1, pp 53-80.

Theobald, S. (2002) 'Gendered bodies recruitment, management and occupational health in Northern Thailand's electronics factories', *Women and Health*, vol 35, no 4, pp 7-26.

UN (United Nations) (1993) *Internal migration of women in developing countries*, New York, NY: UN.

van Esterik, P. (ed) (1996) *Women of Southeast Asia* (revised edn), Occasional Papers Number 17, Northern Illinois: University Center for Southeast Asian Studies.

Vanwey, L.K. (2004) 'Altruistic and contractual remittances between male and female migrants and households in rural Thailand', *Demography*, vol 41, no 4, pp 739-56.

Vichit-Vadakan, J. (1994) 'Women and family in Thailand in the midst of social change', *Law and Society Review*, vol 28, no 3, pp 515-24.

Warr, P. and Nidhiprabha, B. (1996) *Thailand's macroeconomic miracle: Stable adjustment and sustained growth*, Washington, DC: The World Bank.

Primary sources in translation

Dialogues of the Buddha (Dīgha Nikāya)
Walshe, M. (translator) (1987/1995) *The long discourses of the Buddha: A translation of the Dīgha Nikāya*, Somerville, MA: Wisdom Publications.

Middle-length discourses of the Buddha (Majjhima Nikāya)
Ñānamoli, B. and Bodhi, B. (1995) *The middle length discourses of the Buddha: A translation of the Majjhima Nikāya*, Somerville, MA: Wisdom Publications.

Connected discourses of the Buddha (Samyutta Nikāya)
Bodhi, Ven. B. (translator) (2002) *Connected discourses of the Buddha*, vol I, London: Pali Text Society.

Bodhi, Ven. B. (translator) (2002) *Connected discourses of the Buddha*, vol II, London: Pali Text Society.

Lesser discourses (Khuddaka Nikāya)

Norman, K.R. (translator) (2001) *The group of discourses* (Suttanipāta) (2nd edn with notes), London: Pali Text Society.

Cowell, E.B. (ed) *The Jataka or stories of the Buddha's former births* (six volumes, 1895–1907 and index 1913, all reprinted 1990), London: Pali Text Society.

EIGHT

Reciprocity in intergenerational relationships in stepfamilies

Lawrence H. Ganong and Marilyn Coleman

Introduction

The rising costs of healthcare and other social welfare programmes and the efforts of the federal, state and local governments to reduce services that are provided by governmental agencies have increased the importance of distinguishing personal and familial responsibilities from public (that is, governmental) obligations to dependent individuals. Societal debates about collective, familial and individual responsibility for dependent individuals are not new, but demographic and social changes have made the issue of who will assist dependent family members an increasingly important topic.

Increased longevity and reduced fertility in the past few decades have profoundly affected the structure of families in the US. Just as in other industrialised nations, life expectancies in the US have been increasing (Vaupel and Kistowski, 2005), which has resulted in more multiple-generation extended families than ever before (Uhlenberg and Kirby, 1998). These multiple-generation families are different than in the distant past, however, because lowered fertility means that there are fewer younger family members to care for greater numbers of older people than was true just a couple of generations ago. Younger adults are therefore likely to have more older kin who potentially need aid, which has fuelled societal concerns about the well-being of older adults.

Unlike many other industrialised nations, the US lacks a comprehensive system of government-sponsored social programmes for its citizens. Although there are a few federal support programmes for older adults (that is, Medicare, which provides funds for health-related needs), and even fewer state programmes that are primarily for low-income older people, for the most part responsibilities for the care and support of older adults have been seen in the US as belonging primarily to families.

The belief that families are obligated to care and support older kin is so widespread that 30 of the 50 states have filial responsibility laws that define which family members are obligated to provide care and what care they are obligated to provide (Bulcroft et al, 1989). Critics have argued that these laws and other US social policies about intergenerational care and assistance are based on the outdated and questionable assumptions that kin networks are unwaveringly emotionally close and loving, families have readily available members to assist older kin and family membership is stable (Hooyman and Gonyea, 1995). These assumptions do not reflect the experiences of many, if not most, families in the 21st century. For instance, families vary in the degree to which members are emotionally involved in each other's lives and, with most adult men and women in the paid workforce, there are fewer families with available kin to provide aid. Moreover, family membership is not always constant; families in the US have experienced decades of structural changes due to divorce, remarriage and cohabitation, and these changes make kinship more ephemeral than in the past.

Although the divorce rate has levelled off after years of increasing (Kreider, 2005), many US families have been and will continue to be affected by divorce and subsequent family transitions. An increasing proportion of older adults have been divorced, and it can reasonably be expected that the number of ever-divorced older people will be higher in the future than it is now (Kreider, 2005; Cornman and Kingson, 1996). Moreover, most divorced people remarry (Kreider, 2005), as do many widowed individuals. Consequently, nearly half of all US marriages are remarriages for one or both partners (US Census Bureau, 2000), and in many of these remarriages one or both partners have offspring from prior relationships. About 17 per cent of minor children reside in a household with a stepparent (Fields, 2001), and approximately 40 per cent of adult women will reside in a remarried or cohabiting stepfamily household as a parent or stepparent during their lifecourse (Bumpass et al, 1995). Many of these individuals will remarry and be in stepfamilies later in life – in 2001, 58 per cent of ever-divorced men and 41 per cent of ever-divorced women over the age of 49 were remarried (Kreider, 2005) – and this number is likely to grow, given extensions in the life span and improvements in the quality of later life.

US policy makers are therefore faced with laws and social policies that are designed for a mid-20th-century extended family at a time when multigenerational family structures are becoming increasingly more complex. In addition, it is probable that beliefs and attitudes about intergenerational responsibilities are also more complex than they were in the last century (Ganong and Coleman, 1999). For instance, although most North Americans usually agree with the statement that 'adult children should take care of their parents when they get old' (for example Lee et al, 1994), a sentiment suggesting that there is consistency among attitudes and social policy about intergenerational aid and support, researchers have reported far less agreement about intergenerational assistance when individuals are asked to consider real-life contexts (for example Rossi and Rossi, 1990; Ganong and Coleman, 1999). Divorce, remarriage and non-marital repartnering are among the relevant contexts that affect beliefs about intergenerational assistance.

Motives for making intergenerational resource exchanges

Several rationales have been offered to explain why people do or do not make intergenerational transfers of resources. Among them are:

- *A norm of family obligation:* this norm asserts that intergenerational transfers are duties that must be performed because individuals are related to each other (Silverstein et al, 2002). Obligations to help kin exist regardless of other factors, such as resource availability, responsibility for the problem or closeness of the relationship.
- *Altruism based on kinship ties:* evolutionary theory contends that there is a genetic predisposition to care for those with whom one is genetically related (Cheal, 1988). Economists also propose altruism as a motive for intergenerational transfers because it makes the donor happier than alternative uses of those resources would (Becker, 1981).
- *A norm of reciprocity:* this is the belief that children owe debts to their parents that should be repaid when the parents are elderly and in need of aid and the children are grown up (Cheal, 1988; Bengtson et al, 2000). This norm is consistent with exchange theories of relationships, which would propose that middle-generation households transfer resources to their children because they expect some type of reciprocity from their children in the future (*delayed restricted exchange*; Ribar and Wilhelm, 2002). A variation of this reciprocity norm has been called the *downstream strategy of obligation* (Boyd and Richerson, 1989), or the *generational chain of obligations*; in this version of reciprocity norms, adult children transfer resources to older generations because, if they do not, they believe it would be less likely that they themselves will receive support in the future from successive generations. In other words, the middle generation aids the older generations, and for those actions they will be repaid by the next generation of kin.
- *A norm of gratitude:* this is the belief that offspring want to help parents because they are grateful for parents' past help and sacrifices (Brakman, 1995). This norm is contingent on whether or not the parents are deserving of offspring gratitude for their childrearing sacrifices.
- *A moral duty:* in this view, intergenerational resource exchanges must be performed if one is to meet personal or religious moral standards of what a good person should do (Finch, 1989). Intergenerational transfers are made because that is what a moral person does, regardless of whether or not the recipient *deserves* the help.
- *Emotional attachments:* if relationships are emotionally close, then intergenerational transfers are more likely than if they are distant (Cicirelli, 1991).
- *As a function of intergenerational solidarity:* in an early model of intergenerational solidarity, transfers between generations are based on familistic norms, affection, an opportunity structure that facilitates interactions between generations and perceptions that intergenerational exchanges have been reciprocal (Bengtson

and Roberts, 1991). Another early model of intergenerational solidarity proposes that transfers are based on frequent contact, positive sentiments, agreement on values and beliefs, a perceived commitment to meeting family obligations and the opportunity structure for interaction (Rossi and Rossi, 1990).

Most of these rationales for intergenerational transfers are based on the assumption that parents take care of and nurture children when the children are young and helpless, behaviours that elicit aid from the younger generation when they become adults, and the older generation is relatively more dependent. Some of these explanations (that is, *reciprocity*, *altruism* based on kinship ties, *gratitude*, *intergenerational solidarity*) are explicit in asserting that intergenerational transfers of adult children are based on repaying debts to parents for past help. This repayment assumption is more implicit in the *emotional attachment* explanations for intergenerational transfers, but it is present in most of the other explanations. For example, attachments to parents are stronger when children's needs have been met by parents throughout the lifecourse. An adult child who is securely attached to a parent who has been a supportive and loving caretaker is more likely to allocate resources to that parent than a less securely attached adult will help an unsupportive parent. Only in the *normative family obligations*, *altruism* and *moral duty* arguments is the assumption of reciprocity absent.

Many of these models of intergenerational assistance have been criticised as not recognising inherent ambivalences in intergenerational relationships (Connidis and McMullin, 2002; Ha and Ingersoll-Dayton, 2008). Much of the criticism has been directed towards the intergenerational solidarity and normative family obligations models, but the critique also applies to other explanations.

Divorce, remarriage and intergenerational assistance

Divorce and intergenerational exchanges

Researchers in the US have consistently found that divorced parents and their adult offspring exchange fewer resources with each other than continuously married parents and their adult offspring (for example Amato et al, 1995). Parental divorce, and the parent–child relationships that evolve after separation and divorce, may have the effect of giving adult offspring fewer reasons to help their parents, especially parents who did not live with them when they were children. Reduced contact over time may lead to decisions not to allocate resources to help parents when children reach adulthood and parents reach old age (Cooney, 1994). There is evidence for this in that divorced fathers, who are less likely to have physical custody of children after divorce than mothers, have been found to be less likely to exchange financial support with their children than divorced mothers (White, 1992; Curran et al, 1998). It may be that frequent contact between parents and children following divorce is necessary for there to be feelings of kinship, gratitude, attachment to the parent, family solidarity and a sense that there are debts to be repaid. Children may be seen as having a lesser debt to repay than they would have had if parents had maintained contact with the child and continued to provide financial, tangible and emotional support to them. Moreover, the desire to help an older parent may be reduced if the definition of kinship is altered when parents divorce (Johnson, 1988). Non-residential parents who have little contact with their children following divorce may not be seen as family members by the children when they grow up. A filial sense of duty to them may be eliminated because of this redefinition (Cooney, 1994).

A few researchers have found that continuously married parents and adult children exchange more resources than divorced parent–child pairs, regardless of the amount of contact between parents and children after the divorce (White, 1992; Aquilino, 1994). Perhaps divorce strains family ties and lowers relationship quality and emotional closeness between parents and children, regardless of residence or frequency of interactions. If so, motivation to exchange resources would be reduced.

Later-life divorce and intergenerational exchanges: there has been relatively little research on the effects of later-life divorce on intergenerational exchanges. One study found that later-life divorce is associated with sons receiving less financial help from parents than daughters (Aquilino, 1994). Motivation to exchange resources across generations may be less affected by later-life divorce, but there is little empirical evidence that has addressed this issue.

Offspring divorce and exchanges: divorce also affects intergenerational transfers between divorced adults and their older parents, although it is not clear if these effects are long lasting or temporary. Research findings on the effects of offspring divorce on resource exchanges have been mixed. Researchers who found that divorced offspring help their parents less than married children speculated that divorced offspring think their parents have fewer needs, feel less filial obligation and perceive more limits to their abilities to help than married offspring (Cicirelli, 1983). The divorce of adult children is thought to increase the demands they make on their parents for aid while reducing their capacities to lend aid to their parents (Spitze et al, 1994). This pattern of exchanges is presumably due to the economic demands of divorce on adult children (that is, greater expenses, working more) and parents' reluctance or unwillingness to request help from them (Johnson, 1988).

However, not all studies have found that divorced children give less help and support to parents than married children (Spitze et al, 1994), nor do divorced children feel less obligated to assist parents (Brody et al, 1994). A relational *continuity perspective* argues that parent–child relationships over the lifecourse are characterised by continuity (Rossi and Rossi, 1990; Spitze et al, 1994). Divorce of offspring may result in temporary alteration in exchange patterns, with parents helping their children more and adult children helping their parents less, but eventually long-term patterns of exchange resume.

The gender of the divorcing child and the presence of grandchildren are factors that may influence exchanges between generations. Daughters generally maintain contact with parents more than sons; daughters are more likely to have custody of children than sons, so parents and daughters are more likely to exchange resources than are parents and sons (Johnson, 1988; Spitze et al, 1994).

Remarriage and intergenerational exchanges

Remarried parents (White, 1992) provided less support to adult children than parents in first marriages, but remarried mothers gave some types of support as much as married mothers (Amato et al, 1995; Marks, 1995). Remarried mothers also exchanged more with children than remarried fathers (White, 1994a; Amato et al, 1995). Amato et al (1995) found that even though remarried mothers gave as much to adult children as first-marriage mothers, they received less support from children than first-marriage mothers. Reasons offered to explain these findings (see White, 1994a, 1994b) include: differences between remarried adults and adults in first marriages in attitudes about their financial obligations to assist children (Marks, 1995); normative beliefs about intergenerational responsibilities after remarriage (Ganong and Coleman, 1998a, 1998b); and differences in family solidarity. It should be noted that the studies mentioned here focus on adult child–parent relationships in families in which the parental remarriage occurred when children were minors. Little is known about the effects of remarriages on parent–adult child relationships when the remarriages occur after the offspring are grown.

After they remarry, non-residential parents of minor aged children often had less contact with those children than they did before (King and Heard, 1999), although some parents had more or similar levels of involvement (Manning and Smock, 2000). Remarriage of a parent with physical custody of children had inconsistent effects, with some researchers finding that it reduced child support payments (for example Folk et al, 1992), and some finding no relation between remarriage and child support (for example Lin, 2000).

Older parent–adult child relationships after remarriage: there is growing evidence that parents who remarry have less contact with their adult children than non-divorced parents (Aquilino, 1994; Bulcroft and Bulcroft, 1991). This may lead to fewer exchanges of resources.

Remarriage and step-relationships: most studies have found that stepparents do not provide as much instrumental and financial support for young children as parents for their children in first marriages (for example Pezzin and Schone, 1999). In general, stepparents are less involved in raising their stepchildren than either parents in stepfamilies or parents in first-marriage families are in raising their children, so they may have built less social capital when the children were young. Stepparents with children from prior relationships may also have a financial obligation to those children that lowers their ability to support stepchildren. However, some researchers have found no differences in resources exchanged between stepparents and stepchildren and biological parent–child ties in first marriages (Aquilino, 1994).

Motives to assist after remarriage

Familial responsibilities become more ambiguous following marital transitions; divorces and remarriages cause family members to rethink whether certain individuals continue to be relatives or not. For example, after divorce, parents may lose contact with their children, and remarriage potentially adds members to the pool of kin (new partners, their children and extended family). Step-kin acquired through remarriage may be seen as replacements for relatives lost via divorce (with family-based obligations transferred from old kin to new step-kin), as additional family members, or they may not be seen as kin (thus no obligations to allocate resources across generations are added). For some individuals, family members are only people who share genetic or legal ties (Schneider, 1980).

Decisions about making intergenerational transfers between stepparents and stepchildren may not involve the same factors as decisions regarding resource allocations between children and parents. Stepparent–stepchild bonds are ambiguous, and cultural guidelines regarding appropriate behaviour for mutual responsibilities and interactions in stepchildren–stepparent relationships are either absent or unclear (Cherlin, 1978). There are also few legally mandated responsibilities between stepchildren and stepparents. The emotional bonds between stepparents and stepchildren tend to be less cohesive than parent–child bonds because: (a) stepparents and stepchildren often have spent little time together, reducing chances to develop close bonds; (b) stepchildren may feel loyalty to their parents that prevents them from trying to get close to the stepparent; and (c) some stepparents rush into parental (that is, disciplinary) roles before they have developed an emotional bond, which deters them from establishing warm relationships with stepchildren (Coleman et al, 2000). The weaker emotional bonds in stepfamilies may contribute to structurally weaker social networks than in first-marriage families (White, 1994b; Widmer, 2006), resulting in lower family solidarity and fewer felt obligations between stepfamily members. Even when stepparents develop close relationships with stepchildren, and many do, most stepparents are additional adults in the lives of adult children, rather than substitutes for deceased or absent divorced parents, which may mean that stepparents are perceived as having less claim for assistance from adult stepchildren. Rossi and Rossi (1990) found that people perceived greater family obligations to parents than to stepparents. Consequently, in some families resources may not be adequate to include stepparents. If stepparents are seen as having less right to receive aid than parents, then they will be more likely to have to seek assistance from non-familial sources.

However, several of the explanations proposed for intergenerational transfers between parents and children may be applied to intergenerational transfers between stepchildren and stepparents. For example, *norms of reciprocity*, *gratitude* and *emotional attachments* could be the bases for decisions about intergenerational transfers between stepchildren and stepparents. It may be that the more closely step-relationships resemble parent–child relationships, the more likely similar decisions will apply. For example, when step-relationships resemble close parent–child bonds, when the stepparent and stepchild have spent years together in the relationship, and when stepparents have served as the functional equivalents of parents, then decisions about intergenerational transfers may apply to step-relationships. The more step-relationships deviate from parent–child ties, the less likely it is that similar decisions about intergenerational transfers between stepchildren and stepparents will be made.

There are several reasons to expect that older parents and adult offspring from stepfamilies may differ from parents and adult children from first-marriage families in the amount of intergenerational transfers of resources. Differences between remarried or cohabiting repartnered parents and parents in first marriages in support of adult children have been attributed to a number of factors. For example, parental divorce and separation of cohabiting couple relationships when children are young, and the relationships between children and parents that subsequently evolve, may result in adult offspring having fewer reasons to help parents later in life, especially parents who did not live with them when they were children.

Parents' remarriage/repartnering also may disrupt parent–child bonds when children are young. In a series of studies about normative beliefs about intergenerational obligations following divorce and remarriage, Ganong, Coleman and colleagues found that (a) kinship, (b) intergenerational closeness or relationship quality and (c) prior patterns of assistance between generations (that is, reciprocity) were significant influences on judgements about whether intergenerational responsibilities existed, and, if so, how much help should be given (Coleman and Ganong, 1998; Coleman et al, 2005; Ganong and Coleman, 1998a, 1998b, 1999, 2006a). Other contextual factors were important for attributing how much help to give, such as available resources and other demands on kin, but these were not as important as perceiving kinship bonds, closeness and reciprocity.

The Family Obligations Project

In research that we have conducted over the past 15 years we have examined cultural beliefs about intergenerational relationships when families have been affected by marital transitions in either older or younger generations. In our work, we have focused on how divorce and remarriage affect beliefs about intergenerational assistance. We have examined perceived obligations to both genetic and step-kin, and have examined beliefs about aid given to both older and younger family members. In this chapter we discuss the findings of this programme of research, focusing mostly on beliefs about intergenerational reciprocity in stepfamilies.

Consensual beliefs about intergenerational family relationships and support are important to examine because such beliefs function as parameters within which individuals define and negotiate their responsibilities to kin, they serve as criteria to measure how well individuals are functioning as family members and they provide a framework that people use to justify and explain their conduct to others. What people actually do in relationships is based partly on personal beliefs about appropriate actions between kin and partly on widely held expectations about what should be done regarding family responsibilities (Finch and Mason, 1993; Ganong and Coleman, 1999). Normative beliefs about intergenerational responsibilities are also important to understand because such beliefs influence the development and application of public policy (Finch and Mason, 1993).

Overview of the Intergenerational Obligations Project

We have completed about 24 studies that focused on intergenerational obligations. All of these studies used multiple segment factorial vignettes (MSFV) (Ganong and Coleman, 2005), which is an elaboration of factorial survey methods (Rossi and Nock, 1982). Factorial surveys combine elements of survey research and experiments in that participants are randomly sampled and presented with brief vignettes in which the researcher has randomly manipulated levels of the independent variables (Rossi and Nock, 1982). Using this experimental method, researchers can examine the effects of different levels of the featured dimensions of the vignettes on participants' attitudes and beliefs. In our adaptation of the factorial surveys, MSFV surveys, participants are presented with vignettes that are divided into several separate units, or segments, that together form a story to which people are asked to respond. The MSFV in our studies contained two to five segments and respondents were asked questions after each segment. Additionally, new independent variables were randomly added in subsequent segments. Each segment thus contained a unique set of independent variables.

In each study several hypotheses were examined. Each study contained different independent and dependent variables, although over time some variables were included in more than one investigation as we sought to determine if varying contexts elicited different responses. Independent variables in the vignettes usually included the type of relationship between the adults (for example parent–child or stepparent–stepchild; stepgrandparent–stepgrandchild or grandparent–grandchild). Other frequently measured independent variables included relationship quality, prior patterns of resources exchanged between the adults (for example reciprocity in resources exchanged or non-reciprocated resource exchanges), and the amount of resources available to family members (for example they had many resources or few). In all of the studies there was at least one change in marital status among either the oldest generation or middle-generation adults because we wanted to see how structural transitions in multigenerational families brought about by divorce and remarriage affected beliefs about intergenerational assistance.

The dependent variables in these studies included a variety of ways of providing intergenerational assistance, including helping older adults with activities of daily living (ADL), physical caregiving and providing financial support. The studies were designed to: (a) test the effects of randomly assigned independent variables on dependent variables (beliefs about intergenerational assistance); (b) examine the relations of respondent characteristics and their beliefs about intergenerational assistance; and (c) explore respondents' rationale for their beliefs about intergenerational assistance. In addition to examining the effects of independent variables on the dependent variables (questions about intergenerational assistance), we also asked participants after each segment to explain their answers with open-ended questions.

Although many of our studies were from regionally drawn samples, in this chapter we report primarily on results from a national sample of 3,316 adults that were contacted via telephone interviews. Nearly half (48.5 per cent) were men. The age of the participants ranged from 18 to 89, with a mean of 43.8 years. More than half had children ($n = 573$); 146 had stepchildren. Of the 43 per cent that were married, about one fourth of them were remarried. Nearly one third had never been married, 19 per cent were divorced or separated, and about eight per cent were widowed. The ethnic diversity in this study was comparable to the distribution of the ethnic and racial composition of the US (US Census Bureau, 2000), and the sample resembled North American society as a whole in religious preference, education, household incomes and employment status.

The sample was obtained with a multistage probability sampling design using random digit dialing (RDD) of telephone numbers selected from valid telephone exchanges in the US. The multistage sampling involved three stages. The first stage was grouping of metropolitan areas or counties nationwide. The second grouped smaller areas – cities, towns and rural areas. The third was a random selection of households of each of the first and second stages. To ensure adequate racial and ethnic diversity in the samples, areas known to have high proportions of African American, Asian American and Latino residents were over-sampled. Eligible respondents were people 18 years of age or over. The response rate was 54 per cent.

Respondents were read a MSFV describing a family in which an older adult experienced a dilemma. After each segment was read, respondents were asked questions about what a specific character in the vignette should do about helping another character. The characters' first names and relationships (for example his stepfather, her mother) were read to the participants. At the end of the segment, respondents were asked in an open-ended question to provide a rationale for their answers to the prior questions. After responding to the vignettes, participants were asked demographic questions, including age, sex, marital status, parental status, income, ethnicity, education and religiosity. We also gathered information about personal experiences related to helping or being helped by a family member.

Beliefs about intergenerational reciprocity among stepfamilies in later life

Parent–child relationships in stepfamilies

Kinship counts, but so do reciprocity and relationship quality: traditionally, in most societies, kinship status between adults and offspring is important because intergenerational kinship means that there are special bonds of duty and responsibility between generations. Such cultural expectations have been called family obligation norms, filial obligations, filial piety (in Asian cultures) and filial responsibilities (Ganong and Coleman, 1999). In the past, and in traditional societies now, kinship obligation norms influence what people do when younger or older family members are in need of assistance.

Social scientists have argued that kinship definitions are more flexible than in the past (Scanzoni and Marsiglio, 1993). Instead of limiting family membership to individuals related by the traditional standards of genetic and legal bonds (Schneider, 1980), today's postmodern families are said to rely on more fluid markers of kinship, such as mutual affection and shared interests (Scanzoni and Marsiglio, 1993). Divorce, cohabiting relationship terminations and remarriage/repartnering can result in changes in how family members define who is in and who is out of their kin networks. Individuals who diminish the amount of contact they have with others after separation or divorce may lose kinship status in the eyes of other family members, for instance, as may parents who have conflicted or hostile interactions with children and who are emotionally distant. If remarriage of a parent creates emotional distance between parents and children or if aid to children is reduced by remarriage, then there also may be effects on how kinship between parent and child is perceived.

In our studies of normative beliefs about intergenerational obligations kinship was immutable for only a minority of respondents. That is, for approximately 25 per cent of the participants in multiple studies examining multiple tasks, intergenerational obligations between parents and adult children were unaffected by marital transitions, relationship quality, prior patterns of helping or other factors (Ganong and Coleman, 1998a, 1998b, 1999, 2006a, 2006b; Coleman et al, 2005). The exception was inheritance, where nearly all thought that genetic kin took precedence over step-kin (Coleman and Ganong, 1998).

Most people in our studies, however, thought that kinship alone was inadequate justification for providing intergenerational aid – these individuals perceived lower obligations and suggested less help be given when parent–child relationships were emotionally distant or hostile, contact had not been maintained after divorce or remarriage and parents had not aided children in the past. In such situations, intergenerational exchanges were more discretionary than obligatory. Kinship was still relevant, but did not automatically carry with it special considerations that overrode other relational factors.

Reciprocity: adult children were not thought to be obligated to help parents who did not fulfil expected parental responsibilities to care for the children when they were young (Coleman et al, 1997; Ganong and Coleman, 2006b). Family obligation norms no longer applied when genetic kin had not observed the *norm of reciprocity* between generations (younger family members owe older family members for having raised them). In some studies, we presented families in which the patterns of aid in the past had been reciprocal or unbalanced; however, even in studies in which reciprocity was not a variable, respondents spontaneously mentioned the need for children to repay parents as a rationale for providing assistance to them.

Kinship ties had value and meaning to our samples, but without past histories of mutual helping, it was almost as if the special loyalties and responsibilities attendant to sharing kinship were lost (Coleman et al, 1997; Ganong and Coleman, 1999, 2006b). Children were seen as having a lesser debt to repay than they would have had if parents had maintained contact and continued to provide financial, tangible and emotional support to them. Divorced and remarried older parents who were perceived to have broken the reciprocity 'contract' had lost any 'rights' to be the recipients of help from adult children.

Relationship closeness: more important than genetic ties to judgements about intergenerational aid and support was relationship quality (Ganong and Coleman, 1998a, 1998b, 1999, 2006a). Moreover, marital status of older adults and their adult offspring and the acuity of need for help were far less relevant than how well they got along with each other. In fact, emotional closeness was a key factor for most respondents in our studies. Parents and children were thought to be much more obligated to help each other when the relationship was characterised by emotional closeness than by distance. When relationships were distant or hostile, any help provided was discretionary and much more limited than when parent–child bonds were emotionally close. As with reciprocity, in some studies we manipulated the level of closeness in relationships, but even when we did not, individuals used closeness as a criterion for making judgements about the amount of help to be offered. In some studies, participants interpreted the lack of contact after divorce and remarriage as an indicator of relationship closeness, suggesting that frequent contact between parents and children following divorce, separation or remarriage may be necessary for there to be warm attachment to the parent.

Stepparent–stepchild relationships

Kinship: stepgrandparents, stepparents and stepchildren may become family members, even without legal connections (via adoption) or without sharing genetic ties (Schmeekle et al, 2006; Widmer, 2006). However, several studies have found that the inclusion of step-kin as part of a family network is quite variable (Schmeekle et al, 2006; Widmer, 2006). Young stepchildren identify various configurations of people as members of their families, sometimes including stepparents and sometimes not, and they utilise a broad array of criteria for kinship, such as sharing genetic ties, living together, living with the child's non-residential parent and being important to the child for some reason. Some adolescent stepchildren consider their stepparents to be parents, friends or outsiders, depending on the nature of the relationship (Fine et al, 1998). Adult stepchildren also employ a variety of criteria to decide who is in their family networks (Schmeekle et al, 2006). Stepfathers and stepmothers also have been found to vary greatly in how and when they claim stepchildren as kin. Some stepparents and stepchildren attain/are assigned quasi-kin status (Ganong et al, 2002), which is loosely defined as a type of kinship bond that lacks some of the glue of genetic bonds – affection, loyalty and a sense of obligation exists among quasi-kin, but perhaps not as much as to genetic kin. Relationships with intergenerational step-kin can be considered to be: (a) the same as genetic kin; (b) almost like kinship; (c) close friendships; (d) acquaintances; (e) strangers; or (f) something much more negative. How step-relationships are defined is an important factor in understanding and predicting resource exchanges between older stepparents and adult stepchildren.

In our studies, when step-kin were seen as family, then norms of filial obligations applied just as if there were genetic and legal ties (Ganong and Coleman, 1998a; Coleman et al, 2005). In practice, this means that step-relationships characterised by past mutual exchanges of resources and emotional bonding are generally seen as kinship ties, and intergenerational obligation norms apply. Meeting norms of reciprocity in the past and closeness between step-kin are seen as indicators that the participants think of each other as family. This is easier to achieve when stepparents have helped raise the stepchildren than when remarriage occurred after the stepchildren were grown and gone from parental households.

Reciprocity norms and relationship closeness: stepparents and stepchildren who develop emotionally close relationships or who have helped each other in the past (that is, the stepparent helped raise the stepchild or they mutually assisted each other as adults) were perceived to have obligations to assist each other as much as possible, and at levels similar, but not quite equal, to older parents and adult children who had close ties and reciprocal exchanges (Ganong and Coleman, 1998a, 1998b, 1999; Coleman et al, 2005). When long-term stepfamily relationships are emotionally close, then family members are expected to assist each other in times of need.

Step-relationships formed in later life would not have the opportunities that long-term stepparents and stepchildren would have to build emotional bonds and exchange resources with each other, thus reducing the likelihood that older stepparents and adult stepchildren would exchange resources or perceive each other as kin (Ganong et al, 1998; Ganong and Coleman, 2006a). Although direct reciprocity norms may not apply in later-life step-relationships, other types of reciprocity influenced judgements about intergenerational assistance in our studies – for instance, some people thought that older stepparents should be helped by adult stepchildren as a way to repay the stepparents for help the stepparents provided to the genetic parents or as an indirect way to repay parents for their past aid by helping their new spouses/partners.

In summary, the importance of *norms of kinship obligations* and *reciprocity*, and the relevance of *emotional attachments* between generations help explain decisions about intergenerational transfers between stepchildren and stepparents. It may be that the more closely step-relationships resemble parent–child relationships, the more likely similar decisions will apply. For example, when step-relationships resemble close parent–child bonds, when the stepparent and stepchild have spent years together in the relationship and when stepparents have served as the functional equivalents of parents (for example helping raise children, providing children with resources), then decisions about intergenerational transfers may apply to step-relationships just as they do to genetic parent–child relationships. The more step-relationships deviate from parent–child ties, the less likely that similar decisions about intergenerational transfers between stepchildren and stepparents will be made (Ganong and Coleman, 1999). And these conclusions held true across racial and ethnic groups in the US (Coleman et al, 2006).

Policy implications

Both familism and individualism have been used by US politicians to support the *public burden* perspective of family policy. The public burden model takes the position that the responsibility of caring for dependent older people and children is the duty of family members; policies and laws are designed to make sure that families assume their responsibilities (Hooyman and Gonyea, 1995). The results of our studies do not support the public burden argument that most people believe that families are unconditionally responsible for dependent family members. Given our data, it is questionable that the surge towards personal responsibility regulations in recent years will be met with widespread support. Ambivalence rather than unwavering acceptance appears to be the normative view.

Policies need to reflect the variability of family structures. Criticisms have been levelled at US policies that assume that families change membership relatively rarely, and then only via marriage, birth and death (Hooyman and Gonyea, 1995). Divorce and remarriage are not rare experiences, however, and they result in significant alterations in family membership. Some of these changes in membership involve changes in perceived intergenerational responsibilities, which have implications for family policy. Most US family policy is based on the nuclear family ideology (Hooyman and Gonyea, 1995). If dependent older people are to be well served by society, it is important that beliefs about families become more flexible.

It is hard to establish family policy when kinship is dynamic, based not only on membership changes because of divorce and remarriage, but also on idiosyncratic and personal criteria of kinship rather than on static criteria. On the other hand, it is foolish to base policies on the assumption that family members are seen as unconditionally, or even generally, obligated to help each other. This appears to be an erroneous assumption, particularly for families in which there have been marital transitions. Competing ideologies of kin responsibilities and fluid definitions of kinship make it difficult to establish uniform policies. Do our data give some direction about how policies might be constructed that could reflect such diverse public opinion?

The most elegant policy solution is to employ society-wide safety nets (national health insurance), but these are often derided as public burdens to be avoided. Our data indicate that there is a need for policies that ensure a safety net for childless older people and for divorced older people who are cut off from their children. The lack of a perceived unconditional obligation to assist an older parent with physical care may suggest that there needs to be a safety net for all older people, whether they have grown children or not. Perhaps safety nets such as care insurance and nursing home insurance can fit the niche between familial responsibility and governmental responsibility.

Our results overall suggest that policy makers need to think more broadly and flexibly about families. It would do law makers in other societies well to observe the progress and outcomes of the efforts of other countries, as well as to widen their lens from the nuclear family ideology.

References

Amato, P.R., Rezac, S.J. and Booth, A. (1995) 'Helping between parents and young adult offspring: the role of parental marital quality, divorce, and remarriage', *Journal of Marriage and the Family*, vol 57, pp 363-74.

Aquilino, W.S. (1994) 'Impact of childhood family disruption on young adults' relationships with parents', *Journal of Marriage and the Family*, vol 56, pp 295-313.

Becker, G.S. (1981) *A treatise on the family*, Cambridge: Harvard University Press.

Bengtson, V.L. and Roberts, R.E.L. (1991) 'Intergenerational solidarity in aging families: an example of formal theory construction', *Journal of Marriage and the Family*, vol 53, pp 856-70.

Bengtson, V.L., Giarrusso, R., Silverstein, M. and Wang, H. (2000) 'Families and intergenerational relationships in aging societies', *International Journal of Aging*, vol 2, pp 3-10.

Boyd, R. and Richerson, P.J. (1989) 'The evolution of indirect reciprocity', *Social Networks*, vol 11, pp 213-36.

Brakman, S.V. (1995) 'Filial responsibility and decision-making', in L.B. McCullough and N.L. Wilson (eds) *Long-term care decisions: Ethical and conceptual dimensions*, Baltimore, MD: Johns Hopkins University Press, pp 181-96.

Brody, E., Litvin, S., Albert, S. and Hoffman, C. (1994) 'Marital status of daughters and patterns of parent care', *Journal of Gerontology*, vol 49, S95-S103.

Bulcroft, K.A. and Bulcroft, R.A. (1991) 'The timing of divorce: effects on parent–child relationships in later life', *Research on Aging*, vol 13, pp 226-43.

Bulcroft, K., Bulcroft, R., Hatch, L. and Borgatta, E. (1989) 'Antecedents and consequences of remarriage in later life', *Research on Aging*, vol 11, pp 82-106.

Bumpass, L., Raley, R.K. and Sweet, J. (1995) 'The changing character of stepfamilies: implications of cohabitation and nonmarital childbearing', *Demography*, vol 32, pp 425-36.

Cheal, D.J. (1988) 'Theories of serial flow in intergenerational transfers', *International Journal of Aging and Human Development*, vol 26, pp 261-73.

Cherlin, A. (1978) 'Remarriage as an incomplete institution', *American Journal of Sociology*, vol 84, pp 634-50.

Cicirelli, V.G. (1983) 'A comparison of helping behavior to elderly parents of adult children with intact and disrupted marriages', *The Gerontologist*, vol 23, pp 619-25.

Cicirelli, V.G. (1991) 'Attachment theory in old age: protection of the attached figure', in K. Pillemer and K. McCartney (eds) *Parent–child relations throughout life*, Hillsdale, NJ: Erlbaum, pp 25-42.

Coleman, M. and Ganong, L. (1998) 'Attitudes toward men's intergenerational financial obligations to older and younger male family members following divorce', *Personal Relationships*, vol 5, pp 293-309.

Coleman, M., Ganong, L. and Cable, S. (1997) 'Beliefs about women's intergenerational family obligations to provide support prior to parents and stepparents following divorce and remarriage', *Journal of Marriage and the Family*, vol 59, pp 165-76.

Coleman, M., Ganong, L. and Fine, M. (2000) 'Reinvestigating remarriage: another decade of progress', *Journal of Marriage and Family*, vol 52, pp 1288-1307.

Coleman, M., Ganong, L. and Rothrauff, T. (2006) 'Racial and ethnic similarities and differences in beliefs about intergenerational assistance to older adults after divorce and remarriage', *Family Relations*, vol 55, pp 576-87.

Coleman, M., Ganong, L., Hans, J., Sharp, E.A. and Rothrauff, T. (2005) 'Filial obligations in post-divorce stepfamilies', *Journal of Divorce and Remarriage*, vol 43, nos 3/4, pp 1-27.

Connidis, I.A. and McMullin, J.A. (2002) 'Sociological ambivalence and family ties: a critical perspective', *Journal of Marriage and Family*, vol 64, pp 558-67.

Cooney, T.M. (1994) 'Young adults' relations with parents: the influence of recent parental divorce', *Journal of Marriage and the Family*, vol 56, pp 45-56.

Cornman, J.M. and Kingson, E.R. (1996) 'Trends, issues, perspectives, and values for the aging of the baby boom cohorts', *The Gerontologist*, vol 36, pp 15-26.

Curran, S., McLanahan, S. and Knab, J. (1998) *Ties that bind: Marital history, kinship ties and social support among older Americans*, Office of Population Research Working Paper No 98-1, Princeton, NJ: Princeton University.

Fields, J. (2001) 'Living arrangements of children', *Current Population Reports*, Washington, DC: US Census Bureau, pp 70-74.

Finch, J. (1989) *Family obligations and social change*, Oxford: Polity Press.

Finch, J. and Mason, J. (1993) *Negotiating family responsibilities*, London: Tavistock/ Routledge.

Fine, M., Coleman, M. and Ganong, L. (1998) 'Consistency in perceptions of the stepparent role among stepparents, parents, and stepchildren', *Journal of Social and Personal Relationships*, vol 15, pp 810-28.

Folk, K.F., Graham, J.W. and Beller, A.H. (1992) 'Child support and remarriage: implications for the economic well-being of children', *Journal of Family Issues*, vol 13, pp 142-57.

Ganong, L. and Coleman, M. (1998a) 'Attitudes regarding filial responsibilities to help elderly divorced parents and stepparents', *Journal of Aging Studies*, vol 12, pp 271-90.

Ganong, L. and Coleman, M. (1998b) 'An exploratory study of grandparents' and stepgrandparents' perceived financial obligations to grandchildren and stepgrandchildren', *Journal of Social and Personal Relationships*, vol 15, pp 39-58.

Ganong, L. and Coleman, M. (1999) *Changing families, changing responsibilities*, Englewood, NJ: Erlbaum.

Ganong, L. and Coleman, M. (2005) 'Measuring intergenerational family obligations', *Journal of Marriage and Family*, vol 67, pp 1003-11.

Ganong, L. and Coleman, M. (2006a) 'Responsibilities to stepparents acquired in later life: relationship quality and acuity of needs', *Journal of Gerontology: Social Sciences*, vol 61B, S80-S88.

Ganong, L. and Coleman, M. (2006b) 'Patterns of exchanges and intergenerational obligations after divorce and remarriage', *Journal of Aging Studies*, vol 20, pp 265-78.

Ganong, L., Coleman, M. and Weaver, S. (2002) 'Maintenance and enhancement in remarried families: clinical applications', in J. Harvey and A. Wenzel (eds) *A clinicians' guide to maintaining and enhancing close relationships*, Hillsdale, NJ: Erlbaum, pp 105-29.

Ganong, L., Coleman, M., Killian, T. and McDaniel, A.K. (1998) 'Attitudes toward obligations to assist an elderly parent or stepparent after later-life remarriage', *Journal of Marriage and the Family*, vol 60, pp 595-610.

Ha, J.-H. and Ingersoll-Dayton, B. (2008) 'The effect of widowhood on intergenerational ambivalence', *The Journal of Gerontology*, vol 63, S49-S58.

Hooyman, N.R. and Gonyea, J. (1995) *Feminist perspectives on family care*, Thousand Oaks, CA: Sage Publications.

Johnson, C.L. (1988) *Ex familia*, New Brunswick, NJ: Rutgers University.

King, V. and Heard, H. (1999) 'Nonresident father visitation, parental conflict, and mother's satisfaction: what's best for child well-being?', *Journal of Marriage and the Family*, vol 61, pp 385-96.

Kreider, R. (2005) 'Number, timing and duration of marriages and divorces: 2001', Washington, DC: US Census Bureau (www.census.gov/prod/2005pubs/p70-97.pdf).

Lee, G.R., Netzer, J.K. and Coward, R.T. (1994) 'Filial responsibility expectations and patterns of intergenerational assistance', *Journal of Marriage and the Family*, vol 56, pp 559-65.

Lin, I.-F. (2000) 'Perceived fairness and compliance with child support obligations', *Journal of Marriage and Family*, vol 62, pp 388-98.

Manning, W. and Smock, P. (2000) 'New families and nonresident father–child visitation', *Social Forces*, vol 78, pp 87-116.

Marks, N.F. (1995) 'Midlife marital status differences in social support relationships with adult children and psychological well-being', *Journal of Family Issues*, vol 16, pp 5-28.

Pezzin, L.E. and Schone, B.S. (1999) 'Parental marital disruption and intergenerational transfers: an analysis of lone elderly parents and their children', *Demography*, vol 36, pp 287-97.

Ribar, D.C. and Wilhelm, M.O. (2002) 'Socialization, exchange and the intergenerational transmission of elder support attitudes: evidence from the three generations of Mexican–Americans', manuscript, George Washington University, Washington, DC.

Rossi, P. and Nock, P. (1982) *Measuring social judgments*, Beverly Hills, CA: Sage Publications.

Rossi, A. and Rossi, P. (1990) *Of human bonding*, New York, NY: Aldine de Gruyter.

Scanzoni, J. and Marsiglio, W. (1993) 'New action theory and contemporary families', *Journal of Family Issues*, vol 14, pp 105-32.

Schmeekle, M., Giarrusso, R., Feng, D. and Bengtson, V.L. (2006) 'What makes someone family? Adult children's perceptions of current and former stepparents', *Journal of Marriage and Family*, vol 67, pp 595-610.

Schneider, D. (1980) *American kinship*, New York, NY: Prentice Hall.

Silverstein, M., Conroy, S., Wang, H., Giarrusso, R. and Bengtson, V.L. (2002) 'Reciprocity in parent–child relations over the adult lifecourse', *Journals of Gerontology-Psychological Sciences & Social Sciences*, vol 57B, S3-S13.

Spitze, G., Logan, J.R., Deane, G. and Zerger, S. (1994) 'Adult children's divorce and intergenerational relationships', *Journal of Marriage and the Family*, vol 56, pp 279-93.

Uhlenberg, P. and Kirby, J.B. (1998) 'Grandparenthood over time: historical and demographic trends', in M. Szinovacz (ed) *Handbook on grandparenthood*, Hartford, CT: Greenwood, pp 23-39.

US Census Bureau (2000) *Statistical abstract of the United States: 2000* (120th edn).

Vaupel, J.W. and Kistowski, K.G. (2005) 'Broken limits to life expectancy', *Ageing Horizons*, vol 3, pp 6-13.

White, L. (1992) 'The effects of parental divorce and remarriage on parental support for adult children', *Journal of Family Issues*, vol 13, pp 234-50.

White, L. (1994a) 'Stepfamilies over the lifecourse: social support', in A. Booth and J. Dunn (eds) *Stepfamilies: Who benefits? Who does not?*, Hillsdale, NJ: Erlbaum, pp 109-38.

White, L. (1994b) 'Growing up with single parents and stepparents: long-term effects on family solidarity', *Journal of Marriage and the Family*, vol 56, pp 935-48.

Widmer, E.D. (2006) 'Who are my family members? Bridging and binding social capital in family configurations', *Journal of Social and Personal Relationships*, vol 23, pp 979-98.

NINE

New patterns of family reciprocity? Policy challenges in ageing societies

Misa Izuhara

Are new patterns of family reciprocity emerging?

The chapters in this volume investigated various trends in relation to changing patterns and functions of intergenerational relationships. Returning to one of the key questions posed in the introduction to this volume – 'whether new forms or patterns of family reciprocity are emerging' – this concluding chapter first summarises what we have learned from the previous chapters. What evidence did we find regarding 'new patterns' of family reciprocity at the beginning of the 21st century? How 'new' are those patterns that we have recently been witnessing in comparison to conventional ones? To what extent and in which contexts are new patterns likely to be emerging – in any particular family context or socioeconomic circumstances? Or are there adaptations of culturally and institutionally ascribed norms of relations between generations?

Some chapters have highlighted new trends more vividly, in particular new patterns of intergenerational exchange of support, while others have described previously known systems and networks of intergenerational relations that have been reinforced rather than transformed under more recent global pressures. Transformation could be pro-active or passive, and changes could be either temporary or more permanent. This chapter considers each of the chapters in turn to evaluate how each has demonstrated continuity and change of resource transfers and exchange over the generations.

Chapter Two by Chris Phillipson and Chapter Three by Ruth Katz and Ariela Lowenstein presented some solid theoretical and conceptual frameworks for the analysis of change in families and their relationships. The theories adopted from various disciplines of economic, sociological or psychological backgrounds provided useful analytical 'tools' to understand and examine the empirical chapters that followed. Phillipson first explained how demographic changes were embedded in a wider social and economic structure with a specific concern regarding globalisation as an influential force to help transform family relations in later life in contemporary societies. The role of international organisations, for example, influences various aspects of social policy when increasing 'individualisation of risks' in relation to older people and their families; and accelerated urbanisation as well as domestic and international migration under globalisation also has an inevitably high impact on the life of families, especially those 'global families' in old age. There was evidence that the structure(s) of families has changed, which often accompanied a change in their functions and relationships. Despite the transformation of the population and family structure, however, Phillipson argues that families have maintained existing patterns of reciprocity and support networks, although the norms and assumptions underpinning intergenerational reciprocity may have been challenged under demographic change and globalisation. Chapter Three, on the other hand, reviewed the development of theoretical bases such as social psychology and family sociology approaches identified as the contribution to the study of family cohesion. This chapter aimed to present and explore how theoretical frameworks themselves needed to evolve to capture and accommodate the complexity and multifaceted nature of intergenerational family relations in later life since the emergence of the 'solidarity paradigm' in the 1970s. As Katz and Lowenstein highlighted in Chapter Three, families might develop varied patterns of intergenerational solidarity and this requires further study, especially in a comparative perspective.

In Chapter Four, Ricky Joseph presented the empirical analysis of the theory – the impact of a contemporary phenomenon, globalisation – on intergenerational relations explored by Phillipson in Chapter Two. The increased flow of intergenerational migration is a phenomenon that has indeed been transforming family and intergenerational relations. However, the research subject in this chapter is not the recent migration in a globalising world that Phillipson explored, but the first wave of postwar large-scale migrants who moved from the Caribbean to the UK in the 1950s (through to the 1970s). This first generation of postwar migration has now reached the retirement age and has experienced or started to experience inheritance of 'family land' cross-nationally. Family reciprocity in this chapter is therefore focused around the importance of housing wealth accumulation, especially passing down 'family land' in the context of globalised intergenerational transfers over the generations separated by global migration. In their culture, 'collective well-being of family members' features strongly in the exchange and family relations in general. 'Family land' tends to be owned and inherited communally across extended kinships among Caribbean families. It is particularly important in societies in which homeownership plays a key role in family wealth accumulation, both ideologically and financially, since housing/home is the locus of kinship ties as a source of financial well-being for households and their families'. Symbolised as 'cultural remittance', culture and financial ties are strongly embedded with intergenerational exchanges. The migrants use kinship links to maintain cultural connections to the place of origin as for them a UK home provides investment and economic security, while their Caribbean home signifies their emotional ties. Due to the strong emphasis on 'family collectivity', wealth transfers do not appear to be significantly based on reciprocal arrangements. These transfers form strong ideologies and self-identities. Overall, this chapter highlighted the pattern of intergenerational transfers separate and distinct from the international migration. If this is the new pattern created by the first generation of migrants, inevitable changes in intergenerational reciprocity (and generational transfers) are likely to follow when the subsequent generations move up in their lifecourse. There are enough uncertainties in areas such as return migration and the degree of commitment and attachments to the original society among the subsequent generations born in the UK that may break down the established link.

Chapter Five highlighted particular East Asian practices of family support, although these are not necessarily distinctive since families in many other societies, both developed and developing, practise similar support exchanges around care and sharing accommodation. This chapter emphasised the 'strong continuity' of support exchange over the generations in postwar Japan and urban China. Within such continuity, however, certain shifts are also evident. As the respective economies have grown and the societies have modernised with differing levels of state and occupational welfare, the various types of support provided by families have shifted to adopt new social contexts, mainly away from the direct provision of practical support to more of an emotional, financial and organisational type of support. As Wang and Hsieh (2000) call it, 'from material reciprocity to more psychological interdependency', adult children nowadays are more likely to provide their ageing parents with the organisation and management of available resources and the provision of emotional support rather than the direct provision of long-term care single-handedly through co-residency. Despite the advancement of the market and public policy, however, the active role played by families in the provision of key social policy areas such as housing, education and social care remains unchanged. The shift in social contexts may dictate the flow of support between the generations; and instead of the traditional reciprocal arrangements over their lifecourse, new patterns are visible as there are continuous flows of support from the older to the younger generation for an extended period of time, especially due to greater affluence enjoyed by the middle/older generations and the increasing precariousness of the current labour markets for the younger generation. It is evident that with social change and now more alternative services available in the market economy, generations in both societies are moving away from the previously defined intensive and exclusive self-help approaches to welfare. At the same time, the direction of such changes is quite polarised and the speed and level of changes occurring in the two societies are not uniform. There is an increase in both independence and dependence over the generations to a varying extent. There may be a structural lag between Japan and urban China and change may be more compressed in Shanghai.

Grandparents have always been a great source of family support in a developmental context. In Chapter Six, however, Akpovire and Choja Oduaran demonstrated particular contemporary challenges that grandparents in Sub-Saharan Africa are facing due to the widespread epidemic of HIV and AIDS. HIV and AIDS are quickly eroding the human capital of the middle generation in the region. Although the pattern of family relations between grandparents and grandchildren is not 'new' since grandparents have always helped their younger family members, it is indeed a 'rediscovery' or 're-emphasis' of the traditional role played by grandparents. The missing middle generation in families due to the pandemic, however, has meant that the role of grandparents is no longer 'complementary' to that of their adult children (parents of grandchildren) in a traditional sense, but has often become one of 'substitute' parents entirely. This is an onerous task, not just teaching traditions and cultural values but now being required to be equipped with contemporary knowledge of education, technology and income-earning skills to bring up their grandchildren at an advanced age themselves, while also looking after the infected middle generation with appropriate medical skills and knowledge. The lack of alternatives, for example, through social policy measures, adds severity to their situation in the developmental context as much as the ageing process. Despite the modern trend towards family nuclearisation, the importance of extended kinship has increased. It is questionable, however, whether the role of grandparents stretched beyond their limits socially and economically is sustainable. In this context, the lack of 'family reciprocity' is acute (and much more so at the survival level than in the East Asian cases) – grandparents remain providers throughout their lifecourse not only to their adult children but to their grandchildren, with little hope of receiving support back from the younger generations in old age. The lack of valid data and academic literature in this area is well highlighted by the authors. This chapter clearly demonstrates the break with the past in family reciprocity.

Finding the root of the gendered cultural practice of intergenerational support exchange in Thailand was the main aim of Chapter Seven by Pascale F. Engelmajer and myself. By focusing on how the ancient religious (Buddhist) text has been translated into modern family practice, this chapter examined the rationales behind such family practices more than exploring its changing nature and patterns in recent years. Filial obligations feature as a vital part of social life in Thailand but it is a highly gendered practice. While the rationale and social norms appear to have remained unchanged, however, more recent globalisation has brought women new economic opportunities, resulting in a high volume of urban as well as international migration since the mid-1980s, and this has exacerbated the gendered patterns of filial obligations. This is a phenomenon/pattern new to the traditional intergenerational exchange system and network. What this chapter found was the fact that the discourse of 'dutiful daughters' has grown away from the original more gender-neutral religious teaching. The ancient Buddhist text stresses the importance of 'family reciprocity', especially adult children repaying debts to their parents – the spiritual gift of human life can only be repaid spiritually – but no explicit gender differences are described as the texts recognised the same obligations for sons and daughters and thus the same means to achieve the repayment. We could assume that the gendered discourse and practices may have emerged to fit in with modern socio-cultural and economic needs, and the conditions of families and society since the family system has been more matrilineal in household succession as well as physical and material obligations. The flow of migration appears to continue but the motivations and outcomes of female migrants may be transforming in the current socioeconomic contexts. Their motivations could also be less altruistic and based more on individualised behaviours.

Linking to the 'second demographic transition' (Hughes and Waite, 2007), with changes in family life around marriage and divorce discussed in Chapter Two, the analysis of Chapter Eight focused around the post-divorce relations between generations using examples from the US. Multiple family ties created by an increasing number of divorces, separations and remarriages/repartnering have definitely led to some 'new' patterns of intergenerational relations in contemporary societies. The demographic trends have brought more complexities and variations in family ties and thus support exchanges as an increased number of actors in those families such as divorced parents, divorced children, resident and non-resident parents, step-kinships and grandparents of both birth and stepparents often exist. Lawrence Ganong and Marilyn Coleman found some common patterns of 'complex family' practices: for example adult children tended to exchange fewer resources with their divorced parents, especially with a non-resident parent, than children whose parents remained together. Divorced adult children tend to provide less support to their parents but may receive more support from them. The definition of kinship is likely to be altered when parents divorce/remarry and the filial sense of duty towards particular family members may diminish due to the separation. In such 'complex families', *reciprocity* (along with emotional attachment) can be a key determinant for family support exchange, especially from adult children up to their parents, birth or step. With the multiple ties the younger generation has through separation and repartnering of their parents, 'being helped' in the past may act as an important factor when deciding who to help in the future. The hierarchy of support obligations appears to be dictated by family reciprocity especially when resources, both financial and emotional, are limited.

The five case studies illustrate well how globalisation is transforming family reciprocities and at the same time captures the resilience of their practices. The case studies also provide strong evidence of the persistence of norms in the context of equally strong external pressures for change. New patterns of reciprocity are indeed emerging in families in various contexts. The mixed picture of continuity and change, however, suggests that such newly emerging patterns tend to co-exist with, rather than replace, existing and conventional family practices.

This leads to my final point in this volume to address a missing piece of the puzzle – the *role of social policy*. The interaction between the state and families relating to the changing patterns of intergenerational relations is the area in which many chapters of this volume have touched on but no single chapter has specifically or substantially addressed. The final section of this concluding chapter will thus provide some reflections on the role of governments and policy issues influencing family roles, functions and relationships, and whether and how policy and practice might further support intergenerational reciprocity.

Policy challenges in ageing societies

Micro-level intergenerational relations (the focus of this volume) do not exist on their own, but they always influence and are influenced by more macro-level social structures and public policies (see for example Walker, 1996). Demographic change, for example, affects labour market structures such as how low fertility impacts on the balance between the working and non-working population, and also how increased labour participation by women alters the pool and practice of informal caregivers within (extended) families. Moreover, as Walker (1996) argues, welfare states play a vital role in moderating the relationship between the generations. The availability or lack of policy measures in areas such as public assistance and social services influencing existing family practice is a case in point. Two levels of intergenerational relations – at the family and societal level – are, however, often analysed separately. As Kohli (2005) suggests, there is a clear need and benefit to bring the two different levels together as a unified framework for analysis due to their strong interaction and interlinkages. Indeed Bengtson and Putney (2006, p 27) point out the importance of looking at the impacts of the macro relations:

> In the context of population ageing and rapidly changing economic and geographic conditions, we maintain that issues of micro-level family generational obligations and exchanges have remained relatively similar over time. At the same time, issues of macro-level age-group reciprocities and equities may acquire new urgency as a major concern in domestic social policy and economic discussions in contemporary nation states.

Policy challenges in the shifting economic and demographic contexts are well debated (see for example Williamson et al, 1999, 2003; Lynch, 2006; Vincent et al, 2006; Hill, 2007). With the population ageing, changing social and economic contexts and accompanying shifts in family formation, structure and relations all provide public policy challenges in areas such as pensions, health and social care. The current global demographic shifts mean that family support is predicted to be eroding while increased longevity and the increasing number of marital breakdowns found especially in the global North are likely to increase the need and demand for old age care (Walker, 1996). Moreover, a mismatch of available informal resources and rising demand for care has been occurring alongside the global trend of the retrenchment of the role of the states on welfare. The question posed here is therefore whether welfare states will be able to maintain pre-existing social and generational contracts.

Furthermore, the consensus on the 'social contract' including redistribution by the welfare state is argued to be crucial to maintain age integration in society and thus social cohesion (Lynch, 2006). Although not necessarily consistent across policy fields and programmes, different welfare states tend to allocate resources differently to different age groups by means of direct expenditures, indirect (tax) expenditures, through housing, social security and education policy and so on. According to Lynch, based on the available aggregated social spending data, some welfare societies appear to invest more resources in older people (for example Japan, Italy, Greece, Spain, Austria and the US) while others 'lean towards more youth-oriented welfare states' (2006, p 16) (for example Scandinavian and British Commonwealth countries), and continental Europe is located somewhere in the middle. Despite the discourse during the 1980s which brought a moral threat labelling older people as a 'selfish welfare generation', the systems are, however, often contradictory if we look at both societal redistribution and micro-level intergenerational transfers within families. As Vincent (2003, p 86) argues, 'the view of population ageing as a demographic time-bomb has been constructed by those with a particular agenda and a specific way of seeing the world'. However, some of the rhetoric behind the 'generational war' debate had given way to, according to Phillipson (2005, p 505), more realistic appraisals about the nature and implications of demographic change by the end of the 1990s (see also Williamson et al, 2003). In some welfare states, large resources pour into older people through pension programmes and social insurance or tax-based health and social care schemes, while at the same time, a significant amount of intergenerational transfers (both inter vivo and inheritance) takes place from the older generation to their adult children within families. The importance of taking both public and private transfers over generations into account needs to be highlighted here. As Kohli (1999) argues, private transfers tend to flow in the opposite direction to the public transfers of welfare states, and such micro-level redistribution within families tends to offset the direction of resources at the social policy level. In this scenario, however, giving the young public resources directly may help reduce social inequality or recent generational animosity over the 'welfare generation'; and it may also help reduce the perpetuation of family wealth accumulation over generations to advantage more privileged families (see also Silverstein et al, 2000).

Policies on welfare provision tend to draw a boundary between the state and families, but such a boundary is highly contested and shifts over time, according to changes in a nation's social and economic circumstances, demographic patterns and political agenda (for example Fox Harding, 1996; Izuhara, 2009). With the power of law and social and public policies, the state is often a facilitator in drawing such boundaries by encouraging and also discouraging certain family attitudes and behaviours. For example, legislation defines the role of the family and many East Asian societies such as Taiwan, Singapore and mainland China and also in the West including Spain, Israel, and 30 out of 50 states in the US have filial responsibility legalised to define to what extent and which family members are obliged to provide care to older adults. The impact of such institutions on micro-level family relations through a variety of means such as legislation, direct service provision, cash transfers and redistribution are indeed apparent. However, the state can also be a follower of trends and implement some measures to support or confirm the gap vacated by families. Indeed, families and the state co-exist in a welfare mix, in various societies and also in various social policy fields within a society. These two sectors play shared but distinctive roles to replace, substitute, crowd out or interact and complement each other (Kohli, 1999, p 103).

Policies on long-term care provide a good example of state–family boundary shifts. Many developed welfare states have experienced both a pre-welfare state period of predominantly informal family support shifting to a period of high investment on institutional care, and back to home-centred care becoming increasingly more popular, backed up with older people's wishes to stay put as well as the financial viability of governments in more recent years. Policies can actively or implicitly strengthen the role of the family in caring responsibility, again through a variety of policy measures identified by Leitner (2003, p 358) such as time rights (for example care leaves); direct and indirect transfers for caring to provide incentives for families to take up their caring responsibility (for example cash benefits and tax credits); and also social rights (for example individual pension rights). According to Leitner (2003), some societies have a 'familialistic policy' by strengthening the role of families with services and benefit provision; or even the lack of alternatives makes families remain as informal carers, while other welfare states adopt a 'de-familialistic policy' which aims to lift the burden of caring from families through means such as direct public provision of social services and the provision of subsidies enabling families to purchase care services in the market. However, policies in one society may not be so clear-cut, and many welfare states are likely to combine both familialistic and de-familialistic approaches.

The recent Japanese scheme on long-term care highlights well such boundary shifts, where they have opted for a social insurance scheme since 2000 (Ikegami and Campbell, 2002; Izuhara, 2009). Unlike the traditional self-help approach, under this new scheme caring responsibilities are shared in society with a variety of providers. The scheme has been successful in expanding the number of services and providers, and now includes a much wider section of society as recipients, in particular those who used to be excluded from public services owing to their financial and family circumstances. The 'availability of family resources' was removed from the eligibility criteria for older people to provide access to insurance-based public welfare when it was first introduced. However, financial sustainability soon became an issue, resulting at the first five-year review in 2005 in abolishing domiciliary services for those who were granted the lowest need categories (support need 1 and 2) and also re-introducing the 'availability of family resources' as an assessment criterion to cut back on services (Hiraoka, 2006). This shift can be considered a step backwards since the uniform entitlements in return for mandatory contributions were one of the key features of the new scheme.

There has been a long debate about whether the development of welfare states tends to 'crowd out' the role of families in society. In some national contexts, states are in fact filling a gap vacated by families, or replacing some of the traditional functions of family support. There is as such a 'substitution' hypothesis that argues that the generous provision of formal services to support older people 'crowds out' family support, and the provision of care predominantly falls on the responsibility of the state (for example Motel-Klingebiel et al, 2005). Motel-Klingebiel et al's analysis shows that the total quantity of support received by older people is greater in welfare states with a strong infrastructure of formal services, and no evidence of a substantial 'crowding out' of family support was found. Instead, it concluded that in societies 'with well-developed service infrastructures, family support and public services act accumulatively, but that in "familistic" welfare states, similar combinations do not occur' (Künemund and Rein, 1999; Motel-Klingebiel et al, 2005). The crowding-out hypothesis also discusses the compensational role of the state as welfare states move in to compensate the reduced role of families to maintain the total level of welfare in society. However, scholars such as Kohli (1999) and Daatland and Lowenstein (2005) argue for a more complementary role of welfare states to increase the total volume of care in society. For example, instead of crowding out the role of families, public old age security tends to create resources for new links between adult family generations (Kohli, 1999). The European comparative research (Daatland and Lowenstein, 2005) also found that welfare states had not crowded out the family in old age care, but rather helped the generations establish more 'independent relations'. The variation in welfare states is thus more likely to create variation in the characteristics of intergenerational relations.

Finally, as illustrated in this volume, policy issues are becoming increasingly global. There are many structural changes taking place, including demographic change, changes in economy and labour markets and also a shared political agenda towards neoliberalism in many advanced societies, which are likely to produce shared global policy concerns. Families as an agency are also shifting in their structures, roles and functions to adopt wider structural changes. Instead of providing a global solution, however, this volume has illustrated that many cultures appear to have deeply held and widely understood social norms about intergenerational exchange, and intergenerational family practices often fall on such norms. Policy responses adopted by these societies are thus more likely to be sensitive not only to their available national resources and political agenda but also their own cultural understanding of intergenerational relations.

References

Bengtson, V.L. and Putney, N.M. (2006) 'Future "conflicts" across generations and cohorts?', in J.A. Vincent, C.R. Phillipson and M. Downs (eds) *The futures of old age*, London: Sage Publications, pp 20-9.

Daatland, S.O. and Lowenstein, A. (2005) 'Intergenerational solidarity and the family–welfare state balance', *European Journal of Ageing*, vol 2, pp 174-82.

Fox Harding, L. (1996) *Family, state and social policy*, Basingstoke: Macmillan.

Hill, M. (2007) *Pensions*, Bristol: The Policy Press.

Hiraoka, K. (2006) 'Koroni tatus Nihon no kaigo hoken' ['Long-term care insurance in Japan at a turning point'], in S.Takegawa and H.K.Lee (eds) *Fukushi reji-mu no nikkan hikaku: Shakai hosho, jyendaa, rodo sijyo [Comparing Japanese and Korean welfare regimes: Social security, gender, and labour markets]*, Tokyo:Tokyo University Press, pp 123-45 [in Japanese].

Hughes, M.E. and Waite, L. (2007) 'The aging of the second demographic transition', in K.W. Schaie and P. Uhlenburg (eds) *Social structures: Demographic change and the well-being of older adults*, New York, NY: Springer Books, pp 179-212.

Ikegami, N. and Campbell, J.C. (2002) 'Choices, policy logics and problems in the design of long-term care systems', *Social Policy and Administration*, vol 36, no 7, pp 719-34.

Izuhara, M. (2009) *Housing, care and inheritance*, London: Routledge.

Kohli, M. (1999) 'Private and public transfers between generations: linking the family and the state', *European Societies*, vol 1, pp 81-104.

Kohli, M. (2005) 'Generational changes and generational equit', in M. Johnson (ed) *The Cambridge handbook of age and ageing*, Cambridge: Cambridge University Press, pp 518-26.

Künemund, H. and Rein, M. (1999) 'There is more to receiving than needing: theoretical arguments and empirical explorations of crowding in and crowding out', *Ageing and Society*, vol 19, pp 93-121.

Leitner, S. (2003) 'Varieties of familialism: the caring function of the family in comparative perspective', *European Societies*, vol 5, no 4, pp 353-75.

Lynch, J. (2006) *Age in the welfare state: The origins of social spending on pensioners, workers, and children*, New York, NY: Cambridge University Press.

Motel-Klingebiel, A., Tesch-Roemer, C. and Von Kondratowitz, H.J. (2005) 'Welfare states do not crowd out the family: evidence for mixed responsibility from comparative analyses', *Ageing & Society*, vol 25, no 6, pp 863-82.

Phillipson, C. (2005) 'The political economy of old age', in M. Johnson (ed) *The Cambridge handbook of age and ageing*, Cambridge: Cambridge University Press, pp 502-9.

Silverstein, M., Parrott, T.M., Angelelli, J.J. and Cook, F.L. (2000) 'Solidarity and tension between age groups in the United States: challenge for an aging America in the 21st century', *International Journal of Social Welfare*, vol 9, pp 270-84.

Vincent, J.A. (2003) *Old age*, London: Routledge.

Vincent, J.A., Phillipson, C.R. and Downs, M. (eds) (2006) *The futures of old age*, London: Sage Publications.

Walker, A. (ed) (1996) *The new generational contract: Intergenerational relations, old age and welfare*, London: UCL Press.

Wang, Q. and Hsieh, Y. (2000) 'Parent–child interdependence in Chinese families: change and continuity', in C.Violate, E. Oddone-Paolucci and M. Genuis (eds) *The changing family and child development*, Burlington, VT: Ashgate, pp 60-9.

Williamson, J.B., McNamara, T.K. and Howling, S.A. (2003) 'Generational equity, generational interdependence, and the framing of the debate over social security reform', *Journal of Sociology and Social Welfare*, vol 30, pp 3-13.

Williamson, J.B., Watts-Roy, D.M. and Kingson, E.R. (eds) (1999) *The generational equity debate*, New York, NY: Columbia University Press.

Index

Page references for notes are followed by n